TRADE ISSUES, POLICIES AND LAWS

THE ANDEAN TRADE PREFERENCE ACT (ATPA)

TRADE ISSUES, POLICIES AND LAWS

Additional books in this series can be found on Nova's website
under the Series tab.

Additional E-books in this series can be found on Nova's website
under the E-books tab.

TRADE ISSUES, POLICIES AND LAWS

THE ANDEAN TRADE PREFERENCE ACT (ATPA)

AARON J. DOHRNMANN
EDITOR

Nova Science Publishers, Inc.
New York

Library of Congress Cataloging-in-Publication Data

The Andean Trade Preference Act (ATPA) / editors, Aaron J. Dohrnmann.
p. cm.
Includes index.
CRS report for Congress prepared for members and committees of Congress.
ISBN 978-1-61324-386-2 (hardcover)
1. United States. Andean Trade Preference Extension Act of 2008. 2. Tariff preferences--Law and legislation--United States. 3. Tariff preferences--Andes Region. 4. Drug traffic--Andes Region. 5. United States--Foreign economic relations--Andes Region. 6. Andes Region--Foreign economic relations--United States. I. Dohrnmann, Aaron J.
KF6708.P7A85 2011
343.7305'6--dc22

2011013413

Published by Nova Science Publishers, Inc. † New York

Contents

PREFACE

This book examines the developments and impacts of the Andean Trade Preference Act (ATPA), which extends duty-free treatment to certain U.S. imports that meet domestic content and other requirements from designated countries in the Andean region. The purpose of ATPA is to promote economic growth in the Andean region and to encourage a shift away from dependence on illegal drugs by supporting legitimate economic activities. Critics of ATPA argue that unilateral trade programs are ineffective; that the ATPA has forced U.S. producers to compete with lower-cost Andean imports and, in the cases of Bolivia and Ecuador, that trade preferences should not be extended to countries that do not support U.S. foreign and trade policies.

Chapter 1- The Andean Trade Preference Act (ATPA) extends duty-free treatment to certain U.S. imports that meet domestic content and other requirements from designated countries in the Andean region. The purpose of ATPA is to promote economic growth in the Andean region and to encourage a shift away from dependence on illegal drugs by supporting legitimate economic activities. ATPA (Title II of P.L. 102-182) was enacted on December 4, 1991. It was renewed and modified under the Andean Trade Promotion and Drug Eradication Act (ATPDEA; Title XXXI of P.L. 107-210) on August 6, 2002, extending trade preferences until December 31, 2006. Since that time, Congress has provided several short-term extensions of ATPA. The most recent extension took place late in December 2010 when the 111th Congress enacted legislation for a six-week extension of ATPA for Colombia and Ecuador until February 12, 2011 (H.R. 6517).

Chapter 2- Since ATPA was enacted in 1991, it has had a minimal economic impact on the U.S. economy as a whole and on the great majority of U.S. industries and consumers. This continued to be the case during 2008 and 2009. Imports under ATPA of fresh cut roses and fresh-cut chrysanthemums provided the most significant benefits for U.S. consumers through lower prices (as a result of duty-free treatment). For U.S. producers, the most significant adverse impact of ATPA tariff preferences occurred as a result of reduced domestic production in industries producing fresh cut chrysanthemums.

Chapter 3- The Andean Trade Preference Act (ATPA), as amended by the Andean Trade Promotion and Drug Eradication Act (ATPDEA) (jointly referred to as ATPA/ATPDEA), requires the U.S. Trade Representative (USTR) to submit a report to Congress on the operation of the program no later than June 30, 2010,[1] and every two years thereafter during the period that the program is in effect. Congress directed that these reports include a general review of the ATPA/ATPDEA beneficiary countries based on the eligibility criteria and considerations described in the statute. This is the fifth USTR report to Congress on the ATPA/ATPDEA, and covers the year 2009, unless otherwise indicated.

In: The Andean Trade Preference Act (ATPA)
Editor: Aaron J. Dohrnmann
ISBN: 978-1-61324-386-2

Chapter 1

ATPA RENEWAL: BACKGROUND AND ISSUES*

M. Angeles Villarreal

SUMMARY

The Andean Trade Preference Act (ATPA) extends duty-free treatment to certain U.S. imports that meet domestic content and other requirements from designated countries in the Andean region. The purpose of ATPA is to promote economic growth in the Andean region and to encourage a shift away from dependence on illegal drugs by supporting legitimate economic activities. ATPA (Title II of P.L. 102-182) was enacted on December 4, 1991. It was renewed and modified under the Andean Trade Promotion and Drug Eradication Act (ATPDEA; Title XXXI of P.L. 107-210) on August 6, 2002, extending trade preferences until December 31, 2006. Since that time, Congress has provided several short-term extensions of ATPA. The most recent extension took place late in December 2010 when the 111th Congress enacted legislation for a six-week extension of ATPA for Colombia and Ecuador until February 12, 2011 (H.R. 6517).

The countries originally designated to qualify for trade preferences under ATPA were Bolivia, Colombia, Ecuador, and Peru. Trade preferences for Peru were not renewed in 2010 because Peru has a free trade agreement with the United States, which entered into force in February 2009. In the case of Bolivia, trade preferences were suspended in December 2008 because Bolivia failed to meet ATPA eligibility criteria related to counter-narcotics cooperation. Bolivia may only be reinstated as a beneficiary country under ATPA if Congress approves legislation to do so.

The impact of the ATPA on coca production in Andean countries has been small and mostly indirect, according to a 2010 study by the U.S. International Trade Commission. The study reports that illegal coca cultivation fell substantially in Andean countries from a 20-year peak of 232,500 hectares in 2007 to 192,000 in 2008. The study also reports that the ATPA, in combination with other alternative development programs, may indirectly have helped support job growth in certain exports from Andean countries, such as fresh-cut flowers, asparagus, bananas, and pineapples.

The trade effects of ATPA on the U.S. economy have been minimal because the amount of U.S. trade with the Andean region is low. The value of duty-free U.S. imports

---

* This is an edited, reformatted and augmented version of a Congressional Research Services publication, dated January 21, 2011.

under ATPA accounts for about 0.7% of total U.S. imports, or 0.1% of the U.S. gross domestic product (GDP). Nearly 90% of U.S. imports from ATPA countries enter duty-free under various trade preference programs or through normal trade relations. Duty-free imports under ATPA account for 45.8% of total U.S. imports from ATPA countries. Leading U.S. ATPA imports in 2009 were crude petroleum oil, cut flowers, petroleum-oil products (other than crude), refined copper, and knitted or crocheted apparel.

The 112th Congress may reevaluate the extension of ATPA trade preferences for Ecuador and Colombia, and could decide to reconsider the suspension of preferences for Bolivia. Policymakers may also consider broader reform of U.S. trade preference programs, including the Generalized System of Preferences. Some Members of Congress maintain that if ATPA trade preferences are not extended, the United States and the Andean countries risk losing some of the economic progress that has been achieved over the eighteen-year life of the program. Supporters of ATPA argue that the program should continue to reinforce the U.S. commitment to the "alternative development" counternarcotics strategy. Critics of ATPA argue that unilateral trade programs are ineffective; that the ATPA has forced U.S. producers to compete with lower-cost Andean imports; and, in the cases of Bolivia and Ecuador, that trade preferences should not be extended to countries that do not support U.S. foreign and trade policies.

ATPA Overview

The United States extends duty-free treatment to certain imports from Colombia and Ecuador under a regional trade preference program that began under the Andean Trade Preference Act (ATPA). ATPA was enacted on December 4, 1991 (Title II of P.L. 102-182) and was originally authorized for ten years with Bolivia, Colombia, Ecuador, and Peru as designated beneficiary countries.[1] It lapsed on December 4, 2001 and was renewed and modified on August 6, 2002 under the Andean Trade Promotion and Drug Eradication Act (ATPDEA; Title XXXI of P.L. 107- 210). ATPDEA amended ATPA by expanding trade preferences to include additional products that were previously excluded under ATPA. These products include certain items in the following categories: petroleum and petroleum products, textiles and apparel products, footwear, tuna in flexible containers, and others. Since the enactment of ATPDEA, Congress has extended ATPA several times for short-term periods. The most recent extension of ATPA continues preferential duty treatment for Colombia and Ecuador through February 12, 2011 (P.L. 111-124). Without this six-week extension, approved late in the 111th Congress, trade preferences under ATPA would have expired on December 31, 2010.

The 112th Congress may consider legislation to extended ATPA for Colombia and Ecuador, and may address the issue of reinstating Bolivia as a beneficiary country under ATPA. Under the most recent ATPA extension, Peru was dropped from the list of designated beneficiaries because the United States and Peru have a free trade agreement, which entered into force on February 1, 2009 (P.L. 110-138). The previous extension of ATPA provided trade preferences for Colombia, Ecuador, and Peru until the end of 2010 (P.L. 111-124). In the case of Bolivia, President George W. Bush suspended Bolivia's designation in November 2008, stating that Bolivia failed to meet the eligibility criteria because of its lack of cooperation with the United States on counter-narcotics efforts. In 2009, President Barack Obama continued the Bush Administration's determination that Bolivia was not meeting the eligibility criteria. The President's option of reinstating Bolivia as an ATPA beneficiary country expired on June 30, 2009. Bolivia can only be reinstated as a beneficiary country under ATPA if Congress approves legislation to do so.

ATPA, as amended by ATPDEA, is part of a broader U.S. initiative with Andean countries to address the drug trade problem with Latin America. The act (as a complement to crop eradication, interdiction, and other counter-narcotics efforts) was intended to promote economic growth in the Andean region and to encourage a shift away from dependence on illegal drugs by supporting legitimate economic activities. Increased access to the U.S. market was expected to help create jobs and expand legitimate opportunities for workers in the Andean countries in alternative export sectors.

U.S. Trade with Andean Countries

U.S. Total Trade with Bolivia, Colombia, Ecuador, and Peru

In 2009, the United States imported $21.2 billion (1.4% of total U.S. imports) from the four Andean countries that were originally designated as ATPA beneficiaries (Bolivia, Colombia, Ecuador, and Peru). U.S. exports to these countries in 2009 totaled $17.1 billion (1.8% of total U.S. exports). The four countries collectively were the 16th leading supplier of U.S. imports. The United States is a leading market for exports from all four countries. Colombia and Ecuador have the highest market share of exports going to the United States, with 39.2% of Colombia's and 33.2% of Ecuador's exports headed to the United States. For the United States, Colombia is the leading trading partner in the region, accounting for 52.9% of U.S. imports from and 51.3% of U.S. exports to all four countries (see Table 1). The leading U.S. imports from this region in 2009 were crude petroleum oil, gold, and coal. Leading U.S. exports to the region were petroleum oil products (other than crude), machinery parts, and corn (maize).

U.S. ATPA Imports

The year 2008 marked the sixth full year that ATPA provisions were in effect after its renewal under ATPDEA and also the last year that trade preferences were in effect for the four countries originally designated as ATPA beneficiaries: Bolivia, Colombia, Ecuador, and Peru. Between 2001 and 2008, U.S. imports from the region receiving ATPA preferential duty treatment increased from $1.7 billion (17% of total imports from ATPA countries) to $17.2 billion (61% of total U.S. imports from ATPA countries), an increase of more than 900%. Between 2008 and 2009, however, U.S. ATPA imports fell from $17.2 billion to $9.7 billion, a decrease of $7.5 billion, or 43.7%. The decline in 2009 was mostly due to the downturn in the U.S. economy, but the removal of Bolivia as an ATPA-designated country also contributed to the decline.

Duty-free imports accounted for 87.7% of U.S. imports from the region in 2009. ATPA duty-free imports accounted for 45.8% of total U.S. imports from the region. Of the remaining duty-free imports, a small share (1.9%) entered into the United States under GSP and the remainder entered under normal trade relations, which applies on a nondiscriminatory

Table 1. U.S. Trade with ATPA Countries, 2008

		U.S. Exports[a]		U.S. Imports[b]		
Country	US Billions	Region Share	Leading U.S. Export Items	US Billions	Region Share	Leading U.S. Import Items
Bolivia[c]	$0.4	1.8%	Jewelry, machinery parts, motor cars and vehicles	$0.5	1.9%	Petroleum oils (other than crude), tin, jewelry
Colombia	$10.6	53.5%	Petroleum oils (other than crude), corn, machinery parts	$13.1	45.9%	Crude petroleum oil, coal, coffee
Ecuador	$3.2	15.9%	Petroleum oils (other than crude), polymers of ethylene, machinery parts	$9.0	31.8%	Crude petroleum oil, crustaceans, bananas and plantains
Peru	$5.7	28.8%	Petroleum oils (other than crude), machinery parts, polymers of ethylene	$5.8	20.5%	Copper, petroleum oils (other than crude), silver
Total	$19.8			$28.5		

Source: U.S. International Trade Commission, Interactive Tariff and Trade DataWeb at http://dataweb.usitc.gov.
Compiled by CRS.

Notes:

a. Exports at the HTS 4-digit level.

b. Imports at the HTS 4-digit level.

c. Bolivia's designation as an ATPA beneficiary country was suspended on December 15, 2008.

basis to almost all U.S. trading partners. Only 12.3% of the value of U.S. imports from the four countries was dutiable in 2009. Leading U.S. ATPA imports in 2009 were crude petroleum oil, cut flowers, petroleum oil products (other than crude), refined copper, and knitted or crocheted apparel.

ATPA IMPACT

The trade effects of ATPA on the U.S. economy are minimal because the amount of U.S. trade with the region is low. The value of duty-free U.S. imports under ATPA accounts for about 0.7% of total U.S. imports, or 0.1% of the U.S. gross domestic product (GDP). A 2010 U.S. International Trade Commission (USITC) study on the ATPA states that the overall effect of ATPA-eligible imports on the U.S. economy continued to be minimal in 2008 and 2009.

Table 2. U.S. Imports from ATPA Countries: 2001, 2008, and 2009 ($ in millions)

	Bolivia[a]	Colombia	Ecuador	Peru	Total	% of Total
2001 Total Imports	165.1	5,622.6	1,975.4	1,805.5	9,568.7	
Duty-Free Imports	137.3	3,281.0	1,038.1	1,221.0	5,677.3	59.3%
ATPA	53.2	696.6	216.1	686.3	1,652.2	17.3%
GSP	9.5	68.2	33.0	73.4	184.2	1.9%
Other duty-free	74.5	2,516.1	789.0	461.3	3,840.9	40.1%
2008 Total Imports	540.4	13,058.8	9,043.8	5,839.9	28,483.0	
Duty-Free Imports	471.2	12,001.2	7,915.4	5,507.9	25,895.7	90.9%
Total ATPA (including ATPDEA)	140.0	7,339.2	6,594.8	3,168.7	17,242.7	60.5%
ATPDEA	83.0	6,527.8	6,311.1	1,648.6	14,544.4	51.1%
ATPA	57.0	811.5	283.7	1,520.1	2,698.2	9.5%
GSP	47.6	235.8	57.1	271.0	611.6	2.1%
Other duty-free	283.6	4,426.2	1,263.5	2,068.1	8,041.4	28.2%
2009 Total Imports	504.0	11,209.4	5,245.9	4,234.6	21,192.9	
Duty-Free Imports	406.5	9,962.9	989.8	3,960.3	18,585.7	87.7%
Total ATPA (including ATPDEA)	0.0	5,589.5	2,748.4	1,376.3	9,714.2	45.8%
ATPDEA	0.0	4,792.6	2,476.9	793.0	8,062.6	38.0%
ATPA	0.0	796.9	271.5	583.3	1,651.7	7.8%
GSP	123.9	188.7	52.3	30.7	395.6	1.9%
Other duty-free	282.6	4,184.7	1,455.4	2,553.2	8,475.9	40.0%

Source: United States International Trade Commission, Interactive Tariff and Trade Data Web http://dataweb.usitc.gov. Compiled by CRS.

a. Bolivia's designation as an ATPA beneficiary country was suspended on December 15, 2008.

The study estimates that U.S. imports under ATPA of fresh-cut roses and fresh-cut chrysanthemums provided the most significant impact on U.S. consumers through lower prices. For U.S. producers, the study estimates that the most significant adverse impact of ATPA tariff preferences occurred in 2008 and 2009 as a result of reduced domestic production in fresh-cut chrysanthemums.[2]

The impact of the ATPA on coca production in Andean countries has been small and mostly indirect, according to the USITC study.[3] The ATPA, combined with U.S. economic assistance through alternative development programs,[4] may have contributed to the U.S. counter-narcotics effort. The USITC study states that, in 2008 and 2009, ATPA continued to have a small, indirect effect in support of illicit coca eradication and crop substitution efforts in the Andean region. The study reports that, according to U.S. State Department data, illegal coca cultivation fell substantially in the Andean countries of Bolivia, Colombia, and Peru, from a 20-year peak of 232,500 hectares (ha) in 2007 to 192,000 ha in 2008. The study also states that Ecuador effectively eradicated its coca cultivation by 1992, but remains a major transit country for illegal drugs trafficked from Colombia and Peru.[5]

The rapid rise in the value of imports from ATPA countries since it was modified by ATPDEA was primarily due to an increase in the value of imports of petroleum-related products. Imports of crude petroleum oils accounted for over 70% of U.S. imports under ATPA in 2009. The ATPA, in combination with other alternative development programs, may have helped support job growth in certain export sectors, such as fresh-cut flowers and legal crops (asparagus, bananas, pineapples, and other crops), and expanded alternatives to workers who may have otherwise engaged in drug-crop production.[6]

Possible Sectoral Effects

The USITC study identified the fresh-cut chrysanthemum flower industry as the one U.S. sector that had an estimated displacement of five percent or more due to the ATPA in 2009. In 2007, the two industries that were identified as having an estimated displacement of 5 percent or more were asparagus and fresh-cut flowers (roses and chrysanthemums). ATPA countries supplied 82% of the total value of U.S. imports of fresh cut flowers and 99% of the total value of U.S. imports of chrysanthemums in 2009. U.S. imports of fresh-cut flowers from ATPA countries are primarily sourced from Colombia, and to a much lesser extent, from Ecuador. [7] Almost all imports in this category enter the United States duty-free under ATPA. The United States is an important fresh-cut flower export market for ATPA countries, accounting for 80% of the total value of Colombian exports ($1.02 billion) and 42% of Ecuadorian exports ($471 million) in 2009. The USITC reports that U.S. companies have invested more than $250 million in the Colombian flower industry and own approximately 17% of total Colombian cut-flower production.[8] Colombia's association of flower exporters estimates that the industry provided for 220,000 jobs in Colombia in 2010 and that the U.S. government has recognized the Colombian flower industry as an important ally in efforts to combat the illegal drug trade. The flower industry also provides for jobs in the United States, including airline industry employees, customs personnel, custom brokers, flower importers, retail flower shops employees, and others. However, some U.S. producers of fresh-cut flowers have been adversely affected by ATPA imports and contend that many U.S. flower farmers in California have been forced to give up their farms due to increased flower imports from Colombia and Ecuador. [9]

Another sector that has been affected is the asparagus industry. Peru is the leading exporter of asparagus in the world and, by far, the major Andean supplier of fresh asparagus to the U.S. market. In 2009, Peru supplied nearly all U.S. asparagus imports under ATPA and 57% of all U.S. fresh asparagus imports. Asparagus imports from ATPA countries in 2007 totaled $162.7 million, an increase of 24% from 2006. U.S. asparagus imports from ATPA countries increased in 2008 to $153.5 million and then increased to $162.3 million in 2009.[10] Although U.S. producers may have been adversely affected by lower prices resulting from ATPA, U.S. consumers have benefitted from a greater availability of fresh asparagus throughout the year and from lower retail prices. The Peruvian Asparagus Importers Association states that U.S. consumers have benefited from asparagus imports from Peru because there is now greater availability of fresh asparagus throughout the year. The Association also states that most imports from Peru are destined predominantly to the Eastern United States in areas where local production is minimal. The Peruvian asparagus industry provides jobs for an estimated 60,000 workers in Peru and is considered to be an important part of overall economic development in Peru. The Peruvian Asparagus and Vegetables Institute (IPEH) estimated that nearly 40% of the workers in the asparagus industry in 2006 came from areas that formerly supplied workers to illegal coca cultivation.[11]

Since the ATPA was amended by ATPDEA, investment in the textiles and apparel industries has increased in the Andean region. Textiles and apparel production has been a leading source of economic activity, particularly in Colombia and Peru. In 2009, the textiles and apparel industries provided jobs for 129,434 workers and accounted for 20% of Colombia's manufacturing jobs. Peru has been the leading Andean textile and apparel supplier to the United States for the past several years. In 2009, Peru accounted for 70% ($620 million) of U.S. textiles and apparel imports from the region.[12]

Effects of Bolivia's Suspension under ATPA

The effect of the suspension of trade preferences for Bolivia is difficult to measure because of other factors that affect the economy. A major impact has likely been a loss of investor confidence and reduced private investment, which would subsequently affect jobs. However, investment in Bolivia is also affected by other economic factors and by the internal political situation. [13] The policies of current Bolivian President Evo Morales, an indigenous leader elected in December 2005, have restricted foreign direct investment (FDI) in Bolivia and subsequently caused a great deal of uncertainty for foreign investors. President Morales has nationalized a number of industries since 2006, including hydrocarbons, telecommunications and electricity. Bolivia has stringent rules on foreign ownership and profit repatriation. In addition, U.S.-Bolivian relations have been strained by the Morales government's drug policy and its increasing ties with Venezuela. In September 2008, Bolivia broke off diplomatic ties with the United States over accusations of political interference. Restoring diplomatic ties with the United States remains challenging.[14] The resulting political uncertainty in Bolivia has likely affected the potential for long-term investments in Bolivia and probably contributed to volatility in Bolivia's FDI flows as well as potential ATPA-related investment. Though foreign investment flows to Bolivia are relatively low, any negative impact on the economy could be significant because the size of the Bolivian economy is so small.

The losses due to the suspension of ATPA trade preferences would likely be concentrated in certain sectors or regions of the country and, therefore, could come at a significant cost to certain communities. Some reports on Bolivia's economy and the effect of the removal of ATPA trade preferences for Bolivia conclude that one of the main impacts will be a loss of investor confidence and reduced private investment, which subsequently affects jobs. The government of Bolivia estimated that before Bolivia's suspension, ATPA trade preferences created 19,300 jobs, mostly in the clothing sector. One report cited by the USITC study estimates that the suspension of trade preferences for Bolivia resulted in thousands of job losses in the textiles and leather sectors. Another report estimates that employment in the textile sector fell 30% since trade preferences were suspended.[15]

A 2008 private sector report by a group of Bolivian business owners called the *Confederacin de Empresarios Privados de Bolivia* (CEPB) stated that the Bolivian economy is going through a major crisis due to the political situation and a weakening of free trade practices in the country.[16] The report argued that the suspension of ATPA benefits for Bolivia would increase investor uncertainty, increase unemployment, and have a detrimental effect on attempts to reduce the production of drugs in Bolivia.[17] According to the report, the suspension of ATPA duty benefits for Bolivian exports would mostly affect Bolivia's manufacturing industry because such a high percentage (55%) of Bolivia's total exports in this industry are headed to the United States. The report estimated that the removal of duty-free benefits for Bolivian exports to the United States could eliminate 12,000 direct jobs in the textile sector and up to 85,000 other jobs indirectly.[18] The report also stated that the La Paz region in Bolivia would be the most affected region, especially within the El Alto area, which has high levels of poverty. The study argued that any negative effects in this region can add to political instability and pose a high risk for democracy in Bolivia.[19]

Another report, by the Université de Lausanne (Unil), estimated the effects of ATPA suspension on Bolivian real incomes.[20] The Unil study stated that most industries affected by the removal of ATPA duty benefits are mostly situated in La Paz and El Alto in Bolivia. It estimated that the effect of ATPA termination on households with employees in the manufacturing industry is sizable, but the proportion of those households to the economy as a whole is very small. The study estimated that the termination of ATPA duty benefits would cause a 0.13% drop in manufacturing employment in Bolivia, in general, and a 2% decline in the textile and apparel sector, the most affected sector according to the authors of the study. However, the study's projected job losses fall more than proportionately on indigenous people and the authors argue that indigenous people would have fewer "outside opportunities" for earning money once they lose their job.[21]

Policy Implications

During the 112th Congress, policymakers may consider another extension of ATPA trade preferences for Ecuador and Colombia, which expire on February 12, 2011, and may address the issue of reinstating Bolivia as a designated beneficiary. If ATPA preferences are not renewed before February 12, duty-free treatment of U.S. imports of eligible products under ATPA will end.

Some policymakers believe that if ATPA trade preferences are not extended, the United States and the Andean countries risk losing some of the economic progress that has been achieved over the life of the program. Supporters of ATPA argue that the program should continue to reinforce the U.S. commitment to the "alternative development" counternarcotics strategy. Critics of ATPA argue that unilateral trade programs are ineffective; that the ATPA has forced U.S. producers to compete with lower-cost Andean imports; and that trade preferences should not be extended to countries that do not support U.S. foreign and trade policies. In the Andean countries, ATPA supporters state that the program has had a positive impact in the region by increasing investor confidence; creating thousands of jobs in alternative sectors; preventing organized crime; and reducing the production of drugs. They believe that maintaining confidence in the trade relationship with the United States is key to the long-term stability of the region.

Issues Regarding Suspension of Bolivia

Bolivia can only be reinstated as a beneficiary under an act of Congress. Numerous Members of Congress believe that there is no reason to consider a reinstatement of Bolivia as a beneficiary country because of Bolivia's continued lack of progress on the issue of counternarcotics and because of the lack of support for U.S. trade and foreign policies in Bolivia. Other policymakers, however, have been opposed to the suspension of trade preferences for Bolivia and contend that the suspension would do more harm than good by empowering champions of anti-Americanism; make the United States less and less relevant in Bolivia; and leave thousands of people unemployed.[22] In a hearing held on March 3, 2009, by the House Western Hemisphere Subcommittee on the future of U.S.-Bolivia relations, Representative Engel called for the administrations of Evo Morales and Barack Obama to initiate a high level bilateral dialogue between the United States and Bolivia to consider a renewed strategy for joint counternarcotics efforts and the possible reinstatement of ATPA preferences for Bolivia.[23]

The United States and Bolivia began bilateral talks under the auspices of the U.S.-Bolivia Dialogue in La Paz, Bolivia, in May 2009, which could have implications for future U.S. trade policy concerning Bolivia.[24] The talks were led by the U.S. State Department and Bolivia's Ministry of Foreign Affairs with the objective of reviewing and improving relations between the two countries. The second meeting took place on October 27, 2009, in Washington, DC.[25] The talks, which continued in 2010 and are expected to conclude in 2011, have focused on a framework covering trade, counternarcotics, human rights, economic development, and environmental issues.

Issues Regarding Investment Dispute in Ecuador

Some business groups have called for a reconsideration of trade preferences for Ecuador. One group of business associations stated in October 2010 that Congress should, at a minimum, require periodic reviews of Ecuador's fulfillment of ATPA eligibility criteria. The group contends that Ecuador is falling short of ATPA criteria related to rule of law, foreign investment, and intellectual property rights protection.[26]

A major issue that may be related to the concerns of business groups has to do with a long-running, multibillion-dollar lawsuit brought against the U.S. oil company Chevron by Ecuadorian indigenous peoples in which they claim they are the victims of toxic waste. The case goes back to a period between 1964 and 1990 in which Texaco (which has since merged with Chevron) is accused of dumping more than 18 billion gallons of toxic wastewater into Ecuador's waterways and forests. Chevron claims that the environmental damage was caused by Texaco and that the government of Ecuador exempted the oil companies from liability in exchange for a cleanup and payment in the early 1990s. Chevron reportedly has claimed that the legal system in Ecuador is corrupt and will not provide a fair forum, and that Ecuador's courts are politically influenced.[27]

Chevron filed a claim with the Permanent Court of Arbitration in The Hague to look into whether Ecuador breached international law under the Rules of the United Nations (U.N.) Commission on International Trade Law. In March 2010, the U.N. arbitration panel ruled that the Ecuadorian government violated the Bilateral Investment Treaty (BIT) with the United States with a series of unnecessary court delays in the long-running battle. The panel ruled in Chevron's favor with monetary compensation for the "failure of the Ecuadorian courts to adjudge" the company's claims.[28] Chevron has since filed a motion with the Superior Court in Lago Agrio, Ecuador, to have the case dismissed.[29]

Some Members of Congress have asked the Office of the United States Trade Representative (USTR) to reject Chevron's efforts to suspend trade preferences for Ecuador. They argue that the USTR should not use trade policy "as leverage to interfere in private claims processing through Ecuador's legal process."[30] The USTR has reportedly rejected similar requests made by Chevron in previous years. Other Members of Congress who would like to see a continuation of trade preferences for Bolivia have argued that renewing ATPA is a pragmatic means to urge President Correa of Ecuador to maintain open market and democratic policies.

Colombia

With regard to Colombia, a key issue related to ATPA trade preference renewal is the pending U.S.-Colombia FTA. The 112th Congress may consider whether or not to continue renewing ATPA trade preferences in the absence of a U.S.-Colombia FTA. Implementing legislation for a U.S.- Colombia FTA was introduced on April 8, 2008, but it is unclear whether the 112th Congress will consider implementing legislation for the agreement.[31]

Possible Trade Preference Program Reform

The 112th Congress may consider legislative action on broader reform of the preference programs based on comprehensive reviews in hearings held in both the House and the Senate in the 111th Congress. In the 111th Congress, numerous Members of Congress expressed interest in examining the possibility of reforming U.S. trade preference programs.[32] Congress has established four other trade preference programs, in addition to ATPA: the Generalized

System of Preferences (GSP), which applies to developing countries as a whole; the Caribbean Basin Economic Recovery Act (CBERA); the Caribbean Trade Partnership Act (CBTPA), the African Growth and Opportunity Act (AGOA), and the Haitian Opportunity through Partnership Encouragement (HOPE).

End Notes

[1] Bolivia and Peru were originally designated as beneficiary countries under the Andean Trade Preference Act (ATPA). Peru is no longer a beneficiary country because of the U.S.-Peru free trade agreement which entered into force in February 2009. Bolivia's designation as a beneficiary country was suspended by the President as of December 2008 because the country failed to meet the requirements set forth by the ATPA.

[2] United States International Trade Commission, *Andean Trade Preference Act: Impact on U.S. Industries and Consumers and on Drug Crop Eradication and Crop Substitution, 2009: Fourteenth Report,* USITC Publication 4188, September 2010 (hereinafter USITC Publication 4188).

[3] USITC Publication 4188, pp. 4-1 and 4-2.

[4] The Alternative Development program is a program funded under the U.S. Agency for International Development's Andean Counterdrug Initiative (ACI).

[5] USITC Publication 4188, pp. 4-2 and 4-3.

[6] Ibid, pp. x and xi.

[7] Ibid, pp. 3-10 through 3-13.

[8] Ibid.

[9] USITC Publication 4188, pp. 5-8 through 5-11.

[10] Based on data from the United States International Trade Commission trade database.

[11] Peruvian Asparagus Importers Association, *Written Statement for the House Committee on Ways and Means,* July 12, 2006.

[12] USITC Publication 4188, pp. 3-22 and 3-23.

[13] EIU, *Country Report: Bolivia,* January 2010.

[14] Ibid, p. 5.

[15] USITC Publication 4188, pp. 3-15 through 3-17.

[16] Confederación de Empresarios Privados de Bolivia, *The Importance of ATPDEA for Bolivia,* October 2008.

[17] Ibid., p. 1.

[18] The study does not present a methodology explaining how it estimated job losses.

[19] Confederación de Empresarios Privados de Bolivia, *The Importance of ATPDEA for Bolivia,* October 2008, p. 6.

[20] Université de Lausanne (Unil), *ATPDEA's End: Effects on Bolivian Real Incomes,* by Olivier Cadot, Etchel M. Fonseca, and Synabout Yaye Sakho, February 2008.

[21] Ibid.

[22] Press Release from the Office of Representative Eliot Engel, "Engel Objects to Suspension of Bolivia from Andean Trade Preferences," October 23, 2009.

[23] Press Release from the Office of Representative Eliot Engel, "Engel Calls for Immediate High Level Bilateral Dialogue Between U.S. and Bolivia," March 3, 2009.

[24] U.S. Department of State, "United States-Bolivia Bilateral Dialogue," Press Release, October 26, 2009.

[25] Ibid.

[26] Rosella Brevetti, "Business Groups Urge Renewal of GSP and ATPA for Peru, Colombia," *International Trade Reporter,* October 7, 2010.

[27] Rosella Brevetti, "Chevron Brings Arbitration Claim Against Ecuador in Long-Standing Dispute," *International Trade Reporter,* October 1, 2009.

[28] Lucien O. Chauvin, "U.N. Panel Says Ecuador Violated U.S. BIT Because of Undue Delays in Chevron Case," *International Trade Reporter,* April 8, 2010.

[29] Lucien O. Chauvin, "In Ecuador, Chevron Files for Dismissal of Long-Running Lawsuit Over Pollution," *International Trade Reporter,* August 19, 2010.

[30] Rosella Brevetti, "Sanchez, 25 House Members Urge USTR to Reject Chevron ATPA Lobbying," *International Trade Reporter,* December 24, 2009.

[31] For more information, see CRS Report RL34470, *The Proposed U.S.-Colombia Free Trade Agreement,* by M. Angeles Villarreal.

[32] See CRS Report R41429, *Trade Preferences: Economic Issues and Policy Options*, coordinated by Vivian C. Jones.

In: The Andean Trade Preference Act (ATPA)
Editor: Aaron J. Dohrnmann
ISBN: 978-1-61324-386-2

Chapter 2

ANDEAN TRADE PREFERENCE ACT: IMPACT ON U.S. INDUSTRIES AND CONSUMERS AND ON DRUG CROP ERADICATION AND CROP SUBSTITUTION, 2009, FOURTEENTH REPORT*

United States International Trade Commission

PREFACE

The submission of this study to Congress continues a series of reports by the U.S. International Trade Commission ("the Commission" or "USITC") on the impact of the Andean Trade Preference Act (ATPA) on U.S. industries and consumers. The current study fulfills the Commissions reporting requirement for calendar year 2009 and represents the 14th in the series.

ATPA, enacted on December 4, 1991, authorized the President to proclaim duty-free treatment for eligible articles from Bolivia, Colombia, Ecuador, and Peru. ATPA has been amended and the authority to provide preferential treatment has been extended several times, most recently by Public Law 110-124. The authority to provide preferential treatment is scheduled to expire on December 31, 2010. Bolivia was suspended as an ATPA beneficiary country effective December 15, 2008. The United States-Peru Trade Promotion Agreement entered into force on February 1, 2009, but Peru's status as an ATPA beneficiary country continued.

Section 206 of ATPA requires the Commission to assess the economic impact of the Act "on United States industries and consumers, and in conjunction with other agencies, the effectiveness of this Act in promoting drug-related crop eradication and crop substitution efforts of beneficiary countries." The Commission is required to submit its report to Congress biennially by September 30 of the year following the period covered in each report.

---

* This is an edited, reformatted and augmented version of the United States International Trade Commission's publication, dated September 2010.

LIST OF FREQUENTLY USED ABBREVIATIONS AND ACRONYMS

ATPA	Andean Trade Preference Act (original 1991 legislation)
ATPDEA	Andean Trade Promotion and Drug Eradication Act (2002 amendments)
ATPEA	Andean Trade Preferences Extension Act (2006 amendments)
CBERA	Caribbean Basin Economic Recovery Act
c.i.f.	cost, insurance, and freight
CNC	Crime and Narcotics Center, Central Intelligence Agency
Commission, the	U.S. International Trade Commission
FDI	foreign direct investment
FTA	free trade agreement
FY	fiscal year
GDP	gross domestic product
GSP	Generalized System of Preferences
ha	hectare
HS	Harmonized System
HTS	Harmonized Tariff Schedule of the United States
INCSR	International Narcotics Control Strategy Report
IPR	intellectual property rights
NAFTA	North American Free Trade Agreement
n.e.s.o.i.	not elsewhere specified or otherwise included
NTR	normal trade relations (commonly and historically called most-favored- nation status)
ONDCP	Office of National Drug Control Policy
OTEXA	Office of Textiles and Apparel, U.S. Department of Commerce
SME	square meter equivalents
TPA	Trade Promotion Agreement (term for U.S. FTAs with the Andean countries)
TRQ	tariff-rate quota
UNODC	United Nations Office on Drugs and Crime
USAID	United States Agency for International Development
USDOC	U.S. Department of Commerce
USDOS	U.S. Department of State
USITC	U.S. International Trade Commission
U.S.-Peru TPA	United States-Peru Trade Promotion Agreement
USTR	United States Trade Representative
WTO	World Trade Organization

EXECUTIVE SUMMARY

Since ATPA was enacted in 1991, it has had a minimal economic impact on the U.S. economy as a whole and on the great majority of U.S. industries and consumers. This continued to be the case during 2008 and 2009. Imports under ATPA of fresh cut roses and fresh-cut chrysanthemums provided the most significant benefits for U.S. consumers through lower prices (as a result of duty-free treatment). For U.S. producers, the most significant adverse impact of ATPA tariff preferences occurred as a result of reduced domestic production in industries producing fresh cut chrysanthemums.

The probable future effects of ATPA are likely to be minimal, as the global economic downturn and uncertainty over ATPA renewal dampened investment to produce ATPA-eligible exports. Investments made in Colombia and Ecuador are expected to generate most future exports to the United States under ATPA, because Bolivia is currently suspended from ATPA and most investment in Peru will likely affect exports to the United States under the U.S.-Peru TPA, rather than ATPA.

In 2008–09, the effectiveness of ATPA in reducing illicit coca cultivation and promoting crop substitution efforts in the Andean countries continued to be small and mostly indirect. Although land area under coca cultivation increased in Bolivia in 2009 and Peru in 2008, coca cultivation in Colombia decreased substantially in 2008 (using the most recent data available). U.S. and foreign government agencies continue to recognize that ATPA contributes to U.S. counternarcotics and economic assistance objectives, albeit indirectly, by providing sustainable economic alternatives to drug-crop production in beneficiary countries.

The Andean Trade Preference Act (ATPA) was enacted in 1991 to promote the development of viable economic alternatives to coca cultivation and cocaine production by offering duty-free or other preferential treatment to imports of eligible goods from Bolivia, Colombia, Ecuador, and Peru. [1] Section 206 of ATPA requires the U.S. International Trade Commission (the Commission) to prepare a biennial report assessing the actual and the probable future effects of ATPA on the U.S. economy generally, on U.S. industries, and on U.S. consumers, as well as the estimated effect of ATPA on drug-related crop eradication and crop substitution efforts of the beneficiary countries. ATPA has been amended, and the President's authority to provide preferential treatment has expired and been extended, several times.[2] The authority to provide preferential treatment under ATPA is currently set to expire on December 31, 2010.

This report, the 14th in this series, discusses the estimated impact of ATPA during the calendar year 2009.[3] Since the 13th report, there have been two major changes having an impact on ATPA: (1) Bolivia was suspended from ATPA eligibility as of December 15, 2008, and (2) the U.S.-Peru Trade Promotion Agreement (TPA) entered into force on February 1, 2009. Peru retained its ATPA eligibility after the TPA entered into force.

ATPA tariff preferences can potentially affect (1) U.S. consumers, by providing lower prices and increased product variety; (2) the U.S. Treasury, by reducing tariff revenue; and (3) U.S. producers, by displacing potential U.S. production of competing products, or by increasing the demand for U.S. inputs into the production of goods produced in Andean countries that receive preferential treatment under ATPA (e.g., use of U.S. cotton in the production of Andean textiles exported to the United States). In addition, ATPA potentially provides alternatives to illicit coca production by increasing U.S. market access for Andean countries' exports. This report assesses the impact of ATPA by examining the effect on the U.S. economy as a whole and on U.S. industries and consumers. The Commission's quantitative analysis focuses on the 20 leading products that benefited exclusively from ATPA in 2009, which accounted for 97 percent of imports that benefited exclusively from ATPA in that year.

Key Findings

- **Imports under ATPA:** Of the $9.7 billion in U.S. imports entered under ATPA in 2009, $8.0 billion, or 82 percent, could not have received tariff preferences under any other program. The five leading products benefiting exclusively from ATPA in 2009 were heavy crude oil; light crude oil; fresh-cut roses; heavy fuel oil; and fresh-cut chrysanthemums. Since U.S. duties on petroleum products such as crude and heavy fuel oil are low (well below 1 percent ad valorem equivalent), ATPA tariff preferences likely had little impact on total U.S. imports of those products.
- **Impact on U.S. economy as a whole:** The Andean countries collectively accounted for 1.3 percent of total U.S. imports in 2009. The value of duty-free imports that benefited exclusively from ATPA in 2009 accounted for about 0.5 percent of the value of total U.S. imports, or 0.06 percent of the U.S. GDP. Hence, the overall impact of ATPAexclusive imports on the U.S. economy continued to be negligible in 2009.
- **Impact on U.S. consumers:** Commission analysis found that imports of fresh-cut roses provided U.S. consumers with the largest benefit, and fresh-cut chrysanthemums the second-largest (benefits were valued at up to $20.1 million and $4.7 million, respectively) through lower prices, increased product variety, and higher consumption. U.S. imports of the 20 leading ATPA-exclusive products produced net consumer gains (i.e., net welfare gains, which equal benefits to consumers net of U.S. Treasury losses due to lower ATPA tariffs) for U.S. consumers in 2009. Pouched tuna yielded the largest net benefit to U.S. consumers (valued at up to $1.0 million), followed by fresh-cut roses (valued up to $670,000), and fresh or chilled asparagus (up to $448,000). Apparel products would probably lead in net welfare gains, given the relatively high duty rates on these products, but lack of U.S. production data at the detailed product level precludes making such estimates.
- **Impact on U.S. industries:** Imports of fresh-cut chrysanthemums benefiting exclusively from ATPA may have displaced 5 percent or more of the value of U.S. production in this industry in 2009. This displacement is attributable to the very high share of the U.S. market (91.0 percent) accounted for by these ATPA imports. The Commission estimates the resulting displacement at 1.0-6.4 percent, valued at $116,000– $722,000.
- **The probable future effects of ATPA on the United States:** Future effects of ATPA are expected to be minimal on the overall U.S. economy, because U.S. imports from Colombia, Ecuador, and Peru represent such a small portion of total U.S. imports (1.3 percent in 2009). Future effects in most economic sectors are also likely to be minimal, because foreign and domestic investments in Colombia and Ecuador that could generate future exports to the United States under ATPA were small in 2009. The low level of investment in 2009 was largely because of the global economic downturn; officials in these countries also indicated that the repeated expirations and short-term renewals of ATPA discouraged ATPA-related investment. With the exception of a portion of investment in textiles and apparel, investments in ATPA-eligible products in Peru are expected to generate future exports to the United States under the TPA, rather than ATPA. Despite these developments, the

Commission was able to identify small investments in the textile and apparel, broccoli, flowers, pineapple, and plywood sectors in Colombia and Ecuador. Future exports of textiles and apparel are uncertain because Colombia, Ecuador, and Peru have established regional production chains that depend on cumulation of inputs from more than one ATPA country for the purposes of establishing origin among the beneficiary countries to qualify for ATPA preferences; the U.S.-Peru TPA does not permit ATPA regional cumulation.

- **Impact on drug crop eradication and crop substitution efforts:** In 2009, ATPA continued to have a small, indirect effect in support of illicit coca eradication and crop substitution efforts in the Andean region. According to U.S. government data, net land area under coca cultivation decreased substantially in Colombia in 2008, but it increased in Bolivia in 2009 and in Peru in 2008 (most recent data available). Alternative development programs in these countries continued to provide the infrastructure and job creation needed to generate export sales of new or improved legal crops—such as bananas, pineapples, hearts of palm, coffee, and cacao—which are eligible for duty-free treatment under ATPA or NTR provisions.

U.S.-Andean Trade in 2009

- U.S. imports from the Andean countries: Since ATPA was enacted in 1991, U.S. trade with the Andean countries has grown significantly. Total U.S. imports from the Andean countries have quadrupled, growing from $5.0 billion in 1991 to $20.7 billion in 2009. Leading imports under ATPA and the leading suppliers of these products are shown in figure ES.1.
- **Leading imports entered under ATPA:** In 2009, U.S. imports entered under ATPA totaled $9.7 billion, down from $17.2 billion in 2008. This decline was driven largely by a $6.0 billion decrease in imports of petroleum and petroleum products.

    - Petroleum and petroleum products (mostly crude oil) were the leading ATPA import category in 2009, with imports valued at $7.4 billion, or 75.8 percent of total imports under ATPA. Colombia and Ecuador were the main suppliers. Largely because of lower average prices in 2009, U.S. imports from both countries declined in value from 2008 to 2009, though imports of crude oil from Colombia increased in volume.
    - Several categories of cut flowers combined (including roses, chrysanthemums, alstroemeria, and carnations) made up the second leading ATPA import category, with imports valued at $625 million in 2009, or 26.6 percent of non-oil ATPA imports. Colombia and Ecuador were the main suppliers.
    - Knitted apparel was the third leading ATPA import category in 2009, with imports valued at $490 million or 20.9 percent of non-oil ATPA imports. Peru and Colombia were the leading suppliers.

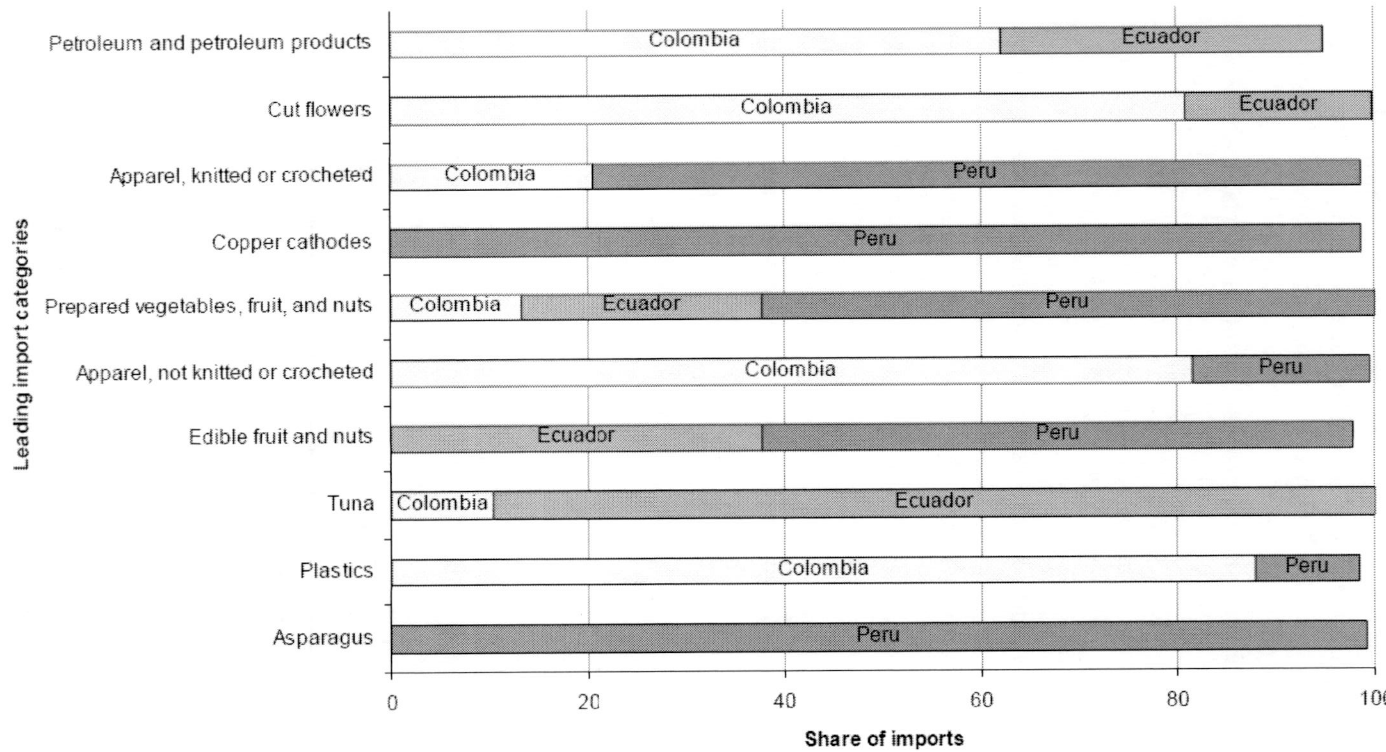

Source: Compiled from official statistics of the U.S. Department of Commerce.
Note: Bars shown may not total 100 percent because figure shows only leading suppliers.
Figure Es.1 Share of selected imports entered under ATPA by leading suppliers, 2009.

- ATPA imports by supplying country in 2009:
    - ATPA imports from Colombia were valued at $5.6 billion, or 57.5 percent of the total. Petroleum and petroleum products made up 81.7 percent of ATPA imports from Colombia. Other leading ATPA imports from Colombia included cut flowers (roses, chrysanthemums, and carnations), apparel, and plastic products (largely industrial plastics such as polyvinyl chloride (PVC)). Colombia was the third-largest global supplier of PVC for the U.S. market in 2009.
    - ATPA imports from Ecuador were valued at $2.7 billion, or 28.3 percent of the total. Petroleum and petroleum products made up 87.8 percent of ATPA imports from Ecuador in 2009. Other leading ATPA imports from Ecuador included cut flowers (roses, chrysanthemums, and carnations) and tuna. Almost 90 percent of tuna imports entered under ATPA were shipped from Ecuador.
    - ATPA imports from Peru were valued at $1.4 billion, or 14.2 percent of the total. Leading ATPA imports from Peru included copper cathodes (Peru was the only supplier of imports entered under ATPA), knitted apparel, petroleum and petroleum products (mostly crude oil), and fresh or chilled asparagus. Peru was the leading global supplier of asparagus for the U.S. market in 2009.

- **U.S. exports to the Andean countries:** U.S. exports to the Andean countries have more than quadrupled since ATPA was enacted, growing from $3.8 billion in 1991 to $16.7 billion in 2009. The United States is the leading supplier to Colombia, Ecuador, and Peru. Economic growth in the Andean countries has led to increased demand for U.S. capital and consumer goods, resulting in growth of U.S. exports to the region that has outpaced import growth, thereby reducing the U.S. trade deficit with the Andean countries. The United States is also an important supplier of inputs used by Andean apparel and jewelry manufacturers to produce ATPA-eligible exports.

Positions of Interested Parties

The Commission held a public hearing in connection with the investigation on July 7, 2010, in Washington, DC. The Commission also received written public submissions in connection with this investigation in response to a *Federal Register* notice. [4] The testimony and the submissions generally related to one of four topics:

- **Several industry and government representatives cited mixed economic effects of ATPA on specific U.S. sectors, but a minimal effect on the overall U.S. economy:** Several foreign officials stated that ATPA has never had a substantial adverse impact on U.S. industry. Some industry and government representatives cited positive effects resulting from ATPA, including increased U.S. exports of capital equipment and inputs used in the production of ATPA-eligible products; benefits to U.S. industries and services that provide support for ATPA-related imports; benefits to U.S. consumers such as greater choice, broader availability, and lower prices; and company-specific benefits. On the other hand, representatives of the California Cut Flower Commission and Bumble Bee Foods asserted that ATPA has had a negative economic impact on their specific industries.

- **ATPA has had a positive effect on beneficiary countries:** Interested parties said that ATPA has promoted exports and investment, which have generated economic growth and employment in the beneficiary countries. One such party stated that ATPA has promoted investment, export-oriented production, and the development of regional and intra-regional supply chain integration, all of which have stimulated job creation.
- **ATPA has had a positive effect on drug crop eradication and crop substitution:** Foreign government and industry representatives commented that through increased exports and investment, ATPA has created employment opportunities for workers who might otherwise engage in drug crop production.
- **Uncertainties regarding the future of ATPA have adversely affected investment and trade:** A number of the public comments received claimed that the uncertainties related to the repeated expiration and short-term renewals of ATPA since2006 have negatively affected the investment environment and bilateral trade. Several government and industry officials stated their opposition to the "graduation" of Peru from ATPA because it would undermine the competitive advantage presently afforded to the Colombian garment industry. If Peru is graduated, it will lose the privilege of being part of the cumulated supply chain for apparel exports, along with Colombia and Ecuador, under ATPA rules of origin; as a result, some of Colombia's apparel exports to the United States that now use significant quantities of Peruvian inputs of yarn and fabric would no longer receive duty-free access.

INTRODUCTION

The Andean Trade Preference Act (ATPA)[1] was enacted in 1991 to encourage the Andean countries of Bolivia, Colombia, Ecuador, and Peru to reduce drug-crop cultivation and production by authorizing the U.S. President to grant tariff preferences to qualifying Andean products in order to foster trade, including the production and export of nontraditional products. In 2002, ATPA was extended and the scope was expanded by the Andean Trade Promotion and Drug Eradication Act (ATPDEA).[2] ATPA, as amended by ATPDEA, authorizes the President to grant duty-free treatment to many Andean products entering the United States. The President's authority to provide duty-free treatment under the act is currently set to expire at the end of 2010.[3]

The United States began bilateral free trade agreement (FTA) negotiations with three ATPA beneficiary countries in 2004—Peru, Colombia, and Ecuador.[4] The United States and Peru concluded work on a bilateral FTA (known as the U.S.-Peru Trade Promotion Agreement, or U.S.-Peru TPA) in December 2005. The agreement was signed in April 2006 and entered into force on February 1, 2009.[5] The United States and Colombia reached agreement on a bilateral FTA (the U.S.-Colombia Trade Promotion Agreement) in February 2006,[6] but the U.S. Congress has not yet enacted legislation to approve and implement the agreement.[7] FTA negotiations with Ecuador were suspended in 2006. In addition, Bolivia was suspended as an ATPA beneficiary country effective December 15, 2008. More information about the status of ATPA countries is provided below.

Section 206 of ATPA requires that the U.S. International Trade Commission (the Commission or USITC) report biennially to Congress on the economic impact of ATPA on U.S. industries, U.S. consumers, and the U.S. economy in general, as well as on the estimated effect of ATPA on drug-related crop eradication and crop substitution efforts of the beneficiary countries.[8] This report is the 14th in the series and covers the period since the previous report, focusing on developments in 2009. Throughout this report, the term "ATPA" refers to ATPA as amended by ATPDEA. The term "original ATPA" will be used to identify the original ATPA program that expired in December 2001, so that the scope and requirements of that statute can be discussed appropriately.

Summary of the ATPA Program

ATPA authorizes the President to grant certain unilateral preferential trade benefits to Bolivia, Colombia, Ecuador, and Peru in the form of duty-free treatment of eligible products imported into the customs territory of the United States, based on importer claims for this treatment. ATPDEA amended the original ATPA to expand the number of products eligible for duty-free treatment. On October 31, 2002, the President designated all four original ATPA beneficiary countries as ATPDEA beneficiary countries and designated most of the additional ATPDEA-eligible products as eligible for duty-free treatment.[9] The following sections summarize ATPA provisions concerning beneficiaries, trade benefits, and qualifying rules, and the relationship between ATPA and the Generalized System of Preferences (GSP).

Beneficiaries

Under the statute as originally enacted and as amended in 2002, only Bolivia, Colombia, Ecuador, and Peru are eligible to be designated as beneficiary countries. Designations are made by the President, subject to certain statutory limitations and after taking into account certain statutory factors.[10] Under the original ATPA, the President determined that all four countries met the eligibility requirements of the statute, and all were designated as beneficiary countries. All four designations remained in effect until 2002, when the ATPA provisions were amended by ATPDEA. Among other things, ATPDEA specified additional criteria for eligibility,[11] which required the President to make new determinations of eligibility for each of the four countries under the expanded list of limitations and factors. The President subsequently redesignated each of the four countries in 2002.[12]

Bolivia, however, was suspended as an ATPA beneficiary country in late 2008, following a series of developments that year. On September 25, 2008, the President announced that he proposed to suspend Bolivia's designation as a beneficiary country under ATPA and as an ATPDEA beneficiary country. [13] This announcement followed the President's identification of Bolivia as a major drug transit or major illicit drug-producing country in his report issued on September 15, 2008, pursuant to section 706(1) of the Foreign Relations Authorization Act, Fiscal Year 2003 (Public Law 107-228).[14] On November 25, 2008, after statutorily required public notice, acceptance of comments from the public, and a public hearing, the President announced the suspension of Bolivia as an ATPA and ATPDEA beneficiary country, effective December 15, 2008, for failure to adhere to its obligations under international counternarcotics agreements.[15]

ATPA was extended to the end of 2009 on October 16, 2008, with contingency provisions for Bolivia and Ecuador.[16] Continuation of beneficiary status for Bolivia and Ecuador past July 1, 2009, was made contingent on Presidential review of the performance of Bolivia and Ecuador with respect to ATPA's eligibility criteria.[17] As a result of the President's review and determination on June 30, 2009, Bolivia's suspension was effectively continued and Ecuador's eligibility was continued.[18]

The United States-Peru Trade Promotion Implementation Act was signed into law on December 14, 2007.[19] The U.S.-Peru TPA entered into force on February 1, 2009.[20] Peru lost GSP eligibility at this time, but continued to be an ATPA beneficiary.[21]

Eligible Articles

ATPA provides duty-free treatment to qualifying imports from designated beneficiary countries. [22] For some products, duty-free entry under ATPA is subject to certain conditions in addition to basic preference eligibility rules. Imports of sugar, like those of some other agricultural products, remain subject to any applicable and generally imposed U.S. tariff-rate quotas (TRQs) and food-safety requirements.[23] In-quota shipments of such products subject to TRQs are eligible to enter free of duty under ATPA. Under the original ATPA, certain leather handbags, luggage, flat goods (such as wallets and portfolios), work gloves, and leather wearing apparel from ATPA countries were eligible to enter at reduced (but not free) rates of duty.[24] The original ATPA specifically excluded from eligibility most textiles and apparel, certain footwear, canned tuna, petroleum and petroleum derivatives, certain watches and watch parts,[25] certain sugar products, and rum and tafia.[26]

ATPDEA authorizes the President to extend duty-free treatment to some of the products previously ineligible for preferences under the original ATPA, including certain textiles and apparel, footwear, tuna in foil or other flexible airtight packages (not cans), petroleum and petroleum products, and watches and watch parts (including cases, bracelets, and straps). Certain handbags, luggage, flat goods, work gloves, and leather wearing apparel, previously eligible for reduced rates of duty under the original ATPA,[27] are eligible for duty-free treatment under ATPDEA. ATPDEA authorizes the President to proclaim duty-free treatment for qualifying additional articles if he determines that such articles are "not import sensitive in the context of imports from ATPDEA beneficiary countries."[28] When ATPDEA was implemented, the President extended ATPDEA duty-free treatment to most newly eligible products. However, he did not include 17 footwear tariff lines on the basis of their import sensitivity in the context of imports from ATPDEA countries.[29]

Nearly 6,300 tariff lines or products are now covered by ATPA trade preferences, of which about 700 were added by ATPDEA.[30] The following products continue to be excluded by statute from receiving preferential treatment: certain textile and apparel articles; canned tuna; above-quota imports of certain agricultural products subject to TRQs, including sugars, syrups, and sugar-containing products; and rum and tafia.[31]

Qualifying Rules

To be eligible for ATPA treatment, ATPA products must either be wholly grown, produced, or manufactured in a designated ATPA country or be "new or different" articles made from substantially transformed non-ATPA inputs.[32] The cost or value of the local

(ATPA region) materials and the direct costs of processing in one or more ATPA countries must total at least 35 percent of the appraised customs value of the product at the time of entry. ATPA countries are permitted to pool their resources to meet the value-content requirement and to count inputs from Puerto Rico, the U.S. Virgin Islands, and countries designated under the Caribbean Basin Economic Recovery Act (CBERA)[33] toward the value threshold. In addition, goods with an ATPA content of 20 percent of the customs value and the remaining 15 percent attributable to U.S.-made (excluding Puerto Rican) materials or components,[34] as well as goods containing third-country inputs that undergo double substantial transformation within the ATPA countries and are counted with other qualifying inputs to total 35 percent, are deemed to meet the 35 percent value-content requirement.[35]

ATPDEA extended duty-free treatment for the first time to certain textile and apparel articles imported from designated ATPDEA beneficiary countries. ATPDEA authorized unlimited duty-free and quota-free treatment for imports of textile and apparel articles made in beneficiary countries from fabrics or fabric components wholly formed, or components knit-to-shape, in the United States from yarns produced in the United States or one or more ATPDEA beneficiary countries, provided the fabrics are also dyed, printed, and finished in the United States.[36] ATPDEA also includes unlimited preferential treatment for apparel assembled from ATPDEA-country fabrics or fabric components formed, or components knit-to-shape, of llama, alpaca, or vicuña.

Apparel items assembled in ATPDEA countries from fabrics or components formed in, or knit-to-shape from yarns produced in, the United States or one or more ATPDEA beneficiary countries (known as "regional fabrics or components") are also eligible to enter free of duty but are subject to a cap.[37] The principal textile and apparel provisions of ATPDEA are summarized in table 1.1.

Annual Reviews

ATPDEA requires the USTR to conduct an annual review of the eligibility of articles and countries for ATPA benefits similar to the annual reviews performed for GSP.[38] The USTR initiated its 2009 ATPA review on August 26, 2009, requesting the submission of petitions for changes in tariff treatment.[39] Seven parties filed submissions in response to that request, but none of the submissions constituted petitions that were accepted for review.[40]

The USTR submits biennial reports to Congress on the operation of ATPA, including the results of its annual reviews.[41] The most recent USTR report on the operation of the ATPA program was issued in June 2010.[42] No actions have been taken to withdraw, suspend, or limit ATPDEA benefits on the basis of the USTR reviews.[43]

Table 1.1. ATPDEA: Key apparel and textile provisions

Articles eligible to enter free of duty and quota	Criteria
Apparel assembled in one or more ATPDEA beneficiary countries from fabrics or fabric components wholly formed, or components knit-to-shape, in the United States	• Apparel must be made from U.S. or Andean yarn. Knit and woven fabrics must be dyed, printed, and finished in the United States.
Apparel assembled from Andean fabrics or fabric components formed, or components knit-to-shape, of llama, alpaca, or vicuña	• Apparel must be made from Andean yarn. • Fabrics or components must be in chief value of llama, alpaca, or vicuña.

Table 1.1. (Continued)

Articles eligible to enter free of duty and quota	Criteria
Apparel cut and assembled from fabrics or yarns identified in Annex 401 of NAFTA as being not available in commercial quantities (in "short supply") in the United States (HTS 9821.11.10)	• The fabrics and yarns include fine-count cotton knitted fabrics for certain apparel; linen; silk; cotton velveteen; fine-wale corduroy; Harris Tweed; certain woven fabrics made with animal hairs; certain lightweight, high-thread-count polyester-cotton woven fabrics; and certain lightweight, high-thread-count broadwoven fabrics for use in men's and boys' shirts[a]
Apparel assembled in ATPDEA countries from fabrics or yarns deemed not available in commercial quantities at the request of any interested party	• President must determine that such fabrics or yarns cannot be supplied by the domestic industry in commercial quantities in a timely manner based on advice from the appropriate advisory committee and the USITC within 60 days after the request.
Apparel assembled in ATPDEA countries from regional fabrics or regional components formed or knit-to-shape in the region	• Apparel must be made from U.S. or Andean yarn. • Apparel is subject to cap.b
Certified handloomed, handmade, and folklore articles	• Articles must originate in ATPDEA countries.
Certain brassieres cut and sewn or otherwise assembled in the United States, or one or more ATPDEA countries, or both	• Producer must satisfy rule that, in each of four one-year periods starting on Oct. 1, 2003, at least 75 percent of the value of the fabric contained in the firm's brassieres in the preceding year was attributable to fabric components formed in the United States (the 75 percent standard rises to 85 percent for a producer found by Customs not to have met the 75 percent standard in the preceding year).
Apparel assembled in ATPDEA countries from qualifying fabrics that contain findings or trimmings of foreign origin	• Findings or trimmings may not exceed 25 percent of the cost of the components of the assembled product.
Apparel assembled in ATPDEA countries from qualifying fabrics that contain certain interlinings of foreign origin	• Value of such interlinings (and any findings and trimmings) may not exceed 25 percent of the cost of the components of the assembled article.
Apparel assembled in ATPDEA countries from qualifying fabrics that contain yarns not wholly formed in the United States or in one or more ATPDEA countries	• Total weight of such yarns may not exceed 7 percent of the total weight of the good.
Textile luggage assembled in ATPDEA countries from U.S. fabrics	• Luggage must be of U.S. yarn and U.S. fabric.

Source: Compiled by USITC staff from ATPDEA statute.

[a] As described in General Note 12(t), chapter rule 2 to Chapter 62 of the Harmonized Tariff Schedule from the NAFTA rules of origin.

[b] Maximum 2 percent of the aggregate SME of all apparel articles imported into the United States in the preceding 12- month period for which data are available, increased in equal increments in each succeeding one-year period to a maximum of 5 percent beginning Oct. 1, 2006. The 5 percent limit is still in effect.

ATPA and GSP

Colombia and Ecuador are GSP beneficiaries, as is Bolivia.[44] Peru was a GSP beneficiary until the U.S.-Peru TPA entered into force. ATPA and GSP provisions are similar in many ways, and many products can enter the United States free of duty under either program—all of the major imports from ATPA countries that are designated as GSPeligible are also ATPA-eligible. Both programs offer increased access to the U.S. market. Like ATPA, GSP requires that eligible imports (1) be imported directly from beneficiaries into the customs territory of the United States, (2) meet the (usually double) substantial transformation requirement for any foreign inputs, and (3) contain a minimum of 35 percent qualifying value content.

However, the two programs differ in several ways that tend to make ATPA country producers prefer the more comprehensive and liberal ATPA. First, ATPA authorizes duty-free treatment on more tariff categories than GSP, including textile and apparel articles ineligible for GSP treatment. Unless specifically excluded, all products can be designated as having a tariff preference under ATPA. Second, unlike under the U.S. GSP law, U.S. imports under ATPA are not subject to competitive-need and country-income restrictions. This fact means that imports of a product under ATPA will not lose their preferential treatment when they exceed a certain threshold, either in absolute terms or as a percentage of U.S. imports (the competitive need limit under GSP), nor will ATPA countries lose preferential treatment if their national incomes exceed a specified amount. Third, ATPA qualifying rules of origin for products are more liberal than those of GSP. GSP requires that 35 percent of the value of the product be added in a single beneficiary or in a specified association of GSP-eligible countries, whereas ATPA allows regional aggregation within ATPA, plus U.S. and Caribbean content.

Analytical Approach

The core of ATPA is the duty-free treatment importers can claim when entering qualifying products of designated beneficiary countries. The duty elimination for almost all eligible products occurred in single actions (rather than through staged duty reductions) when countries were designated as beneficiaries, first under original ATPA and later under ATPDEA. Direct effects of such a one-time duty elimination can be expected to consist primarily of increased U.S. imports from beneficiary countries resulting from trade and resource diversion to take advantage of lower duties in the U.S. market, including (1) a diversion of beneficiary-country production away from sales to domestic and non-U.S. foreign markets, and (2) a diversion of variable resources (such as labor and materials) away from production of other nonqualifying products for domestic and non-U.S. foreign markets. These direct effects likely occurred within a short time (probably one or two years) after the duty elimination, or by about 1992–93 for the original ATPA, and by about the end of 2004 for ATPDEA.

Over a longer period, the effects of ATPA will likely flow mostly from investment in industries in beneficiary countries that benefit from the U.S. duty elimination. Both the short-term and long-term effects on the United States are limited by the small size of the ATPA beneficiary-country economies relative to the U.S. economy. In addition, the longterm effects of ATPA on the U.S. economy are likely to be difficult to distinguish from other market forces in play, including the expiration—or anticipated expiration—of ATPA benefits, the entry into force of the FTA with Peru, and the uncertainties about whether and when the FTA with Colombia will enter into force. Investment data, therefore, were collected to examine the trends in, and composition of, export-oriented investment in the Andean region to assess the probable future effects of ATPA.

The effects of ATPA on the U.S. economy, industries, and consumers are assessed through (1) an analysis of imports entered under the program and trends in U.S. consumption of those imports; (2) estimates of gains to U.S. consumers due to lower prices or greater availability of goods, losses to the U.S. Treasury resulting from reduced tariff revenues, and potential displacement in U.S. industries competing with the leading U.S. imports that benefited exclusively from the ATPA program in 2009;[45] and (3) an examination of trends in production and other economic factors in the industries identified as likely to be particularly affected by such imports. General economic and trade data come from official statistics of the U.S. Department of Commerce and from materials developed by USITC country/regional and industry analysts. The report also incorporates public comments received in response to the Commission's *Federal Register* notice regarding the investigation, including both hearing testimony and written submissions.[46]

As in previous reports in this series, the effects of ATPA are analyzed by estimating the differences in benefits to U.S. consumers, levels of U.S. tariff revenues, and U.S. industry production that probably would have occurred if normal trade relations (NTR) tariffs[47] had been in place for beneficiary countries in 2009. Actual 2009 market conditions are compared with a hypothetical case in which NTR duties are imposed for the year. The effects of ATPA duty preferences for 2009 are estimated by using a standard economic approach for measuring the impact of a change in the prices of one or more goods. Specifically, a partial-equilibrium model (i.e., a sector-based analysis) is used to estimate the gains to consumers, losses in tariff revenues, and industry displacement for each of the 20 leading U.S. imports that benefited exclusively from ATPA during 2009.[48] Previous analyses in this series have shown that since ATPA went into effect, U.S. consumers have benefited from lower prices and higher consumption, competing U.S. producers have experienced lower sales, and tariff revenues to the U.S. Treasury have been lower.

Generally, the net welfare effect is measured by adding three components: (1) the change in consumer surplus, (2) the change in tariff revenues to the U.S. Treasury resulting from the ATPA duty reduction, and (3) the change in producer surplus.[49] The model used in this analysis assumes that the supply of U.S. domestic production is perfectly elastic; that is, U.S. domestic prices do not fall in response to ATPA duty reductions. Thus, price-related decreases in U.S. producer surplus are not captured in this analysis. However, the effects of ATPA duty reductions on most U.S. industries are expected to be small.

This analysis estimates potential net welfare effects and industry displacement, and these estimates reflect a range of assumed substitutabilities between ATPA products and competing U.S. output. The upper estimates reflect the assumption of high substitution elasticities,[50] whereas the lower estimates reflect the assumption of low substitution elasticities. Upper estimates are used to identify items that could be most affected by ATPA.

The Commission's analysis covers the 20 leading items that benefited exclusively from ATPA tariff preferences.[51] The analysis provides estimates of welfare and potential U.S. industry displacement. Industries for which estimated upper potential displacement is more than 5 percent of the value of U.S. production were selected for further analysis.

Commission analysis of the probable future effects of ATPA is based on a qualitative analysis of economic trends and investment patterns in beneficiary countries and in competing U.S. industries. The primary sources for information on investment in ATPA-related production facilities are U.S. embassies in the region, hearing testimony and written submissions, and published sources.

To assess the estimated effect of ATPA on the drug-crop eradication and crop substitution efforts of the beneficiary countries, the Commission relied primarily on information from other U.S. Government agencies, such as the U.S. Department of State and the Office of National Drug Control Policy.

Organization of the Report

This chapter summarizes the provisions of ATPA and describes the analytical approach used in the report. Chapter 2 analyzes U.S. merchandise trade with Bolivia, Colombia, Ecuador, and Peru during 2009, and general changes in trends since 2005; it also provides information on total U.S. imports from Andean countries, U.S. imports under ATPA,[52] and U.S. exports to the Andean countries. Chapter 3 analyzes imports that benefit exclusively from ATPA to estimate the impact of ATPA in 2009 on the U.S. economy generally, as well as on U.S. industries and consumers. Chapter 3 also examines the probable future effects of ATPA. Chapter 4 assesses the estimated effect of ATPA on the drug-crop eradication and crop substitution efforts of the Andean countries. Chapter 5 summarizes the positions of interested parties who appeared as witnesses at the July 7, 2010, public hearing or who provided written submissions in connection with this investigation.

Appendix A reproduces the *Federal Register* notice by which the Commission provided notice of a public hearing and solicited public comments. Appendix B provides the calendar of the public hearing held in connection with this investigation on July 7, 2010. Appendix C explains the economic model used to derive the findings presented in chapter 3. Appendix D provides additional statistical tables.

Data Sources

General economic and trade data come from official statistics of the U.S. Department of Commerce and from relevant information developed by country/regional and industry analysts of the Commission. Other primary sources of information include U.S. embassies in the Andean countries; other published sources for information on ATPArelated investment and production; and other U.S. government departments and offices, including the U.S. Department of State and the White House Office of National Drug Control Policy, for information on drug-crop eradication and crop substitution efforts. The report also incorporates testimony presented at the Commission's July 7, 2010, public hearing for this investigation as well as written public comments received in response to the Commission's *Federal Register* notice regarding the investigation.[53]

U.S. TRADE WITH THE ATPA COUNTRIES

Introduction

This chapter describes and analyzes U.S. imports under ATPA.[1] Total U.S. imports from the ATPA countries and U.S. exports to the ATPA countries are also examined. As indicated in chapter 1, calendar year 2009 was the seventh full year that ATPDEA was in effect. Since the 13th report, there have been two major changes that affected ATPA: (1) Bolivia lost ATPA eligibility as of December 15, 2008, and (2) the U.S.-Peru TPA entered into force on February 1, 2009.[2] Given the predominance of oil imports among products benefiting from ATPA and the relatively small preference margin provided by ATPA to imports of oil products, total imports and non-oil shares of imports under ATPA will be discussed separately.

The chapter is organized as follows. First, it presents trends in overall U.S. imports from the ATPA countries and the dutiable share of total imports from these countries. Next is an analysis of the leading U.S. imports under ATPA (which include imports eligible under the original ATPA, those eligible under ATPDEA, and those eligible under GSP or the U.S.-Peru TPA but entered under ATPA). Finally, the chapter examines the composition of, and trends in, U.S. exports to the ATPA countries. Data are also presented for U.S. trade with individual beneficiary countries. Data on imports that are entered exclusively under ATPA are examined in chapter 3.

Trade Overview

Since ATPA was enacted in 1991, U.S. trade with the ATPA countries has grown significantly. The value of U.S. imports from the ATPA countries was more than 300 percent larger in 2009 than in 1991, increasing from $5.0 billion in 1991 to $20.7 billion in 2009 (table 2.1), while the value of U.S. imports from the world increased 220 percent during the same period. Total U.S. imports from the ATPA countries more than doubled in value during the nine years from 1991 to 2000, increasing from $5.0 billion to $11.1 billion. Since the October 2002 implementation of ATPDEA, which significantly expanded the list of products eligible for duty-free treatment under ATPA, U.S. imports from ATPA countries more than doubled in value again, increasing from $11.6 billion in 2003 to $20.9 billion in 2007 and $28.5 billion in 2008, before declining 27.4 percent to $20.7 billion in 2009 (figure 2.1). U.S. imports from ATPA countries were about the same in 2009 as they were in 2007, reflecting the drop in commodity prices during 2009 after they spiked in 2008. The ATPA countries collectively accounted for 1.3 percent of U.S. imports in 2009, compared to 1.4 percent in 2008.

U.S. exports to the ATPA countries in 2009 were more than four times their value in 1991, while U.S. exports to the world increased by less than 150 percent. Exports to ATPA countries increased from $3.8 billion in 1991 to $14.6 billion in 2007 and $19.8 billion in 2008, before declining 15.5 percent to $16.7 billion in 2009. The ATPA countries collectively accounted for 1.8 percent of total U.S. exports in 2009, their highest share during the period covered in table 2.1. The U.S. merchandise trade deficit with the ATPA countries narrowed to $4.0 billion in 2009, compared to $8.7 billion in 2008 (table 2.1). The steep decline in the value of trade between the United States and the ATPA countries in 2009 can most likely be attributed to the global financial crisis and subsequent global recession, which led to a reduction in the volume of trade, as well as lower commodity prices.

Table 2.1. U.S. trade with ATPA countries, 1991–2009

Year	Exports to ATPA countries	Imports from ATPA countries	Trade balance with ATPA countries	ATPA countries' share of U.S exports to the world	ATPA countries' share of U.S. imports from the world	Average U.S. tariff[a] for ATPA countries
	Value (millions of $)				Percent	
1991	3,798	4,969	-1,171	0.9	1.0	1.9
1992	5,320	5,059	261	1.3	1.0	1.7
1993	5,359	5,282	77	1.2	0.9	1.5
1994	6,445	5,880	566	1.3	0.9	1.5
1995	7,820	6,969	851	1.4	0.9	1.2
1996	7,719	7,868	-149	1.3	1.0	1.1
1997	8,682	8,674	8	1.3	1.0	1.1
1998	8,670	8,361	309	1.4	0.9	1.3
1999	6,263	9,830	-3,567	1.0	1.0	1.3
2000	6,295	11,117	-4,822	0.9	0.9	1.3
2001	6,363	9,569	-3,205	1.0	0.8	1.5
2002	6,464	9,611	-3,148	1.0	0.8	1.8
2003	6,526	11,639	-5,114	1.0	0.9	0.6
2004	7,664	15,490	-7,826	1.1	1.1	0.3
2005	8,919	20,060	-11,141	1.1	1.2	0.2
2006	11,637	22,511	-10,874	1.3	1.2	0.1
2007	14,621	20,923	-6,302	1.4	1.1	0.1
2008	19,763	28,483	-8,720	1.7	1.4	0.1
2009[b]	16,697	20,690	-3,993	1.8	1.3	0.1

Source: Compiled from official statistics of the U.S. Department of Commerce.

a Trade-weighted average duty (total duties/total imports).

b Bolivia was not included in 2009.

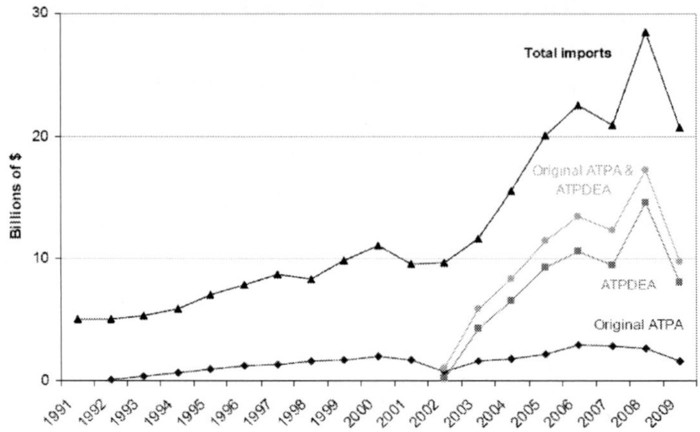

Source: Compiled from official statistics of the U.S. Department of Commerce.
[a] Bolivia was not included in 2009.
Figure 2.1. U.S. imports from Andean countries, under original ATPA, and ATPDEA, 1991–2009.

U.S. Imports from the ATPA Countries

In 2009, total U.S. imports from the ATPA countries collectively were $20.7 billion.[3] The United States continued to be the leading destination for exports from Colombia, Ecuador, and Peru.[4] U.S. imports from the ATPA countries consisted primarily of raw materials and their derivatives, agricultural and horticultural products, apparel, and seafood. Table 2.2 shows the composition of total U.S. imports from the ATPA countries by HS chapter during the years 2005–09. Mineral fuels and oils (HS chapter 27), precious stones and metals (HS 71), and coffee (HS 09) represented almost two-thirds of total U.S. imports from the ATPA countries in 2009. Mineral fuels and oils—mostly petroleum and coal—have accounted for around 50 percent of the value of total imports from ATPA countries in each of the last five years, with the exception of 2008, a year of historically high average oil prices, when the share was 59.4 percent. Imports of precious stones and metals, consisting mostly of gold bullion, but also including precious stones, metals, and jewelry, accounted for 9.9 percent of total imports from the ATPA countries in 2009 (or 20.2 percent of non-oil imports). Imports of coffee decreased 11.8 percent in 2009 to $941.6 million, and represented 4.6 percent of total imports in 2009 (or 9.3 percent of non-oil imports). In 2009, the value of imports of edible fruits and nuts (HS 08), 72.2 percent of which were bananas, increased by 17.9 percent to $821 million, or 4.0 percent of total imports (or 8.1 percent of non-oil imports). This latest increase in the edible fruit and nut imports is part of a 42.6 percent increase since 2005, mainly stemming from a 50 percent increase in imports of bananas.

Table 2.3 lists the leading U.S. imports from the ATPA countries in 2009 on an 8-digit HTS subheading basis. Since ATPDEA entered into effect in 2002, all of these products from the ATPA countries have been eligible for duty-free entry under ATPA, under GSP or the U.S.-Peru TPA, or at NTR duty rates. Products that have NTR duty rates of free include many traditional imports from the Andean countries: gold and silver bullion, coffee, coal, bananas, shrimp, unalloyed tin, and cocoa beans. Most of the products in table 2.3 decreased in import value in 2009, though imports of gold, bananas, cocoa beans, and petroleum coke all increased considerably.

Table 2.2. Leading U.S. imports for consumption from ATPA countries, by HS chapter, in value and share of non-oil imports for consumption, 2005–09

HS chapter	Description	2005	2006	2007	2008	2009[a]	Change 2008–09
		Value (millions of $)					Percent
27	Mineral fuels, mineral oils and products of their distillation; bituminous substances; mineral waxes	10,053.8	11,355.8	10,410.3	16,930.0	10,583.5	-37.5
71	Natural or cultured pearls, precious or semiprecious stones, precious metals; precious metal clad metals, articles thereof; imitation jewelry; coin	2,317.5	2,261.4	1,533.9	1,930.4	2,038.0	5.6
09	Coffee, tea, mate and spices	738.2	788.8	890.4	1,067.0	941.6	-11.8
08	Edible fruit and nuts; peel of citrus fruit or melons	575.9	646.1	597.1	696.2	821.0	17.9
61	Articles of apparel and clothing accessories, knitted or crocheted	978.8	1,024.7	949.0	915.7	678.5	-25.9
06	Live trees and other plants; bulbs, roots and the like; cut flowers and ornamental foliage	557.2	601.5	668.1	653.0	637.2	-2.4
03	Fish and crustaceans, molluscs and other aquatic invertebrates	483.1	537.2	574.2	603.2	612.4	1.5
74	Copper and articles thereof	593.9	1,050.8	1,073.4	937.9	589.5	-37.1
07	Edible vegetables and certain roots and tubers	193.9	223.0	272.9	286.3	289.6	1.2
80	Tin and articles thereof	195.9	270.8	326.7	460.2	266.1	-42.2
	Subtotal	16,688.1	18,760.2	17,296.0	24,479.8	17,457.5	-28.7
	All other	3,372.0	3,750.4	3,627.0	4,003.2	3,232.3	-19.3
	Total	20,060.1	22,510.6	20,922.9	28,483.0	20,689.9	-27.4
		Percent of total imports					In percentage points
27	Mineral fuels, mineral oils and products of their distillation; bituminous substances; mineral waxes	50.1	50.4	49.8	59.4	51.2	-8.3
			Percent of non-oil total				
71	Natural or cultured pearls, precious or semiprecious stones, precious metals; precious metal clad metals, articles thereof; imitation jewelry; coin	23.2	20.3	14.6	16.7	20.2	3.5
09	Coffee, tea, mate and spices	7.4	7.1	8.5	9.2	9.3	0.1
08	Edible fruit and nuts; peel of citrus fruit or melons	5.8	5.8	5.7	6.0	8.1	2.1
61	Articles of apparel and clothing accessories, knitted or crocheted	9.8	9.2	9.0	7.9	6.7	-1.2

Table 2.2. (Continued)

HS chapter	Description	2005	2006	2007	2008	2009[a]	Change 2008–09
06	Live trees and other plants; bulbs, roots and the like; cut flowers and ornamental foliage	5.6	5.4	6.4	5.7	6.3	0.7
03	Fish and crustaceans, molluscs and other aquatic invertebrates	4.8	4.8	5.5	5.2	6.1	0.8
74	Copper and articles thereof	5.9	9.4	10.2	8.1	5.8	-
07	Edible vegetables and certain roots and tubers	1.9	2.0	2.6	2.5	2.9	0.4
80	Tin and articles thereof	2.0	2.4	3.1	4.0	2.6	-
	Subtotal	66.3	66.4	65.5	65.3	68.0	2.7
	All other	33.7	33.6	34.5	34.7	32.0	-
	Total	100.0	100.0	100.0	100.0	100.0	

Source: Compiled from official statistics of the U.S. Department of Commerce. a Bolivia was not included in 2009.
a Bolivia was not included in 2009.

Table 2.3. Leading U.S. imports for consumption from ATPA countries, by HTS provisions, 2005–09

HTS	Description	2005	2006	2007	2008	2009[a]	Change
			Millions of $				Percent
2709.00.10	Petroleum oils and oils from bituminous minerals, crude, testing under 25 degrees A.P.I.	5,584.4	6,193.4	5,999.1	11,042.9	7,273.7	-34.1
7108.12.10	Gold, nonmonetary, bullion and dore	1,856.	1,565.	632.1	867.0	1,643.	89.6
2709.00.20	Petroleum oils and oils from bituminous minerals, crude, testing 25 degrees A.P.I. or more	1,961.7	2,416.5	1,819.3	2,147.6	1,049.4	-51.1
2701.12.00	Coal, bituminous, whether or not pulverized, but not agglomerated	637.9	769.4	771.7	1,001.	802.1	-19.9
0901.11.00	Coffee, not roasted, not decaffeinated	638.0	678.5	766.1	902.8	780.0	-13.6
0803.00.20	Bananas, fresh or dried	394.2	445.6	385.8	446.6	592.9	32.8
7403.11.00	Refined copper cathodes and sections of cathodes	556.4	993.0	989.1	844.4	548.3	-35.1

HTS	Description	2005	2006	2007	2008	2009[a]	Change
			Millions of $				Percent
2710.19.05	Distillate and residual fuel oil (including blends) derived from petroleum or oils from bituminous minerals, testing under 25 degrees a.p.i.	797.2	602.0	712.8	938.1	474.2	-49.5
0306.13.00	Shrimps and prawns, cooked in shell or uncooked, dried, salted or in brine, frozen	309.4	365.0	355.9	392.0	376.8	-3.9
0603.11.00[b]	Sweetheart, spray and other roses, fresh cut	263.3	288.6	327.6	310.6	305.2	-1.8
2701.19.00	Coal, other than anthracite or bituminous, whether or not pulverized, but not agglomerated	313.0	414.3	467.7	491.8	275.8	-43.9
8001.10.00	Tin (o/than alloy), unwrought	181.7	255.0	324.8	455.4	266.1	-41.6
2710.11.25	Naphthas (exc. motor fuel/mtr fuel blend. stock) fr petroleum oils & bitumen minerals (o/than crude) or preps 70%+ by wt. fr petroleum oils	553.2	723.0	466.7	666.2	248.2	-62.7
6110.20.20	Sweaters, pullovers and similar articles, knitted or crocheted, of cotton, n.e.s.o.i.	297.4	320.9	302.1	244.3	197.8	-19.0
0603.19.00[c]	Fresh cut, anthuriums,alstroemeria,gypsophilia,lilies, snapdragons and flowers, n.e.s.o.i.	159.8	172.3	191.0	196.1	189.0	-3.6
1801.00.00	Cocoa beans, whole or broken, raw or roasted	46.6	32.0	60.8	95.9	177.1	84.7
7106.91.10	Silver bullion and dore	151.7	180.9	340.5	596.1	149.5	-74.9
2713.11.00	Coke, petroleum, not calcined	15.6	48.5	18.6	39.4	144.4	266.8
0709.20.90	Asparagus, n.e.s.o.i., fresh or chilled	87.4	126.8	159.4	145.2	137.5	-5.3
6109.10.00	T-shirts, singlets, tank tops and similar garments, knitted or crocheted, of	165.9	172.6	158.0	166.3	133.9	-19.5
	Subtotal	14,97	16,76	15,24	21,99	15,76	-28.3
	All other	5,089.	5,746.	5,674.	6,492.	4,924.	-24.2
	Total	20,06	22,51	20,92	28,48	20,68	-27.4

Source: Compiled from official statistics of the U.S. Department of Commerce.

Note: The abbreviation "n.e.s.o.i." stands for "not elsewhere specified or otherwise included."

[a] Bolivia was not included in 2009.

[b] Imports of HTS 0603.11.00 were reported under HTS 0603.10.60 during 2005–06.

[c] Imports of HTS 0603.19.00 were reported under HTS 0603.10.80 during 2005–06.

Duty Treatment

While the share of dutiable imports from the ATPA countries declined to 6.0 percent in 2006, they have since more than doubled to 12.2 percent in 2009 (table 2.4).[5] In 2009, dutiable imports from the region included principally those petroleum products that were not entered under ATPA preferences.

Duty-free imports from the ATPA countries entered in one of the following ways in 2009: (1) conditionally free of duty under ATPA (47.0 percent of all imports from the ATPA countries); (2) unconditionally free of duty under NTR tariff rates (35.0 percent); (3) conditionally free of duty under GSP or other special programs (1.3 percent); and most recently (4) conditionally free of duty under the Peru TPA (4.3 percent).[6]

Table 2.4. U.S. imports for consumption from ATPA countries, by duty treatments, 2005–09

Duty treatment	2005	2006	2007	2008	2009[a]
		Value (millions of $)			
Dutiable imports	1,561.8	1,344.6	1,292.8	2,587.3	2,515.0
Duty-free value:					
NTR duty-free	6,379.8	6,958.9	6,462.9	7,818.8	7,235.8
ATPA:					
Exclusive	10,648.1	12,531.1	11,488.3	16,360.8	7,963.5
Non-exclusive	815.6	953.2	818.5	881.9	1,750.8
Total ATPA	11,463.7	13,484.4	12,306.8	17,242.7	9,714.2
GSP	448.2	453.9	599.3	611.6	271.7
Peru FTA	0.0	0.0	0.0	0.0	898.1
Other duty-free	([b])	0.0	0.0	0.0	898.1
Total duty-free value	18,291.7	20,897.4	19,369.6	25,673.9	18,121.5
U.S. Virgin Islands[c]	206.5	268.6	260.5	221.8	53.4
Total imports	20,060.1	22,510.6	20,922.9	28,483.0	20,689.9
		Percent of total			
Dutiable imports	7.8	6.0	6.2	9.1	12.2
Duty-free value:					
NTR duty-free	31.8	30.9	30.9	27.5	35.0
ATPA:					
Exclusive	53.1	55.7	54.9	57.4	38.5
Non-exclusive	4.1	4.2	3.9	3.1	8.5
Total ATPA	57.1	59.9	58.8	60.5	47.0

Duty treatment	2005	2006	2007	2008	2009a
		Value (millions of $)			
GSP	2.2	2.0	2.9	2.1	1.3
Peru FTA	0.0	0.0	0.0	0.0	4.3
Other duty-free	([d])	([d])	([d])	([d])	([d])
Total duty-free value	91.2	92.8	92.6	90.1	87.6
U.S. Virgin Islands[c]	1.0	1.2	1.2	0.8	0.3
Total imports	100.0	100.0	100.0	100.0	100.0

Source: Compiled from official statistics of the U.S. Department of Commerce.

a Bolivia was not included in 2009.

b Value is less than 50,000.

c The U.S. Virgin Islands has its own tariff schedule and laws separate from the rest of the United States and is outside the U.S. customs territory; therefore, imports that enter the U.S. Virgin Islands are not identified as either dutiable or free of duty.

d Value is less than 0.05 percent.

Imports under ATPA

U.S. imports under ATPA in 2009 were $9.7 billion, compared to $17.2 billion in 2008 and $12.3 billion in 2007 (figure 2.2). Although the decline in the value of U.S. imports entered under ATPA in 2009 was mostly attributable to a $6.0 billion decline in the value of imports of petroleum and petroleum products (HS 2709 and 2710), the entry into force of the U.S.-Peru TPA had a fairly large impact, while Bolivia's ineligibility in 2009 had a much smaller impact. Imports under ATPA accounted for a 0.6 percent share of total U.S. imports in 2009, or about the same as in 2007.

Product Composition and Leading Import Categories

In 2009, imports under ATPA were primarily in three broad categories: natural resources, apparel, and agricultural and fisheries products. Natural resources included petroleum and petroleum products (HS 2709 and 2710, hereafter also referred to as "oil") and copper cathodes (HTS 7403.11.00). Apparel products consisted mostly of knitted (HS 61) and nonknitted apparel (HS 62). Agricultural products included primarily cut flowers (HS 0603); fresh asparagus (HS 0709.20); edible fruit and nuts (HS 08); prepared vegetables, fruits, and nuts (HS 20); and tuna (HS 1604.14). Plastics (HS 39) was also a significant import product category. Taken together, these goods accounted for more than 95 percent of total imports under ATPA in 2009, and are analyzed in more detail below.

Figure 2.3 and table 2.5 illustrate the dominance of petroleum and petroleum products (HS 2709 and 2710) in imports under ATPA during the period 2005–2009. In 2009, imports of petroleum and petroleum products under ATPA were $7.4 billion and accounted for 75.8 percent of imports under ATPA. This represents a decrease of $6.0 billion, or a 44.9 percent decline compared to 2008, and a decrease of $861 million, or a 10.5 percent decline compared to 2007. Petroleum and petroleum products accounted for more than 95 percent of the total increase in imports under ATPA from 2007 to 2008. Likewise, petroleum and petroleum products accounted for about 80 percent of the total decline in imports under ATPA from 2008 to 2009. As shown in figure 2.4, a 40.5 percent decline in unit values from 2008 to 2009 led the value of imports of crude oil (HTS 2709.00.10 and 2709.00.20) to decline 43.0 percent from $12.2 billion in 2008 to $7.0 billion in 2009, while imports decreased 4.2 percent to 128 million barrels in terms of quantity. Imports of crude oil under ATPA have not been lower in value since 2005, when the import value was also $7.0 billion.

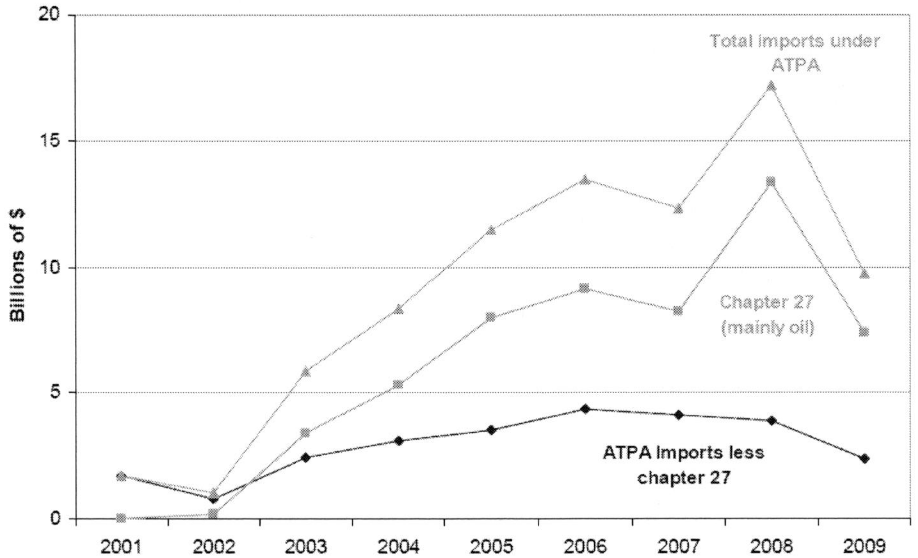

Source: Compiled from official statistics of the U.S. Department of Commerce.
Figure 2.2. U.S. imports under ATPA, 2001–09.

In addition to the steep decline in the value of oil imports from 2008 to 2009, the value and structure of non-oil imports under ATPA changed markedly during that period. For example, although the value of imports of cut flowers (HS 0603) under ATPA declined 1.3 percent in 2009, this decline was much smaller than it was for other major categories. As a result, the cut flowers (HS 0603) share of non-oil imports under ATPA increased from 16.3 percent in 2008 to 26.6 percent in 2009.[7] Imports of knitted or crocheted apparel (HS 61) under ATPA decreased 44.9 percent to $490.3 million in 2009, although knitted or crocheted apparel almost maintained its entire share of non-oil imports under ATPA as compared to 2006 through 2008. Imports of copper cathodes (HTS 7403.11.00), which were more than 20 percent of non-oil imports under ATPA from 2006 to 2008, made up only 9.3 percent of non-oil imports in 2009, primarily because a large portion of imports of copper cathodes were entered under the U.S.-Peru TPA (table 2.5 and figure 2.3). Imports of prepared fruits and vegetables (HS 20) under ATPA declined 16.1 percent in 2009, though their share of non-oil imports continued to increase, from 4.5 percent in 2008 to 6.2 percent in 2009, despite the effects of the U.S.-Peru TPA. Imports under ATPA of nonknitted apparel (HS 62), edible fruits and nuts (HS 08), tuna (HS 1604.14), and plastics (HS 39) all decreased in terms of import value but increased in terms of share of non-oil imports in 2009. However, imports of asparagus (HS 0709.20) under ATPA declined in terms of both value and share of non-oil imports, as the majority were entered under the U.S.-Peru TPA instead of under ATPA.

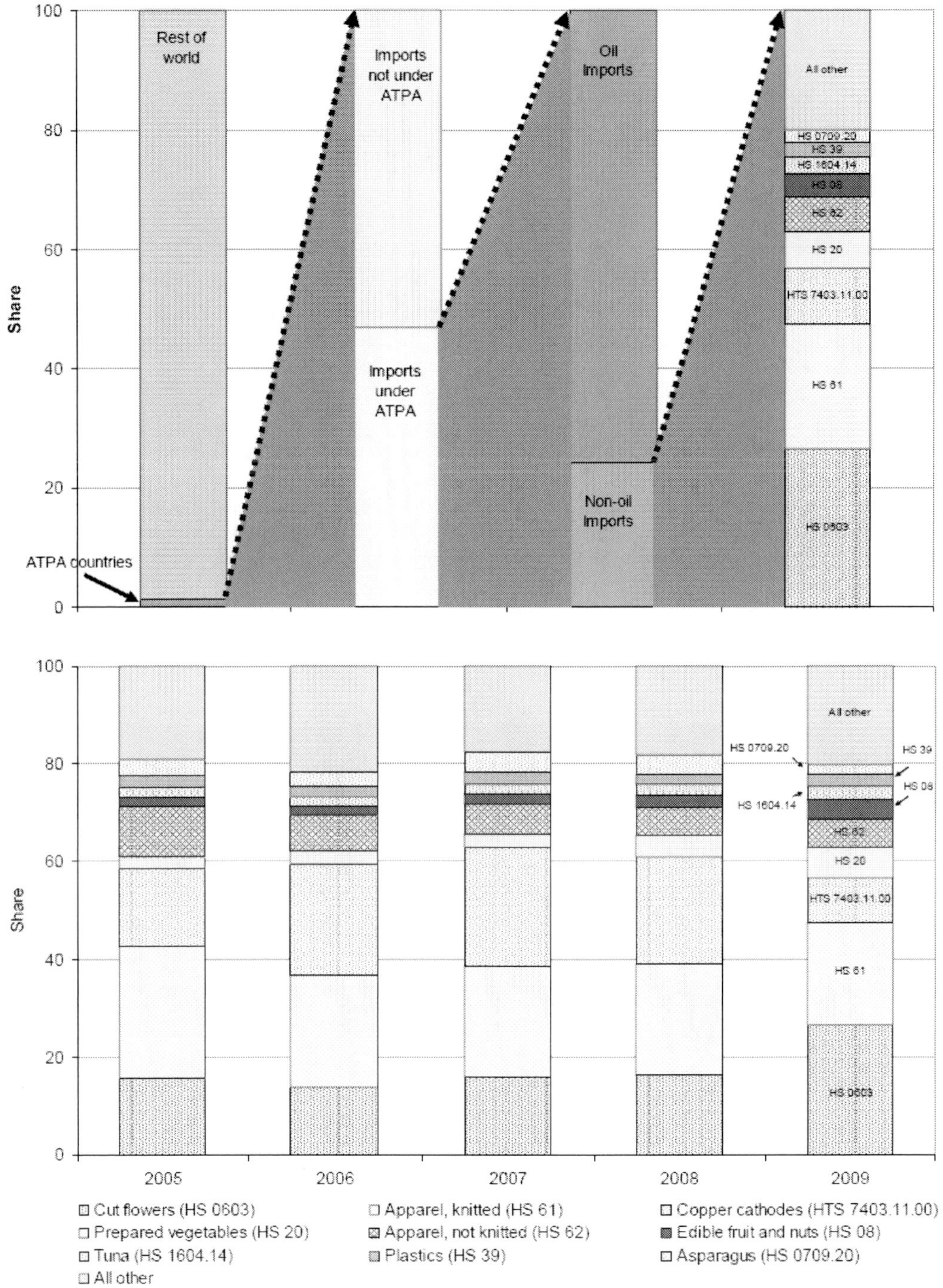

Source: Compiled from official statistics of the U.S. Department of Commerce.

a Bolivia was not included in 2009.

Figure 2.3. U.S. imports for consumption from the world and Andean countries as shares, 2009, and U.S. non-oil imports for consumption under ATPA as shares, 2005–09.

Table 2.5. Leading U.S. imports for consumption entered under ATPA, by major product categories, in value and share of non-oil imports, 2005–09

Product category (HS/HTS code)	2005	2006	2007	2008	2009	Change 2008–09
		Value (millions of $)				Percent
Petroleum oils and oils obtained from bituminous minerals (HS 2709 & 2710)	7,951.8	9,138.4	8,224.9	13,353.	7,363.	-44.9
Cut flowers and buds suitable for bouquets or ornamental purposes, fresh, dried, dyed, bleached, impregnated or otherwise prepared (HS 0603)	548.7	593.0	651.7	633.3	625.1	-1.3
Articles of apparel and clothing accessories, knitted or crocheted (HS 61)	953.6	1,000.0	922.0	889.2	490.3	-44.9
Refined copper cathodes and sections of cathodes (HTS 7403.11.00)	556.4	993.0	989.1	844.4	218.4	-74.1
Preparations of vegetables, fruit, nuts, or other parts of plants (HS 20)	80.4	115.4	118.9	174.8	146.6	-16.1
Articles of apparel and clothing accessories, not knitted or crocheted (HS 62)	364.7	321.3	243.7	219.5	134.3	-38.8
Edible fruit and nuts; peel of citrus fruit or melons (HS 08)	62.7	77.8	87.8	99.2	92.7	-6.5
Tunas, skipjack and bonito (sarda spp), prepared or preserved, whole or in pieces, but not minced (HS 1604.14)	68.2	81.5	76.7	84.2	63.9	-24.2
Plastics and articles thereof (HS 39)	93.3	93.2	111.0	82.7	60.4	-26.9
Asparagus, fresh or chilled (HS 0709.20)	110.7	131.0	162.5	153.5	45.9	-70.1
Subtotal	10,790.	12,544.	11,588.4	16,534.	9,241.	-44.1
All other	673.4	939.9	718.4	708.5	472.9	-33.3
Total	11,463.	13,484.	12,306.8	17,242.	9,714.	-43.7
		Percent of total imports				In
Petroleum oils and oils obtained from bituminous minerals (HS 2709 & 2710)	69.4	67.8	66.8	77.4	75.8	-1.6
		Percent of non-oil total				
Cut flowers and buds suitable for bouquets or ornamental purposes, fresh, dried, dyed, bleached, impregnated or otherwise prepared (HS 0603)	15.6	13.6	16.0	16.3	26.6	10.3
Articles of apparel and clothing accessories, knitted or crocheted (HS 61)	27.2	23.0	22.6	22.9	20.9	-2.0
Refined copper cathodes and sections of cathodes (HTS 7403.11.00)	15.8	22.8	24.2	21.7	9.3	-12.4

Product category (HS/HTS code)	2005	2006	2007	2008	2009	Change
		Value (millions of $)				Percent
Preparations of vegetables, fruit, nuts, or other parts of plants (HS 20)	2.3	2.7	2.9	4.5	6.2	1.7
Articles of apparel and clothing accessories, not knitted or crocheted (HS 62)	10.4	7.4	6.0	5.6	5.7	0.1
Edible fruit and nuts; peel of citrus fruit or melons (HS 08)	1.8	1.8	2.2	2.6	3.9	1.4
Tunas, skipjack and bonito (sarda spp), prepared or preserved, whole or in pieces, but not minced (HS 1604.14)	1.9	1.9	1.9	2.2	2.7	0.6
Plastics and articles thereof (HS 39)	2.7	2.1	2.7	2.1	2.6	0.4
Asparagus, fresh or chilled (HS 0709.20)	3.2	3.0	4.0	3.9	2.0	-2.0
Subtotal	80.8	78.4	82.4	81.8	79.9	-1.9
All other	19.2	21.6	17.6	18.2	20.1	1.9
Total	100.0	100.0	100.0	100.0	100.0	

Source: Compiled from official statistics of the U.S. Department of Commerce.

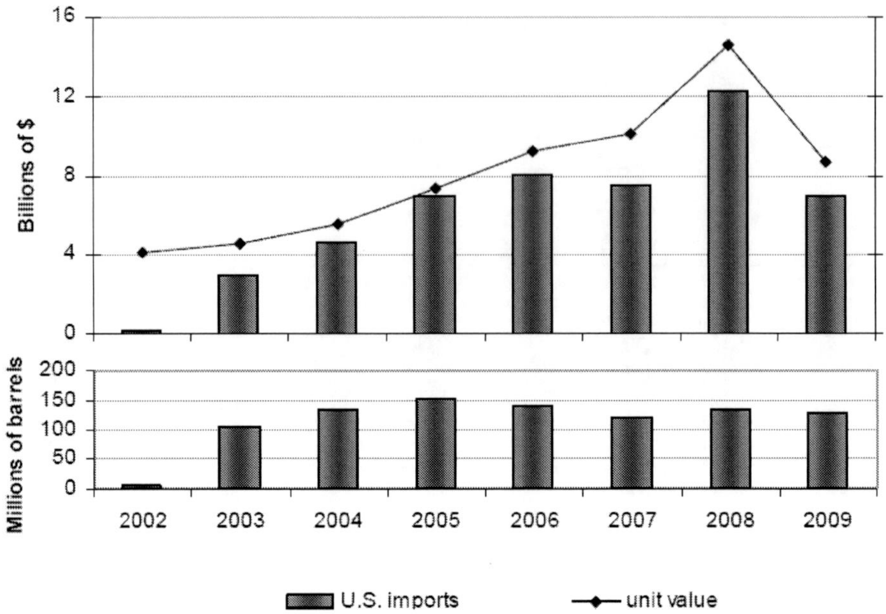

Source: Compiled from official statistics of the U.S. Department of Commerce.

Figure 2.4. U.S. imports of crude oil (HTS 2709.00.10 and 2709.00.20) under ATPA, 2002–09.

Imports under ATPA by Country

The share of imports under ATPA by country shifted considerably in 2009, driven primarily by the entry into force of the U.S.-Peru TPA and, to a small extent, by the suspension of Bolivia as a beneficiary country and the decline in the price of petroleum and petroleum products. For instance, Colombia's share of U.S. imports under the program increased from 42.6 percent in 2008 to 57.5 percent in 2009 mainly because oil imports did not constitute as large a share of imports from Colombia under ATPA (81.7 percent) as they did for Ecuador (87.8 percent, tables 2.6 and 2.7). Conversely, Ecuador's share of U.S. imports under ATPA decreased from 38.2 percent in 2008 to 28.3 percent in 2009 because imports from Ecuador under ATPA are more concentrated in oil (87.8 percent). Peru's share of imports under ATPA decreased from 18.4 percent of total U.S. imports under ATPA in 2008 to 14.2 percent in 2009, because some imports entered under the U.S.-Peru TPA, which entered into force on February 1, 2009. There were no imports under ATPA from Bolivia in 2009 because of its suspension from ATPA; however, the share of imports under ATPA from Bolivia has always been small, accounting for only 0.8 percent of total imports under ATPA in 2008.

Non-oil U.S. imports under ATPA declined 39.6 percent to $2.4 billion in 2009. The share of non-oil imports under ATPA by country also shifted considerably in 2009, driven primarily by the entry into force of the U.S.-Peru TPA. Peru's share of non-oil imports under ATPA decreased from 59.1 percent in 2008 to 42.2 percent in 2009, as at least $730 million in imports that would have formerly entered under ATPA instead entered free of duty under the U.S.-Peru TPA. Colombia's share of U.S. non-oil imports under ATPA increased from 29.6 in 2008 to 42.2 in 2009, mainly because imports of many of its agricultural products such as cut flowers (HS 0603), remained at roughly the same level or increased slightly. Ecuador's share of non-oil imports under ATPA increased from 9.6 percent in 2008 to 14.3

percent in 2009. The country-specific sections below give more information about selected imports under ATPA. Leading U.S. imports entered under ATPA, by country, are shown in table 2.8.

Table 2.6. Leading U.S. imports for consumption entered under ATPA, by major product categories, by source, in value and share of non-oil imports, 2009

Product category (HS/HTS code)	Colombi	Ecuador	Peru	ATPA
		Value (millions of $)		
Petroleum oils and oils obtained from bituminous minerals (HS 2709 & 2710)	4,567.2	2,412.5	384.1	7,363.8
Cut flowers and buds suitable for bouquets or ornamental purposes, fresh, dried, dyed, bleached, impregnated or otherwise prepared (HS 0603)	505.9	118.3	1.0	625.1
Articles of apparel and clothing accessories, knitted or crocheted (HS 61)	100.4	6.5	383.4	490.3
Refined copper cathodes and sections of cathodes (HTS 7403.11.00)	3.0	0.0	215.5	218.4
Preparations of vegetables, fruit, nuts, or other parts of plants (HS 20)	19.5	35.9	91.1	146.6
Articles of apparel and clothing accessories, not knitted or crocheted (HS 62)	109.5	0.7	24.1	134.3
Edible fruit and nuts; peel of citrus fruit or melons (HS	2.1	35.1	55.6	92.7
Tunas, skipjack and bonito (sarda spp), prepared or preserved, whole or in pieces, but not minced (HS 1604.14)	6.7	57.2	0.0	63.9
Plastics and articles thereof (HS 39)	53.2	0.9	6.4	60.4
Asparagus, fresh or chilled (HS 0709.20)	0.1	0.3	45.5	45.9
Subtotal	5,367.4	2,667.3	1,206.6	9,241.
All other	222.1	81.1	169.7	472.9
Total	5,589.5	2,748.4	1,376.3	9,714.
		Percent of total		
Petroleum oils and oils obtained from bituminous minerals (HS 2709 & 2710)	81.7	87.8	27.9	75.8
		Percent of non-oil		
Cut flowers and buds suitable for bouquets or ornamental purposes, fresh, dried, dyed, bleached, impregnated or otherwise prepared (HS 0603)	49.5	35.2	0.1	26.6
Articles of apparel and clothing accessories, knitted or crocheted (HS 61)	9.8	1.9	38.6	20.9
Refined copper cathodes and sections of cathodes (HTS 7403.11.00)	0.3	0.0	21.7	9.3
Preparations of vegetables, fruit, nuts, or other parts of plants (HS 20)	1.9	10.7	9.2	6.2

Table 2.6. (Continued)

Product category (HS/HTS code)	Colombi	Ecuador	Peru	ATPA
		Value (millions of $)		
Articles of apparel and clothing accessories, not knitted or crocheted (HS 62)	10.7	0.2	2.4	5.7
Edible fruit and nuts; peel of citrus fruit or melons (HS	0.2	10.4	5.6	3.9
Tunas, skipjack and bonito (sarda spp), prepared or preserved, whole or in pieces, but not minced (HS 1604.14)	0.7	17.0	0.0	2.7
Plastics and articles thereof (HS 39)	5.2	0.3	0.6	2.6
Asparagus, fresh or chilled (HS 0709.20)	0.0	0.1	4.6	2.0
Subtotal	78.3	75.9	82.9	79.9
All other	21.7	24.1	17.1	20.1
Total	100.0	100.0	100.0	100.0

Source: Compiled from official statistics of the U.S. Department of Commerce.

Table 2.7. U.S. imports entered under ATPA, by source, 2005–09

Market	2005	2006	2007	2008	2009	Change 2008–09
		Value (millions of $)				Percent
Colombia	4,653	4,791	4,528	7,339	5,589	-23.8
Ecuador	4,371	5,325	4,614	6,595	2,748	-58.3
Peru	2,283	3,202	3,017	3,169	1,376	-56.6
Bolivia	157	166	148	140	([a])	-100.0
Total	11,464	13,484	12,307	17,243	9,714	-43.7
	Percent of total imports under ATPA					In percentage points
Colombia	40.6	35.5	36.8	42.6	57.5	15.0
Ecuador	38.1	39.5	37.5	38.2	28.3	-10.0
Peru	19.9	23.7	24.5	18.4	14.2	-4.2
Bolivia	1.4	1.2	1.2	0.8	([a])	-0.8
Total	100.0	100.0	100.0	100.0	100.0	

Source: Compiled from official statistics of the U.S. Department of Commerce.
a Bolivia was not included in 2009.

Ecuador

The value of U.S. imports from Ecuador under ATPA was $2.7 billion in 2009, down from $6.6 billion in 2008, a decline of 58.3 percent. Imports under ATPA in 2009 consisted primarily of petroleum and petroleum products, cut flowers, tuna, and raw and prepared fruits and vegetables (tables 2.6 and 2.8). Petroleum and petroleum products (HS 2709 and 2710) accounted for 87.8 percent of all imports under ATPA from Ecuador in 2009. Ecuador was the sixth largest source for U.S. imports of heavy crude petroleum (HTS 2709.00.10) in 2009, accounting for 5.0 percent of U.S. imports. The value of imports of heavy crude petroleum decreased 61.7 percent compared to 2008, to $2.3 billion, and accounted for almost all petroleum and petroleum product imports under ATPA from Ecuador. In terms of quantity, imports of heavy crude petroleum under ATPA from Ecuador decreased 32.1 percent to 46.7 million barrels in 2009.

Table 2.8. Leading U.S. imports for consumption entered under ATPA, by major product categories, by source, 2005–09

Source	Product category (HTS code)	2005	2006	2007	2008	2009	Change 2008–09
		Millions of $					Percent
Bolivia	Petroleum oils and oils obtained from bituminous minerals (HS 2709 & 2710)	44.5	27.1	37.3	71.6	0.0	-100.0
	Jewelry and parts thereof, of precious metal other than silver (HS 7113.19)	62.7	71.4	57.3	28.4	0.0	-100.0
	Articles of apparel and clothing accessories, knitted or crocheted (HS 61)	33.9	29.7	17.2	9.9	0.0	-100.0
	Jewelry articles of precious or semiprecious stones, valued over $40 per piece (HTS 7116.20.15)	([b])	0.0	0.0	7.8	0.0	-100.0
	Gold (including gold plated with platinum), nonmonetary, in semimanufactured forms (except gold leaf), n.e.s.o.i. (HTS 7108.13.70)	([b])	0.0	0.2	6.6	0.0	-100.0
	Subtotal	141.2	128.3	112.0	124.3	0.0	-100.0
	All other	16.2	37.9	36.2	15.6	0.0	-100.0
	Total	157.4	166.2	148.1	140.0	0.0	-100.0
Colombia	Petroleum oils and oils obtained from bituminous minerals (HS 2709 & 2710)	3,351.7	3,386.2	3,293.8	6,189.2	4,567.2	-26.2
	Cut flowers and buds suitable for bouquets or ornamental purposes, fresh, dried, dyed, bleached, impregnated or otherwise prepared (HS 0603)	417.5	448.1	506.3	498.6	505.9	1.4
	Articles of apparel and clothing accessories, not knitted or crocheted (HS 62)	311.4	271.2	196.1	177.9	109.5	-38.5
	Articles of apparel and clothing accessories, knitted or crocheted (HS 61)	166.3	181.3	143.4	135.1	100.4	-25.7
	Plastics and articles thereof (HS 39)	89.8	85.3	100.8	74.5	53.2	-28.7
	Subtotal	4,336.7	4,372.1	4,240.3	7,075.4	5,336.1	-24.6
	All other	316.5	419.1	287.4	263.8	253.4	-4.0
	Total	4,653.2	4,791.2	4,527.7	7,339.2	5,589.5	-23.8

Table 2.8. (Continued)

Source	Product category (HTS code)	2005	2006	2007	2008	2009	Change 2008–09
			Millions of $				Percent
Ecuador	Petroleum oils and oils obtained from bituminous minerals (HS 2709 & 2710)	4,025.9	4,916.7	4,235.6	6,221.6	2,412.5	-61.2
	Cut flowers and buds suitable for bouquets or ornamental purposes, fresh, dried, dyed, bleached, impregnated or otherwise prepared (HS 0603)	129.1	141.1	143.2	132.6	118.3	-10.8
	Tunas, skipjack and bonito (*sarda* spp), prepared or preserved, whole or in pieces, but not minced (HS 1604.14)	68.2	81.5	76.7	82.9	57.2	-31.0
	Preparations of vegetables, fruit, nuts, or other parts of plants (HS 20)	20.9	24.4	23.0	28.1	35.9	27.7
	Edible fruit and nuts; peel of citrus fruit or melons (HS 08)	26.3	30.3	31.6	27.5	35.1	27.5
	Subtotal	4,270.4	5,194.1	4,510.1	6,492.7	2,659.0	-59.0
	All other	100.3	131.1	103.7	102.1	89.5	-12.4
	Total	4,370.7	5,325.2	4,613.8	6,594.8	2,748.4	-58.3
Peru	Petroleum oils and oils obtained from bituminous minerals (HS 2709 & 2710)	529.7	808.3	658.3	871.1	384.1	-55.9
	Articles of apparel and clothing accessories, knitted or crocheted (HS 61)	738.9	777.4	746.2	733.9	383.4	-47.8
	Refined copper cathodes and sections of cathodes (HTS 7403.11.00)	556.4	993.0	989.1	844.4	215.5	-74.5
	Preparations of vegetables, fruit, nuts, or other parts of plants (HS 20)	50.2	77.1	81.3	129.2	91.1	-29.5
	Edible fruit and nuts; peel of citrus fruit or melons (HS 08)	31.2	40.2	49.6	66.1	55.6	-15.9
	Subtotal	1,906.3	2,695.9	2,524.4	2,644.7	1,129.7	-57.3
	All other	376.3	505.9	492.8	524.0	246.6	-52.9
	Total	2,282.7	3,201.9	3,017.2	3,168.7	1,376.3	-56.6

Source: Compiled from official statistics of the U.S. Department of Commerce.

Note: The abbreviation "n.e.s.o.i." stands for "not elsewhere specified or otherwise included."

[a] Bolivia was not included in 2009.

[b] Value is less than $50,000.

Cut flowers (HS 0603) was the second-largest category of imports under ATPA from Ecuador in 2009.[8] Cut flowers accounted for $118.3 million in U.S. imports under ATPA from Ecuador in 2009, a decrease of 10.8 percent from 2008. Although cut flowers were only 4.3 percent of U.S. imports under ATPA from Ecuador in 2009, they were 35.2 percent of non-oil imports under ATPA from Ecuador. Imports of Ecuadorian cut flowers under ATPA in 2009 included roses (51.0 percent), carnations (0.2 percent), chrysanthemums (0.2 percent), and other cut flowers (48.5 percent).[9]

The value of imports of tuna (HS 1604.14) under ATPA from Ecuador, 99.6 percent of which were composed of imports of tuna in flexible airtight containers (HS 1604.14.1010, 1604.14.2291, 1604.14.3051, and 1604.14.3091, referred to as "pouched tuna"), decreased 31.0 percent, dropping from $82.9 million in 2008 to $57.2 million in 2009. Such imports constituted 2.1 percent of imports under ATPA from Ecuador (17.0 percent of the non-oil imports under ATPA). Except for in 2009, imports of pouched tuna from Ecuador have increased every year since ATDEA made them eligible for duty-free access in 2002, while imports of tuna not packed in airtight containers (HTS 1604.14.40, referred to as "loins") are near elimination. The reason for this shift is primarily the closing of canneries in the United States and Puerto Rico that had been importing loins for processing.[10] Ecuador is the third-largest source of U.S. tuna imports, after Thailand and the Philippines.

Colombia

U.S. imports from Colombia under ATPA were $5.6 billion in 2009, down from $7.3 billion in 2008. Imports from Colombia under ATPA in 2009 consisted primarily of petroleum and petroleum products, cut flowers, apparel, and plastics (tables 2.6 and 2.8). Petroleum and petroleum products (HS 2709 and 2710) accounted for 81.7 percent ($4.6 billion) of all imports under ATPA from Colombia in 2009, compared to 84.3 percent ($6.2 billion) in 2008. In 2009, Colombia was the fifth-largest U.S. source of heavy crude petroleum (HTS 2709.00.10) and the 13th-largest U.S. source of light crude petroleum (HTS 2709.00.20). From 2008 to 2009, imports of heavy crude under ATPA decreased 9.2 percent to $3.8 billion in terms of value, but increased 49.0 percent to 62.2 million barrels in terms of quantity, while imports of light crude under ATPA decreased 55.8 percent to $914 million in terms of value, and decreased 28.8 percent to 14.3 million barrels in terms of quantity. These declines in the value of imports of crude oil reflect the spike in oil prices that occurred in 2008, as unit values of crude imports declined 35 to 45 percent in 2009.

Imports of cut flowers (HS 0603) were the second-largest category of imports under ATPA from Colombia.[11] Imports of cut flowers under ATPA increased 1.4 percent, from $499 million in 2008 to $506 million in 2009. Cut flowers increased to 9.1 percent of U.S. imports from Colombia under ATPA in 2009 (49.5 percent of non-oil imports under ATPA) from 6.8 percent (43.4 percent of non-oil imports under ATPA) in 2008. Colombian cut flower varieties in 2009 included roses (48.3 percent), chrysanthemums (14.8 percent), carnations (10.9 percent), and other fresh cut flowers (25.9 percent).[12]

Imports of nonknitted apparel (HS 62) under ATPA from Colombia continued to decline in 2009. Nonkitted apparel imports under ATPA fell 38.5 percent to $109.5 million or 2.0 percent of total imports under ATPA (10.7 percent of the non-oil imports under ATPA). Imports of knitted apparel (HS 61) under ATPA also fell for the third consecutive year in 2009 to $100 million, or 1.8 percent of imports under ATPA from Colombia (9.8 percent of non-oil imports under ATPA) after peaking at $181 million in 2006. Several factors contributed to this decrease, including the increased competition from China and other low-cost Asian suppliers, uncertainty about the renewal of ATPA, and uncertainty about possible Congressional action on the pending U.S.-Colombia TPA.[13]

Peru

In 2009, imports under ATPA from Peru were $1.4 billion, down 56.6 percent compared to 2008. While imports under ATPA declined $1.8 billion in 2009, at least $730 million in imports of ATPA-eligible products were entered under the new U.S.-Peru TPA. However, total preferential imports (ATPA and U.S.-Peru TPA) fell 25.6 percent in 2009 (table 2.9). Of the imports under ATPA from Peru, $384 million, or 27.9 percent, were petroleum and petroleum products (HS 2709 and 2710; tables 2.6 and 2.8). The value of imports of petroleum and petroleum products under ATPA decreased 55.9 percent, from $871 million in 2008 to $384 million in 2009.

Table 2.9. U.S. preferential imports for consumption from Peru, by major product categories, by duty treatments, 2007–09

Product category (HS/HTS code)	2007	2008		2009	
	ATPA	ATPA	ATPA	U.S.-PERU	Total
			Millions of $		
Petroleum oils and oils obtained from bituminous minerals (HS 2709 & 2710)	658.3	871.1	384.1	56.2	440.3
Articles of apparel and clothing accessories, knitted or crocheted (HS 61)	746.2	733.9	383.4	174.9	558.3
Refined copper cathodes and sections of cathodes (HTS 7403.11.00)	989.1	844.4	215.5	329.9	545.3
Preparations of vegetables, fruit, nuts, or other parts of plants (HS 20)	81.3	129.2	91.1	54.1	145.2
Edible fruit and nuts; peel of citrus fruit or melons (HS 08)	49.6	66.1	55.6	13.4	69.0
Asparagus, fresh or chilled (HS 0709.20)	161.3	152.5	45.5	116.4	161.
Articles of apparel and clothing accessories, not knitted or crocheted (HS 62)	45.6	40.4	24.1	6.6	30.7
Molybdenum ores and concentrates, not roasted (HTS 2613.90.00)	38.8	53.5	14.6	7.4	22.0
Refined copper, bars and rods (HTS 7407.10.50)	21.0	31.3	14.4	3.6	18.0
Paprika, dried or crushed or ground (HTS 0904.20.20)	26.5	41.1	13.5	13.2	26.7
Subtotal	2,817.	2,963.	1,241.8	775.5	2,01
All other	199.7	205.1	134.5	205.0	339.
Total	3,017.	3,168.	1,376.3	980.5	2,35

Source: Compiled from official statistics of the U.S. Department of Commerce.

The value of imports of heavy crude oil (HTS 2709.00.10) remained essentially unchanged at $301 million from 2008 to 2009, despite a decline in unit values of more than 35 percent, as the quantity increased 57.3 percent. Notably, the United States did not import any heavy fuel oil from Peru (HTS 2710.19.05) under ATPA after imports of $270 million in 2008. Imports of naphthas (HTS 2710.11.25) under ATPA declined 75.9 percent, from $255 million in 2008 to $61.4 million in 2009, although some imports of naphthas shifted to the U.S.-Peru TPA ($23.1 million).

Imports of knitted apparel (HS 61) were $383 million, or 27.9 percent of the imports under ATPA from Peru (38.6 percent of non-oil imports under ATPA) in 2009. Knitted apparel imports under ATPA decreased 47.8 percent, from $734 million in 2008 to $383 million in 2009. The decline in the value of imports of knitted apparel from Peru under ATPA was across the board. Imports of tops, men's and boys' shirts, T-shirts, women's and girls' blouses, and women's and girls' suits all declined 40 to 60 percent from 2008 to 2009. Although $175 million in imports of knitted apparel (HS 61) entered under the U.S.-Peru TPA in 2009, it is not possible to know how much of these imports were ATPA-eligible; some of them might have been ineligible for ATPA, since the rules of origin for most apparel products are more liberal for imports under the U.S.-Peru TPA than under ATPA.

In 2009, imports of refined copper cathodes from Peru were eligible to enter the United States under either ATPA or the U.S.-Peru TPA. Imports of refined copper cathodes (HTS 7403.11.00) under ATPA decreased sharply, falling from $844 million in 2008 to $216 million in 2009, while an additional $330 million in imports of refined copper cathodes entered under the U.S.-Peru TPA. Combined, the value of these imports in 2009 declined $299 million, or 35.4 percent compared to 2008, and $444 million or 44.9 percent compared to 2007. On the other hand, although refined copper cathode import unit values declined sharply in 2009, unit values were still more than double what they were from 2000 to 2003 (figure 2.5).

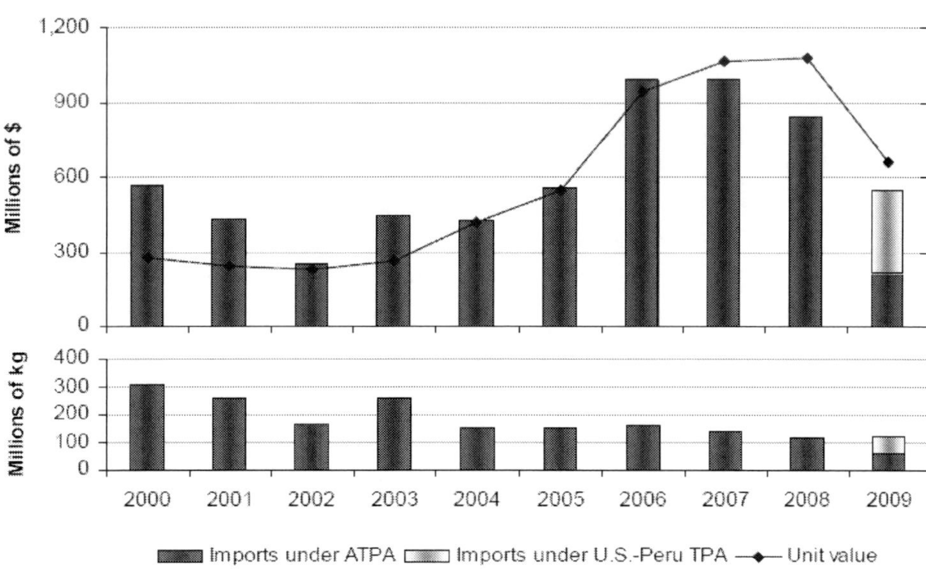

Source: Compiled from official statistics of the U.S. Department of Commerce.

Figure 2.5. U.S. imports of refined copper cathodes (HTS 7403.11.00) under ATPA and the U.S.-Peru TPA, from Peru, 2000–09.

Preferential imports of fruits and vegetables from Peru increased in value in 2009, despite the global recession. While imports of these products under ATPA declined sharply in many cases, declines were offset by imports of ATPA-eligible products that entered under the U.S.-Peru TPA. For example, although imports of fresh asparagus (HS 0709.20) under ATPA decreased 70.2 percent from $153 million in 2008 to $45.5 million, total preferential imports of fresh asparagus were actually higher in 2009 because of $116 million in imports under the U.S.-Peru TPA ($162 million in total preferential imports). Preferential imports of ATPA-eligible prepared vegetables, fruits, and nuts (HS 20)—mostly prepared asparagus and artichokes—increased 12.4 percent, from $129 million in 2008 to $145 million ($91.1 under ATPA and $54.1 under U.S.-Peru TPA) in 2009. Likewise, preferential imports of ATPA-eligible edible fruits and nuts (HS 08), mostly grapes, mangoes, and mandarins, increased 4.3 percent from $66.1 million in 2008 to $69.0 million ($55.6 under ATPA and $13.4 under U.S.-Peru TPA) in 2009.

Bolivia

Bolivia was ineligible for ATPA preferences in 2009, but was able to ship under ATPA in 2008. In 2008, however, U.S. imports under ATPA from Bolivia amounted to only $140 million, or 0.8 percent of all U.S. imports under the program (table 2.7). Petroleum and petroleum products (HS 2709 and 2710) accounted for $71.6 million, or 51.2 percent of all U.S. imports under ATPA from Bolivia in 2008. Imports of jewelry of precious metals other than silver (HS 7113.19) and knitted apparel (HS 61) under ATPA from Bolivia declined in 2008 as compared to 2007.

U.S. Exports to the ATPA Countries

The value of U.S. exports to the ATPA countries decreased 15.5 percent from $19.8 billion in 2008 to $16.7 billion in 2009 (table 2.10).[14] Nonetheless, the United States continued to be the leading supplier of goods to each of the three remaining ATPA countries (Colombia, Ecuador, and Peru). More than one-half of U.S. exports to the ATPA countries in 2009 went to Colombia and over one-quarter to Peru (table 2.10). The ATPA countries collectively accounted for 1.8 percent of total U.S. exports in 2009, which was up from 1.7 percent in 2008 and 1.1 percent in 2005.

Table 2.11 shows the leading exports to ATPA countries by HS chapter.[15] U.S. exports of non-electrical machinery and parts (HS 84) to the ATPA countries decreased 14.4 percent, from $4.3 billion in 2008 to $3.7 billion in 2009, and accounted for 22.0 percent of total U.S. exports to the ATPA countries.

Exports under this HS chapter consisted mostly of machinery intended for use in oil and gas fields, construction, and data processing. Parts for boring or sinking machinery (HS 8431.43), and parts and attachments for heavy equipment (HS 8431.49) were the leading product categories from this sector in 2009 (table 2.12). The ATPA countries received 2.9 percent of all U.S. exports of non-electrical machinery and parts in 2009.

U.S. exports of mineral fuels and oils (HS 27) to the ATPA countries, mostly refined petroleum products (HS 2710), were $2.7 billion in both 2008 and 2009, despite markedly lower unit values (table 2.11). Refined petroleum products (HS 2710) accounted for 15.0 percent of total U.S. exports to the ATPA countries. The ATPA countries received 4.9 percent of all U.S. exports of mineral fuels and oils in 2009.

Table 2.10. U.S. domestic exports to ATPA countries, by market, 2005–09

Market	2005	2006	2007	2008	2009	Change 2008–09
		Value (millions of $)				Percent
Colombia	4,962	6,236	7,884	10,568	8,752	-17.2
Peru	2,038	2,655	3,764	5,687	4,356	-23.4
Ecuador	1,733	2,548	2,709	3,150	3,589	13.9
Bolivia	186	197	263	358	([a])	-100.0
Total	8,919	11,637	14,621	19,763	16,697	-15.5
Percent of total exports						In percentage points
Colombia	55.6	53.6	53.9	53.5	52.4	-1.1
Peru	22.9	22.8	25.7	28.8	26.1	-2.7
Ecuador	19.4	21.9	18.5	15.9	21.5	5.6
Bolivia	2.1	1.7	1.8	1.8	([a])	-1.8
Total	100.0	100.0	100.0	100.0	100.0	0.0

Source: Compiled from official statistics of the U.S. Department of Commerce. a Bolivia was not included in 2009.

U.S. exports of electrical machinery and parts (HS 85) to the ATPA countries decreased 17.2 percent from $1.5 billion in 2008 to $1.3 billion in 2009, and accounted for 7.6 percent of total U.S. exports to the ATPA countries (table 2.11). These exports consisted mostly of telecommunications and computer equipment. Cellular phones (HS 8517.12) and routers and switches (HS 8517.62) were the leading product categories in 2009 (table 2.12). The ATPA countries received 1.5 percent of all U.S. exports of electrical machinery and parts in 2009.

U.S. exports of plastics (HS 39) to the ATPA countries were $1.1 billion in 2009, a decrease of 21.6 percent from 2008 (table 2.11). Polymers of ethylene (HS 3901), polyvinyl chloride (HS 3904), and polyacetals (HS 3907) were the leading products within the plastics chapter in 2009 (table 2.12). The ATPA countries received 2.6 percent of all U.S. exports of plastics in 2009.

U.S. exports of organic chemicals (HS 29) to the ATPA countries were $820.7 million or 4.9 percent of total U.S. exports to the ATPA countries in 2009 (table 2.11). Propylene (HS 2901.22), vinyl chloride (HS 2903.21), and styrene (HS 2902.50) were the leading organic chemicals exported in 2009 (table 2.12). The ATPA countries received 2.7 percent of all U.S. exports of organic chemicals in 2009.

U.S. exports of motor vehicles (HS 87) to the ATPA countries decreased 6.0 percent from $774.8 million in 2008 to $728.4 million in 2009, and accounted for 4.4 percent of total U.S. exports to the ATPA countries (table 2.11). U.S. exports of dumpers (dump trucks) designed for off-highway use (HS 8704.10), parts and accessories for motor vehicles (HS 8708.99), and motor cars and other motor vehicles designed to transport people (HS 8703) were the leading motor vehicle products exported in 2009 (table 2.12). The ATPA countries received 1.1 percent of all U.S. exports of vehicles, parts, and accessories thereof in 2009.

Table 2.11. Leading U.S. domestic exports to ATPA countries, by major product categories, in value and share, 2005–09

HS chapter	Description	2005	2006	2007	2008	2009[a]	Change 2008–09
			Value (millions of $)				Percent
84	Nuclear reactors, boilers, machinery and mechanical appliances; parts	1,913.8	2,556.7	3,089.0	4,289.1	3,669	-14.4
27	Mineral fuels, mineral oils and products of their distillation; bituminous substances; mineral waxes	701.0	1,334.4	1,368.7	2,728.0	2,688 .9	-1.4
85	Electrical machinery and equipment and parts thereof; sound recorders and reproducers, television recorders and reproducers, parts and accessories	851.2	973.5	1,215.1	1,532.0	1,267 .9	-17.2
39	Plastics and articles thereof	567.8	704.2	1,152.8	1,373.9	1,076	-21.6
29	Organic chemicals	791.0	930.9	1,100.7	1,208.9	820.7	-32.1
87	Vehicles, other than railway or tramway rolling stock, and parts and accessories thereof	339.6	491.1	561.6	774.8	728.4	-6.0
90	Optical, photographic, cinematographic, measuring, checking, precision, medical or surgical instruments and apparatus; parts and accessories thereof	341.9	449.9	547.7	704.7	655.9	-6.9
10	Cereals	517.7	582.7	1,085.3	1,232.8	655.2	-46.9
88	Aircraft, spacecraft, and parts thereof	141.8	204.9	239.4	318.9	505.5	58.5
38	Miscellaneous chemical products	207.7	256.7	316.3	383.0	393.7	2.8
	Subtotal	6,373.6	8,484.9	10,676.4	14,546.1	12,46	-14.3
	All other	2,545.5	3,151.6	3,944.1	5,216.7	4,234	-18.8
	Total	8,919.1	11,636.5	14,620.5	19,762.7	16,69	-15.5
		Percent of total exports					In percentage points
84	Nuclear reactors, boilers, machinery and mechanical appliances; parts	21.5	22.0	21.1	21.7	22.0	0.3
27	Mineral fuels, mineral oils and products of their distillation; bituminous substances; mineral waxes	7.9	11.5	9.4	13.8	16.1	2.3

Table 2.11. (Continued)

HS chapter	Description	2005	2006	2007	2008	2009[a]	Change 2008–09
			Value (millions of $)				Percent
85	Electrical machinery and equipment and parts thereof; sound recorders and reproducers, television recorders and reproducers, parts and accessories	9.5	8.4	8.3	7.8	7.6	-0.2
39	Plastics and articles thereof	6.4	6.1	7.9	7.0	6.4	-0.5
29	Organic chemicals	8.9	8.0	7.5	6.1	4.9	-1.2
87	Vehicles, other than railway or tramway rolling stock, and parts and accessories thereof	3.8	4.2	3.8	3.9	4.4	0.4
90	Optical, photographic, cinematographic, measuring, checking, precision, medical or surgical instruments and apparatus; parts and accessories thereof	3.8	3.9	3.7	3.6	3.9	0.4
10	Cereals	5.8	5.0	7.4	6.2	3.9	-2.3
88	Aircraft, spacecraft, and parts thereof	1.6	1.8	1.6	1.6	3.0	1.4
38	Miscellaneous chemical products	2.3	2.2	2.2	1.9	2.4	0.4
	Subtotal	71.5	72.9	73.0	73.6	74.6	1.0
	All other	28.5	27.1	27.0	26.4	25.4	-1.0
	Total	100.0	100.0	100.0	100.0	100.0	

Source: Compiled from official statistics of the U.S. Department of Commerce.

a Bolivia was not included in 2009.

Table 2.12. Leading U.S. domestic exports to ATPA countries, by HS number, 2005–09

HS number	Description	2005	2006	2007	2008	2009	Change 2008–09
		Millions of $					Percent
2710.19	Petroleum oils & oils (not light) from bituminous minerals or preps n.e.s.o.i. 70%+ by wt. from petroleum oils or bitum. min.	639.1	1,247.7	1,181.7	2,519.5	2,113.4	-16.1
8431.43	Parts for boring or sinking machinery, n.e.s.o.i.	249.5	305.8	424.8	573.0	397.6	-30.6
2710.11	Light oils and preparations from petroleum oils & oils from bituminous min. or preps 70%+ by wt. from petro. oils or bitum. min.	33.3	63.7	149.1	91.5	394.1	330.5
1005.90	Corn (maize), other than seed corn	279.2	461.4	679.1	711.9	374.2	-47.4
8800.00 b	Civil aircraft, engines, equipment, and parts	141.8	216.3	219.2	277.7	347.9	25.3
1001.90	Wheat (other than durum wheat), and meslin	222.9	114.1	396.0	503.7	250.8	-50.2
8431.49	Parts and attachments, nesoi, for derricks, cranes, self-propelled bulldozers, graders etc. and other grading, scraping, etc. machinery	148.8	182.0	182.9	294.7	208.6	-29.2
8704.10	Dumpers (dump trucks) designed for off-highway use	35.6	132.7	98.7	186.9	200.2	7.1
8429.52	Mechanical shovels, excavators and shovel loaders with 360 degree revolving superstructure, self-propelled	12.4	17.5	47.6	180.2	190.3	5.6
3901.10	Polyethylene having a specific gravity of less than 0.94, in primary forms	75.7	104.8	190.9	244.2	187.5	-23.2 -
8517.12	Telephones for cellular networks or for other wireless networks	(c)	(c)	114.7	184.8	184.7	0.1
3901.20	Polyethylene having a specific gravity of 0.94 or more, in primary forms	37.8	72.0	206.7	211.8	159.2	-24.9
8411.82	Gas turbines, except turbojets and turbopropellers, of a power exceeding 5,000 kw	8.6	9.0	31.8	85.6	157.7	84.3
5201.00	Cotton, not carded or combed	113.3	127.8	160.3	171.5	152.1	-11.3
2901.22	Propene (propylene)	108.5	146.0	216.9	249.6	137.6	-44.9
2711.12	Propane, liquefied	0.0	14.2	26.3	92.5	136.5	47.6
8471.30	Portable automatic data processing machines, weight not more than 10 kg, consisting of at least a central processing unit, keyboard & a display	15.1	52.4	70.1	117.9	131.1	11.2

Table 2.12. (Continued)

HS number	Description	2005	2006	2007	2008	2009	Change 2008–09
		Millions of $					Percent
8413.91	Parts of pumps for liquids	52.0	49.7	46.6	63.9	129.2	102.0
2304.00	Soybean oilcake and other solid residues resulting from the extraction of soy bean oil, whether or not ground or in the form of pellets	43.8	74.1	93.4	144.0	129.2	-10.3
8414.80	Air pumps and air or other gas compressors, n.e.s.o.i.; ventilating or recycling hoods incorporating a fan, n.e.s.o.i.	16.6	21.4	37.8	40.4	126.4	212.9
Subtotal		2,234.0	3,412.6	4,574.7	6,945.3	6,108.3	-12.1
	All other	6,685.1	8,223.9	10,045.8	12,817.4	10,589.0	-17.4
Total		8,919.1	11,636.5	14,620.5	19,762.7	16,697.3	-15.5

Note: The abbreviation "n.e.s.o.i." stands for "not elsewhere specified or otherwise included."

a Bolivia was not included in 2009.

b 2005–08 Consolidated from Schedule B subheading list.

c Exports for Schedule B subheading 8517.12 were reported under parts of items contained in Schedule B subheading 8525.20 during 2005-06.

Although not a leading export sector, U.S. exports of textiles and apparel play an important role in U.S. exports to the ATPA countries because of special provisions under ATPA. ATPDEA provides duty-free treatment for certain apparel imports using designated U.S. inputs. This provision provides an incentive for the use of U.S. inputs, contributing to U.S. exports of textile and apparel inputs to the ATPA countries. Although U.S. exports of textiles and apparel to the ATPA countries increased steadily between 2002, when ATPDEA's textile provisions went into effect, and 2008, U.S. sector exports to these countries declined 41.2 percent to $139.4 million in 2009. This decrease was roughly in proportion to the drop in U.S. imports of apparel under ATPA.

Economic Impact of ATPA on the United States and Probable Future Effects

This chapter addresses two issues: the economic impact of ATPA on the U.S. economy, industries, and consumers in 2008 and 2009, focusing on 2009 data, and the probable future effects of the program.[1] The economic impact analysis identifies those items most affected by ATPA preferences and examines U.S. industries that are potentially most affected. The chapter also assesses the probable future effects of ATPA based on information about the investment environment in each ATPA beneficiary country as well as ATPA-related investment in these countries. This information was collected from U.S. embassies in the region and from other public sources, as well as testimony provided at the Commission's hearing on July 7, 2010, and written submissions to the Commission.

Impact of ATPA on the United States in 2009

Since its implementation, ATPA has had a minimal effect on the overall economy of the United States. In each year from 1992 through 2002, the value of ATPA duty-free U.S. imports was 0.02 percent or less of U.S. GDP. Following implementation of expanded trade preferences under ATPDEA, imports under ATPA rose to 0.05 percent of U.S. GDP in 2003, peaked at 0.10 percent in 2008, and fell to 0.07 percent in 2009. Furthermore, the total value of U.S. imports from ATPA countries remained small in 2009, amounting to 1.34 percent of total U.S. imports, while imports under ATPA provisions totaled 0.63 percent of total U.S. imports.

ATPDEA sharply increased the number of products and value of imports benefiting from ATPA, especially apparel and petroleum and petroleum products. However, the value of the ATPA program to beneficiary countries and its potential to affect the U.S. economy, consumers, and industries has declined since implementation because the margin of preference for many products has eroded as normal trade relations (NTR) duty rates have fallen (to free in some instances) on many products produced in the region. Also, the advantages of preferential access to the U.S. market have been diluted as more U.S. trading partners have received preferential access under other programs or free trade agreements (FTAs) and as apparel quotas under the Agreement on Textiles and Clothing (ATC) ended in 2005, allowing substantial increases in U.S. imports of apparel from Asian producers.[2] In addition, the potential for ATPA preferences to affect the U.S. economy, consumers, and industries was significantly lower in 2009 because most products from Peru had the option to be entered under the U.S.-Peru TPA starting February 1, 2009, and because Bolivia's beneficiary status was suspended effective December 15, 2008.

To evaluate the impact of ATPA, the Commission considered only that portion of U.S. imports that could receive preferential treatment only under ATPA—that is, imports that benefit exclusively from ATPA. Some ATPA-eligible products are also eligible for duty-free entry under the Generalized System of Preferences (GSP) and therefore are not included in the analysis. Similarly, most ATPA-eligible products are also eligible for duty-free treatment under the U.S.-Peru TPA. Accordingly, practically all imports from Peru entered under ATPA from February 1, 2009, onward, are excluded from the analysis.

Because the original ATPA preferences were enacted for a longer time period (the initial program was for the 10 years from 1991 to 2001) and GSP lapsed several times during this period, ATPA provided greater assurance than the GSP program that GSP-eligible products from ATPA countries would enter the United States free of duty. The greater continuity of the ATPA program in this period made investment related to such products more attractive than would have been the case in the absence of ATPA. Since 2001, however, both ATPA and GSP have been subject to short extensions, so uncertainties remain for both programs. Assessing the quantitative impact of such uncertainties is beyond the scope of the analysis conducted in this study. However, a qualitative assessment is provided in the section below, which addresses the probable future effects of ATPA.

The material that follows in this section defines products that benefit exclusively from ATPA; presents quantitative estimates of the impact of ATPA on U.S. consumers, the U.S. Treasury, and U.S. industries whose goods compete with U.S. imports under ATPA; and describes the U.S. imports that benefited exclusively from ATPA in 2009 and had the largest potential impact on competing U.S. industries.

Products That Benefited Exclusively from ATPA in 2009

U.S. imports of products benefiting exclusively from ATPA in 2009 are defined as those that entered free of duty under ATPA[3] and were not eligible to enter free of duty under NTR rates or under other programs, such as the U.S.-Peru TPA or GSP.[4] Consistent with this definition, GSP-eligible products imported from ATPA countries that were entered under ATPA preferences were considered to benefit exclusively from ATPA only if imports of the product from a designated beneficiary country had exceeded GSP competitive need limits and had therefore lost GSP eligibility.[5]

After increasing more than 50 percent, from $10.6 billion in 2005 to $16.4 billion in 2008, the value of U.S. imports that benefited exclusively from ATPA decreased 51.3 percent to $8.0 billion in 2009, accounting for 38.5 percent of total U.S. imports from ATPA countries (table 3.1). From the implementation of the ATPA program in 1992 until 2002, U.S. imports that benefited exclusively from ATPA accounted for a relatively small portion of total U.S. imports from ATPA countries, ranging from roughly 5 percent in 1993 and 1994 to a high of around 13 percent in 1996.[6] The exclusively benefiting share ranged between 10 percent and 12 percent during 1998–2001, but fell to 7.7 percent in 2002 when the program lapsed. Since petroleum and petroleum products and apparel became eligible for duty-free entry under ATPDEA, the exclusively benefiting share rose sharply, to nearly 45 percent in 2003 and around 55 percent in 2006 and 2007. This share peaked at 57 percent in 2008, mainly because of high oil and copper prices. The exclusively benefiting share fell sharply to 38 percent in 2009 as commodity prices fell, and as all of the major ATPA-eligible products from Peru became eligible for duty-free entry under the U.S.-Peru TPA on February 1, 2009, and hence no longer benefited exclusively from ATPA.

Table 3.1. Total imports from Andean countries, imports entered under ATPA, and imports that benefited exclusively from ATPA, 2005–09

Item	2005	2006	2007	2008	2009[a]
Total imports from Andean countries:					
Value (*million dollars*[b])	20,060	22,511	20,923	24,483	20,690
Imports entered under ATPA:[c]					
Value (*million dollars*[b])	11,464	13,484	12,307	17,243	9,714
Percentage of total	57.1	59.9	58.8	60.5	47.0
Imports that benefited exclusively from ATPA:					
Value (*million dollars*[b])	10,648	12,531	11,488	16,360	7,963
Percentage of total	53.1	55.7	54.9	57.4	38.5

Source: Estimated by the U.S. International Trade Commission from official statistics of the U.S. Department of Commerce.

a Bolivia not included in 2009.

b Customs value.

c Includes articles entered free of duty under ATPA provisions. Those provisions are discussed in chap. 1.

In the years immediately preceding the implementation of ATPDEA, imports of refined copper cathodes from Peru (HTS 7403.11.00) came to dominate this category, accounting for around 40 percent of imports benefiting exclusively from ATPA in 2000 and 2001.[7] Since ATPDEA made petroleum and petroleum products eligible for duty-free treatment in 2002, such products have come to dominate the list of leading imports that benefit exclusively from ATPA in recent years, accounting for 75.8 percent of the value of the 20 leading items in 2007, 84.8 percent in 2008, and 90.9 percent in 2009.

The 20 leading imports that benefited exclusively from ATPA in 2009 are shown in table 3.2. The most notable changes in the value of such imports relative to 2008 were for products originating primarily in Peru—copper cathodes, down $805 million (95 percent); fresh asparagus (HTS 0709.20.90), down $131 million (90 percent); and three apparel products[8]—and for petroleum and petroleum products, down $6.2 billion (47 percent). (See table D.4.) On the other hand, imports of three categories of fresh cut flowers either increased (chrysanthemums, HTS 0603.14.00, up 13 percent) or fell much less than other products among the leading products benefiting exclusively (roses, HTS 0603.11.00, down 2 percent, and other carnations, HTS 0603.12.70, down 10 percent).

Welfare and Displacement Effects of ATPA on U.S. Industries and Consumers in 2009

The analytical approach for estimating the welfare and displacement effects of ATPA was described in chapter 1 and is discussed in more detail in appendix C. Upper estimates and lower estimates are reported in this analysis, reflecting the assumption of higher substitution elasticities and lower substitution elasticities, respectively.

The Commission focused its analysis on the 20 leading imports that benefited exclusively from ATPA in 2009 (table 3.2),[9] and estimated the welfare and potential U.S. industry displacement effects. Industries for which estimated displacement was more than 5 percent of the value of U.S. production, based on upper estimates, were selected for further analysis.

A limited number of U.S. producers benefited from ATPA preferences because they supplied inputs to apparel assembled in ATPA countries. Those producers supplying yarns or fabric are not explicitly analyzed because of data limitations,[10] but U.S. exports of textiles to ATPA countries rose from $100 million in 2002 to $203 million in 2006 before decreasing to $130 million in 2009.[11] The 2008–09 decrease in U.S. textile exports to the region roughly parallels the decrease in U.S. imports of apparel from ATPA countries in 2009.

Items Analyzed

Although a large number of products are eligible for tariff preferences under ATPA, a relatively small group accounts for most of the imports that benefit exclusively from ATPA. Table 3.2 presents the 20 leading products that benefited exclusively from ATPA in 2009; they are ranked and selected on the basis of their cost, insurance, and freight (c.i.f.) import values.[12] Those products totaled $7.7 billion (97 percent) of the $8.0 billion in imports that benefited exclusively from ATPA during 2009.[13] The five leading ATPAexclusive imports in 2009 were (1) heavy crude oil (HTS 2709.00.10), (2) light crude oil (HTS 2709.00.20), (3) fresh cut roses, (4) heavy fuel oil (HTS 2710.19.05), and (5) fresh cut chrysanthemums. Colombia was the leading supplier of all five of these products, although there were also significant imports of heavy crude oil from Ecuador. In 2008, just as in 2009, heavy crude oil ranked first among ATPA-exclusive imports, and light crude oil ranked second.[14]

For any particular product, the U.S. market share accounted for by ATPA-exclusive imports (the value of imports benefiting exclusively from ATPA relative to apparent consumption) was a major factor in determining the estimated impact on competing domestic producers.[15] These market shares varied considerably in 2009 (table 3.3). For instance, the market share of ATPA-exclusive imports of fresh cut roses was approximately 95 percent, whereas the market share of ATPA-exclusive imports of heavy fuel oil was 0.4 percent.

Estimated Effects on Consumers and Producers

Tables 3.4 and 3.5 present the estimated impact of ATPA tariff preferences related to leading imports that benefited exclusively from ATPA in 2009.[16] Estimates of the gains in consumer surplus and the losses in tariff revenue, as well as measures of the potential displacement of U.S. production, are discussed next.

Effects on U.S. consumers

Fresh cut roses provided the largest estimated gain in consumer surplus resulting exclusively from ATPA tariff preferences in 2009, with a range of $20.0 million to $20.1 million (table 3.4). Without ATPA, the price that U.S. consumers (importers) would have paid for imports of fresh cut roses from ATPA countries would have been as much as 5.4 percent higher (the ad valorem duty rate, adjusted for freight and insurance charges).

Fresh cut chrysanthemums provided the second-largest estimated gain in consumer surplus, with a range of $4.6 million to $4.7 million. Without ATPA, the price of imports of such fresh cut roses from ATPA countries would have been as much as 5.2 percent higher. In general, products providing the largest gains in consumer surplus also have either some of the highest NTR tariff rates or the largest volumes of imports, or both.

Table 3.2. Leading imports that benefited exclusively from ATPA, 2009

HTS number	Description	Customs value	C.i.f. value
		Thousands of $	
2709.00.10	Petroleum oils and oils from bituminous minerals, crude, testing under 25 degrees A.P.I. d	5,744,680	5,947,867
2709.00.20	Petroleum oils and oils from bituminous minerals, crude, testing 25 degrees A.P.I. or more	914,001	935,188
0603.11.00	Sweetheart, spray and other roses, fresh cut	304,906	383,780
2710.19.05	Distillate and residual fuel oil (including blends) derived from petroleum or oils from bituminous minerals, testing under 25 degrees A.P.I.	244,655	257,496
0603.14.00[a]	Chrysanthemums, fresh cut	75,121	92,778
2710.11.25	Naphthas (exc. motor fuel/mtr fuel blend. stock) fr petroleum oils & bitumen minerals (o/than crude) or preps 70%+ by wt. fr petroleum oils	85,998	89,289
6203.42.40	Men's or boys' trousers and shorts, not bibs, not knitted or crocheted, of cotton, not containing 15% or more by weight of down, etc	44,205	44,744
1604.14.30	Tunas and skipjack, not in oil, in airtight containers, n/o 7 kg, not of U.S. possessions, over quota	43,400	43,988
0603.12.70[a]	Other carnations, fresh cut	33,621	42,464
7403.11.00[b]	Refined copper cathodes and sections of cathodes	39,442	40,208
6908.90.00	Glazed ceramic flags and paving, hearth or wall tiles; glazed ceramic mosaic cubes and the like, n.e.s.o.i.	20,414	28,567
0710.80.97	Vegetables n.e.s.o.i., uncooked or cooked by steaming or boiling in water, frozen, reduced in size	23,801	27,162
6109.10.00	T-shirts, singlets, tank tops and similar garments, knitted or crocheted, of cotton	24,480	25,123
2710.11.45	Light oil mixt. of hydrocarbons fr petro oils & bitum min (o/than crude) or prep 70%+ wt. fr petro oils, n.e.s.o.i., n/o 50% any single hydrocarbon	22,472	23,761
0709.20.90	Asparagus, n.e.s.o.i., fresh or chilled	14,166	20,369
6110.20.20	Sweaters, pullovers and similar articles, knitted or crocheted, of cotton, n.e.s.o.i.	18,457	19,164

Table 3.2. (Continued)

HTS number	Description	Customs value	C.i.f. value
		Thousands of $	
0804.30.40	Pineapples, fresh or dried, not reduced in size, in crates or other packages	15,411	18,133
6105.10.00	Men's or boys' shirts, knitted or crocheted, of cotton	15,712	16,044
6204.62.40	Women's or girls' trousers, breeches and shorts, not knitted or crocheted, of cotton, n.e.s.o.i.	14,547	15,059
6110.30.30	Sweaters, pullovers and similar articles, knitted or crocheted, of manmade fibers, n.e.s.o.i.	13,779	14,076
Total of above		7,713,268	8,085,261
All other		249,797	261,235
Total		7,963,064	8,346,376

Source: Estimated by the U.S. International Trade Commission from official statistics of the U.S. Department of Commerce.

Notes: The abbreviation, n.e.s.o.i., stands for "not elsewhere specified or otherwise included." Imports from Peru are only included for Jan. 2009.

a Includes only imports from Colombia. Item is GSP-eligible, but imports from Colombia exceeded the competitive need limit and thus were eligible for duty-free entry only under ATPA.

b Includes only imports from Peru. Item is GSP-eligible, but imports from Peru exceeded the competitive need limit and thus were eligible for duty-free entry only under ATPA.

ATPA preferences also reduced U.S. tariff revenues, offsetting much of the gain in consumer surplus. For example, for tuna in airtight containers (HTS 1604.14.30), [17] lower tariff revenues offset 75 percent to 84 percent of the gain in consumer surplus, and for fresh or chilled asparagus, the offset was about 82 percent to 94 percent. For many of the other products listed in table 3.4, reduced tariff revenues offset nearly all of the gain in consumer surplus; this situation typically occurs when NTR duty rates are relatively low, as is the case with many ATPA-exclusive products. Overall, the estimated net welfare effects of ATPA were small. The gain in consumer surplus (column A of table 3.4) was greater than the corresponding decline in tariff revenue (column B) for all of the products analyzed for which data were available. Of the resulting estimated net welfare gains, the largest were for tuna in airtight containers ($0.7 million to $1.0 million), fresh cut roses ($630,000 to $670,000), and fresh or chilled asparagus ($179,000 to $448,000). Apparel products would probably lead in net welfare gains, given the relatively high duty rates on these products, but lack of U.S. production data precludes making such estimates.

Table 3.3. Leading imports that benefited exclusively from ATPA, apparent U.S. consumption, and ATPA exclusive market share, 2009

HTS number	Description	Imports from ATPA countries (c.i.f. value) (A)	Apparent U.S. consumption (B)[a]	Market share (A/B)
		Thousands of $		Percent
2709.00.10	Petroleum oils and oils from bituminous minerals, crude, testing under 25 degrees A.P.I.	5,947,867	98,104,690	6.1
2709.00.20	Petroleum oils and oils from bituminous minerals, crude, testing 25 degrees A.P.I. or more	935,188	164,952,956	0.6
0603.11.00	Sweetheart, spray and other roses, fresh cut	383,780	405,811	94.6
2710.19.05	Distillate and residual fuel oil (including blends) derived from petroleum or oils from bituminous minerals, testing under 25 degrees A.P.I.	257,496	71,167,074	0.4
0603.14.00	Chrysanthemums, fresh cut	92,778	101.962	91.0
2710.11.25	Naphthas (exc. motor fuel/mtr fuel blend. stock) fr petroleum oils & bitumin minerals (o/than crude) or preps 70%+ by wt. fr petroleum oils	89,289	6,673,290	1.3
6203.42.40	Men's or boys' trousers and shorts, not bibs, not knitted or crocheted, of cotton, not containing 15% or more by weight of down, etc	44,744	[b]	[b]
1604.14.30	Tunas and skipjack, not in oil, in airtight containers,			
0603.12.70[c]	n/o 7 kg, not of U.S. possessions, over quota Other carnations, fresh cut	43,988 42,464	1,145,998 [b]	3.8 [b]
7403.11.00	Refined copper cathodes and sections of cathodes	40,208	8,726,311	0.5
6908.90.00	Glazed ceramic flags and paving, hearth or wall tiles; glazed ceramic mosaic cubes and the like, n.e.s.o.i.	28,567	1,547,405	1.8
0710.80.97	Vegetables n.e.s.o.i., uncooked or cooked by steaming or boiling in water, frozen, reduced in size	27,162	[b]	[b]
6109.10.00	T-shirts, singlets, tank tops and similar garments, knitted or crocheted, of cotton	25,123	3,552,774	0.7
2710.11.45	Light oil mixt. of hydrocarbons fr petro oils & bitum min(o/than crude) or prep 70%+ wt. fr petro oils, n.e.s.o.i., n/o 50% any single hydrocarbon	23,761	5,582,586	0.4
0709.20.90	Asparagus, n.e.s.o.i., fresh or chilled	20,369	396,300	5.1

Table 3.3. (Continued)

HTS number	Description	Imports from ATPA countries (c.i.f. value) (A)	Apparent U.S. consumption (B)[a]	Market share (A/B)
		Thousands of $		Percent
6110.20.20	Sweaters, pullovers and similar articles, knitted or crocheted, of cotton, n.e.s.o.i.	19,164	(b)	(b)
0804.30.40	Pineapples, fresh or dried, not reduced in size, in			
6105.10.00	crates or other packages Men's or boys' shirts, knitted or crocheted, of cotton	18,133 16,044	561,372 (b)	3.2 (b)
6204.62.40	Women's or girls' trousers, breeches and shorts, not knitted or crocheted, of cotton, n.e.s.o.i.	15,059	(b)	(b)
6110.30.30	Sweaters, pullovers and similar articles, knitted or crocheted, of manmade fibers, n.e.s.o.i.	14,076	(b)	(b)

Source: Estimated by the U.S. International Trade Commission from official statistics of the U.S. Department of Commerce.

Note: The abbreviation n.e.s.o.i. stands for "not elsewhere specified or otherwise included."

a Apparent U.S. consumption defined as U.S. production plus total imports (landed, duty-paid basis) minus exports.

b U.S. production and/or export data not available.

c Exports of Other carnations not available separately.

Table 3.4. Estimated welfare effects on the United States of leading imports that benefited exclusively from ATPA, 2009

HTS number	Description	Gain in consumer surplus (A)		Loss in tariff revenue (B)		Net welfare effect (A-B)	
		Upper estimate	Lower estimate	Upper estimate	Lower estimate	Upper estimate	Lower estimate
				Thousands of $			
2709.00.10	Petroleum oils and oils from bituminous minerals, crude, testing under 25 degrees A.P.I.	5,732	5,737	5,718	5,729	13	8
2709.00.20	Petroleum oils and oils from bituminous minerals, crude, testing 25 degrees A.P.I. or more	1,819	1,823	1,810	1,817	9	5
0603.11.00	Sweetheart, spray and other roses, fresh cut	20,036	20,078	19,365	19,448	670	630
2710.19.05	Distillate and residual fuel oil (including blends) derived from petroleum or oils from bituminous minerals, testing under 25 degrees A.P.I.	244	244	243	244	1	(a)
0603.14.00	Chrysanthemums, fresh cut	4,645	4,661	4,488	4,519	157	142
2710.11.25	Naphthas (exc. motor fuel/mtr fuel blend. stock) fr petroleum oils & bitumin minerals (o/than crude) or preps 70%+ by wt. fr petroleum oils	171	172	170	171	1	(a)
6203.42.40	Men's or boys' trousers and shorts, not bibs, not knitted or crocheted, of cotton, not containing 15% or more by weight of down, etc	(b)	(b)	(b)	(b)	(b)	(b)
1604.14.30	Tunas and skipjack, not in oil, in airtight containers, n/o 7 kg, not of U.S. possessions, over quota	4,131	4,591	3,097	3,874	1,033	717
0603.12.70	Other carnations, fresh cut	(b)	(b)	(b)	(b)	(b)	(b)
7403.11.00	Refined copper cathodes and sections of cathodes	385	389	376	383	9	6
6908.90.00	Glazed ceramic flags and paving, hearth or wall tiles; glazed ceramic mosaic cubes and the like, n.e.s.o.i.	1,547	1,637	1,376	1,545	171	92

Table 3.4. (Continued)

HTS number	Description	Gain in consumer surplus (A)		Loss in tariff revenue (B)		Net welfare effect (A-B)	
		Upper estimate	Lower estimate	Upper estimate	Lower estimate	Upper estimate	Lower estimate
0710.80.97	Vegetables n.e.s.o.i., uncooked or cooked by steaming or boiling in water, frozen, reduced in size	(b)	(b)	(b)	(b)	(b)	(b)
6109.10.00	T-shirts, singlets, tank tops and similar garments, knitted or crocheted, of cotton	(b)	(b)	(b)	(b)	(b)	(b)
2710.11.45	Light oil mixt. of hydrocarbons fr petro oils & bitum min (o/than crude) or prep 70%+ wt. fr petro oils, n.e.s.o.i., n/o 50% any single hydrocarbon	45	45	45	45	(a)	(a)
0709.20.90	Asparagus, n.e.s.o.i., fresh or chilled	2,482	2,822	2,034	2,643	448	179
6110.20.20	Sweaters, pullovers and similar articles, knitted or crocheted, of cotton, n.e.s.o.i.	(b)	(b)	(b)	(b)	(b)	(b)
0804.30.40 6105.10.00	Pineapples, fresh or dried, not reduced in size, in crates or other packages Men's or boys' shirts, knitted or crocheted, of cotton	227 (b)	230 (b)	223	228	4 (b)	1 (b)
6204.62.40	Women's or girls' trousers, breeches and shorts, not knitted or crocheted, of cotton, n.e.s.o.i.	(b)	(b)	(b)	(b)	(b)	(b)
6110.30.30	Sweaters, pullovers and similar articles, knitted or crocheted, of manmade fibers, n.e.s.o.i.	(b)	(b)	(b)	(b)	(b)	(b)

Source: Estimated by the U.S. International Trade Commission from official statistics of the U.S. Department of Commerce. Note: The abbreviation n.e.s.o.i. stands for "not elsewhere specified or otherwise included."

a Less than $500.

Table 3.5. Estimated displacement effects on the United States of leading imports that benefited exclusively from ATPA, 2009

HTS number	Description	U.S. production	Reduction in U.S. production			
			Value		Share	
			Upper estimate	Lower estimate	Upper estimate	Lower estimate
		Thousands of $			Percent	
2709.00.10	Petroleum oils and oils from bituminous minerals, crude, testing under 25 degrees A.P.I.	32,787,300	8,022	4,184	0.02	0.01
2709.00.20	Petroleum oils and oils from bituminous minerals, crude, testing 25 degrees A.P.I. or more	76,503,738	3,466	1,807	(a)	(a)
0603.11.00	Sweetheart, spray and other roses, fresh cut	17,662 8	07	130	4.57	0.73
2710.19.05	Distillate and residual fuel oil (including blends) derived from petroleum or oils from bituminous minerals, testing under 25 degrees A.P.I.	52,868,471	629	328	(a)	(a)
0603.14.00	Chrysanthemums, fresh cut	11,289	722	116	6.39	1.03
2710.11.25	Naphthas (exc. motor fuel/mtr fuel blend. stock) fr petroleum oils & bitumin minerals (o/than crude) or preps 70%+ by wt. fr petroleum oils	3,006,957	269	140	0.01	(a)
6203.42.40	Men's or boys' trousers and shorts, not bibs, not knitted or crocheted, of cotton, not containing 15% or more by weight of down, etc	(b)	(b)	(b)	(b)	(b)
1604.14.30	Tunas and skipjack, not in oil, in airtight containers, n/o 7 kg, not of U.S. possessions, over quota	475,000	9,944	5,687	2.09	1.2
0603.12.70	Other carnations, fresh cut	440	(b)	(b)	(b)	(b)
7403.11.00	Refined copper cathodes and sections of cathodes	6,034,824	1,150	639	0.02	0.01
6908.90.00	Glazed ceramic flags and paving, hearth or wall tiles; glazed ceramic mosaic cubes and the like, n.e.s.o.i.	594,000	2,136	914	0.36	0.15
0710.80.97	Vegetables n.e.s.o.i., uncooked or cooked by steaming or boiling in water, frozen, reduced in size	(b)	(b)	(b)	(b)	(b)
6109.10.00	T-shirts, singlets, tank tops and similar garments, knitted or crocheted, of cotton	(b)	(b)	(b)	(b)	(b)

Table 3.5. (Continued)

HTS number	Description	U.S. production	Reduction in U.S. production			
			Value		Share	
			Upper estimate	Lower estimate	Upper estimate	Lower estimate
		Thousands of $			Percent	
2710.11.45	Light oil mixt. of hydrocarbons fr petro oils & bitum min (o/than crude) or prep 70%+ wt. fr petro oils, n.e.s.o.i., n/o 50% any single hydrocarbon	3,212,952	88	46	(a)	(a)
0709.20.90	Asparagus, n.e.s.o.i., fresh or chilled	75,827	999	283 (b)	1.32 (b)	0.37
6110.20.20	Sweaters, pullovers and similar articles, knitted or crocheted, of cotton, n.e.s.o.i.	(b)	(E)	(b)	(b)	(b)
0804.30.40	Pineapples, fresh or dried, not reduced in size, in crates or other packages	55,000	49	13	0.09	0.02
6105.10.00	Men's or boys' shirts, knitted or crocheted, of cotton	(b)	(E)	(b)	(b)	(b)
6204.62.40	Women's or girls' trousers, breeches and shorts, not knitted or crocheted, of cotton, n.e.s.o.i.	(b)	(E)	(b)	(b)	(b)
6110.30.30	Sweaters, pullovers and similar articles, knitted or crocheted, of manmade fibers, n.e.s.o.i.	(b)	(E)	(b)	(b)	(b)

Source: Estimated by the U.S. International Trade Commission from official statistics of the U.S. Department of Commerce. Note: The abbreviation n.e.s.o.i. stands for "not elsewhere specified or otherwise included."

a Less than 0.005 percent.

Effects on U.S. producers[18]

Estimates of the potential displacement of domestic production (table 3.5) were small for most of the individual sectors.[19] The analysis indicates that the largest potential relative displacement effects were for chrysanthemums (1.0 percent to 6.4 percent of U.S. domestic production displaced, valued at $116,000 to $722,000) and fresh cut roses (0.7 percent to 4.6 percent displaced, valued at $130,000 to $807,000), mainly because of the very high U.S. market shares enjoyed by these products (see table 3.3). However, even the upper estimates of the displacement share for the majority of the products benefiting exclusively from ATPA were less than 1 percent.

Highlights of U.S. Industries Most Affected by ATPA

Industries having estimated displacements of 5 percent or more, based on upper estimates, were chosen for further analysis. In 2009, one product that benefited exclusively from ATPA met this criterion: fresh cut chrysanthemums, which is discussed in greater detail in the following section. Asparagus and fresh cut flowers (roses and chrysanthemums) were identified as having an estimated displacement of 5 percent or more in 2007.[20]

Fresh Cut Flowers: Chrysanthemums

Fresh cut flowers have been a major component of U.S. imports from ATPA countries since the 1980s, and they continue to represent an important economic activity of ATPA beneficiary countries. ATPA countries supplied 82 percent of the total value of U.S. imports of fresh cut flowers (HTS 0603) and 99 percent of the total value of U.S. imports of chrysanthemums (HTS 0603.14.00) in 2009. Virtually all U.S. imports of fresh cut flowers from beneficiary countries entered free of duty under ATPA. U.S. imports of chrysanthemums from ATPA countries are primarily sourced from Colombia and, to a much lesser extent, from Ecuador.

Fresh cut flowers are a major nontraditional agricultural export product for both Colombia and Ecuador, which were the largest and third-largest exporters of fresh cut flowers in the world in 2009, respectively.[21] Both countries enjoy year-round production and benefit from abundant water, labor, and high-quality land. The United States is an important fresh cut flower export market for ATPA countries, accounting for 80 percent of the total value of Colombian exports ($1.021 billion) and 42 percent of Ecuadorian exports ($471 million) in 2009.[22] U.S. companies have reportedly invested more than $250 million in the Colombian flower industry and owned approximately 17 percent of total Colombian cut flower production in 2009.[23]

The wholesale value of U.S.-produced fresh cut flowers was $359 million in 2009.[24] The number of commercial U.S. cut-flower growers continued to decline in 2009, falling slightly to 362 from 364 the previous year,[25] and U.S. growers continued to face significant competition from cut-flower imports, which represented almost three-quarters of U.S. fresh cut flower sales.

Lower prices for cut flowers have resulted from a trend in the industry toward large-volume production and mass marketing, reflecting increasing sales to supermarkets, home centers, and discount stores. Demand for cut flowers is highly seasonal; sales are highest from February through May and in the autumn and peak at specific occasions, particularly the Valentine's and Mother's Day holidays. Demand for cut flowers in the U.S. market weakened in 2009: both domestic and imported shipments fell 4.3 percent over 2008 as recessionary pressures curbed U.S. consumer spending.[26]

U.S. cut-flower growers increasingly produce high-value, relatively fragile cut varieties with limited import competition (e.g., lilies, tulips, and gerbera daisies), as well as other nursery products such as annual and perennial flowering plants.[27] U.S. production of chrysanthemums accounted for only 3 percent of total U.S. production of cut flowers in 2009. However, imports of chrysanthemums accounted for 92 percent of U.S. consumption of those flowers but only 7 percent of U.S. consumption of cut flowers of all types. Some U.S. growers have differentiated their products from imports to some extent by offering services not available from importers, such as quick turnaround times on special orders.

Increasing import volumes of chrysanthemums from ATPA countries have had a positive impact on U.S. consumers, who are able to purchase high-quality flowers at low prices. Many U.S. importers, distributors, and retail florists depend heavily on moderately priced fresh cut flowers from overseas. Reportedly, imports of cut flowers directly and indirectly contribute nearly 220,000 jobs to the U.S. market.[28] Jobholder include airline employees, Customs and Border Protection personel, U.S. Department of Agriculture (USDA) personnel, customs brokers, importers, truck transporters, wholesalers, retailers, Internet providers, supermarkets, and mass merchandisers. The floral importing industry in the Miami area alone reportedly spends almost $20 million annually on insurance, professional fees, and office expenses.[29]

U.S. market conditions and an oversupply of flowers on the world market have reduced profit margins of cut-flower exporters in ATPA countries to levels of 2–4 percent,[30] less than one-half of the current tariff preference. Transportation costs for cut flowers from ATPA countries are high, especially when transportation costs from Miami (the main port of entry) to other U.S. destinations are included. When these high transportation costs are considered, the roughly 6–7 percent ad valorem U.S. tariff eliminated under ATPA makes up a much smaller portion of the final cost to consumers. The tariff preference is, nevertheless, important to the continued viability of the U.S. market for cut flower exporters in ATPA countries in light of the low profit margins prevalent in the industry.[31]

Although it is possible that some higher-cost producers/exporters in ATPA countries might not be able to compete in the U.S. market absent the duty preferences, the high market share of imports in the decade prior to ATPA[32] indicates that duty preferences are not the sole competitive advantage of the cut flower industries in ATPA countries.[33] Because the high ATPA-country market share of chrysanthemums in the United States has existed for more than two decades, duty-free treatment for chrysanthemums under ATPA alone likely has a modest impact on U.S. growers of chrysanthemums today who have since diversified into other flower varieties, products, and/or services. This diversification over time into other cut varieties and nursery products appears to have lessened the impact of preferential duty treatment under ATPA for chrysanthemums on the U.S. floriculture industry as a whole.

Fresh Cut Chrysanthemums

U.S. imports of fresh cut chrysanthemums were dutiable in 2009 at the NTR rate of 6.4 percent ad valorem.[34] In 2009, virtually all U.S. imports of fresh cut chrysanthemums from the Andean countries entered free of duty under ATPA. U.S. imports of fresh cut chrysanthemums from all sources increased slightly to $94 million in 2009 over the previous year. Among ATPA beneficiary countries, Colombia was by far the leading supplier, accounting for 99 percent of the total import value from all sources in 2009. Ecuador, the next largest ATPA supplier, accounted for less than one-half of 1 percent of total imports. There were no imports of chrysanthemums from Bolivia or Peru in 2009.

U.S. sales of domestically produced fresh cut chrysanthemums fell from $13.428 million in 2008 to $11.298 million in 2009, a decrease of 16 percent.[35] However, total U.S. consumption of fresh cut chrysanthemums increased by 3 percent in 2009 to $102 million. Imports from all sources accounted for 92 percent of the value of consumption in 2009. Imports from ATPA countries, virtually all from Colombia, supplied 91 percent of the value of total U.S. consumption of fresh cut chrysanthemums in 2009, up from 87 percent in 2008.

Probable Future Effects of ATPA [2]

Most of the estimated effects on the U.S. economy and consumers of a one-time elimination of duties under a preference program such as ATPA probably occurred within two years of the program's implementation. However, other effects may occur over time as a result of an increase in export-oriented investment in the Andean countries. Such investment—in new production facilities or in the expansion of existing facilities—may occur in response to the availability of ATPA tariff preferences and may lead to increased exports under ATPA to the United States. Therefore, to the extent possible, the Commission has identified ATPA-related investment in the Andean countries as a proxy for the future trade effects of ATPA on the United States.[36]

The identification of foreign and domestic investment in 2008–09 that could generate future exports to the United States under ATPA has been particularly challenging because of the changing nature of the U.S. trading relationship with the beneficiary countries. In particular, because of the U.S.-Peru TPA, it is expected that most investments in ATPA-eligible products in Peru will likely generate future exports that enter the U.S. market under the TPA, rather than ATPA. Similarly, possible ATPA-related investments in Colombia cannot readily be isolated from investments that may have been made in response to the pending U.S.-Colombia TPA. In the case of Bolivia, the President suspended its designation as an ATPA beneficiary country effective December 15, 2008, and the large uncertainty regarding its future status as an ATPA beneficiary likely discouraged any ATPA-related investments. Because of the U.S.-Peru TPA and Bolivia's suspension from ATPA, the future effects of ATPA are likely to be driven primarily by investments made in Colombia and Ecuador.

Because U.S. imports from Colombia, Ecuador, and Peru represented such a small portion of total U.S. imports in 2009 (1.3 percent), and an even smaller share with respect to U.S. imports of ATPA-exclusive products (0.5 percent), the probable future effects of ATPA on the overall U.S. economy are likely to be minimal.[37] The U.S. embassies in Colombia and Ecuador were able to identify some investments in 2009 that could generate future exports to the United States under ATPA, but many of these were small and remained below 2008 investment levels. Investments were identified in the textile and apparel, broccoli, flower, pineapple, and plywood sectors or subsectors, but most of these investments were made to maintain existing operations and improve production processes to maintain competitiveness, rather than to increase production and exports to the United States. Company closures or declines in cultivation were cited in the case of the textile and apparel, broccoli, flower, pineapple, and mango sectors. Non-ATPA factors that reportedly contributed to these declines included the global economic downturn, as well as exchange rate trends and domestic policies that hurt the investment environment. The U.S. Embassy in Peru anticipates increased exports from Peru to the United States, particularly in agricultural products, but these products can enter the U.S. market under the TPA. The U.S. Embassy in Bolivia was able to identify small investments in the leather and apparel sectors, but as discussed above, Bolivia is currently suspended from ATPA.

In addition to the global economic downturn, which significantly dampened overall foreign direct investment throughout the Andean region, foreign government officials and industry representatives emphasized the adverse impact on ATPA-related investment during 2008–09 of the repeated expirations and short-term renewals of ATPA. The uncertainty about whether ATPA preferences will continue in the future has discouraged ATPA-related investment, especially for products that require larger or longer-term investments. [38] For example, some industries—such as apparel, flowers, and certain agricultural products—require planning as many as 12 to 18 months in advance.[39]

Furthermore, government and industry representatives noted the importance of retaining ATPA preferences even when a beneficiary country implements an FTA with the United States. ATPA permits cumulation of origin of goods among beneficiary countries to meet the value-content requirement, which is not permitted under the U.S.-Peru TPA.[40] In the textile and apparel industry, ATPA regional cumulation of origin is particularly important because Colombia, Ecuador, and Peru have established regional production chains that support their exports to the United States under ATPA. For example, the Colombian textile and apparel industry uses yarns and fabrics from both Peru and Ecuador. Should Peru be graduated from ATPA, Colombian apparel using Peruvian inputs could no longer receive ATPA duty free treatment. Government and industry representatives note that regional cumulation is particularly important for this industry, given the competition it continues to face with China and other Asian countries. Furthermore, the uncertainty about future rules of origin provides another layer of uncertainty regarding future U.S. market access, which affects long-term planning and investment.[41] The country sections below provide more detailed information on ATPA-related investments made during 2008–09 and specifically address the apparel industry, given the importance of ATPA for apparel imports from the Andean countries. Information on ATPA-related investment activity and trends during 2008–09 was drawn largely from official telegrams from U.S. embassies in the Andean region. The Commission's public hearing and written submissions also provided important information. Because disaggregated ATPA-related investment data are not available, overall FDI data are presented to provide context.

Foreign Direct Investment in the Andean Countries

According to preliminary data provided by the UN Economic Commission for Latin America and the Caribbean, FDI inflows to Bolivia, Colombia, Ecuador, and Peru each increased slightly between 2007 and 2008, but declined substantially in 2009 because of the global economic crisis (table 3.6). FDI in the Andean countries continued to be concentrated in natural resource-based industries such as hydrocarbons and mining, and the sudden decline in commodity prices in late 2008 and their slow recovery resulted in a decline in such investment in 2009 in Bolivia, Ecuador, and Peru. In Colombia, the largest recipient of FDI among the ATPA countries, FDI in mining increased (in coal, in particular), but was offset by declines in other sectors, including a 69 percent decline in manufacturing FDI and a 22 percent decline in petroleum FDI. The U.S. recession resulted in a decline in export-oriented investment throughout the region.[42]

Bolivia

Although Bolivia was not eligible for ATPA preferences in 2009, the U.S. Embassy in Bolivia conducted an informal survey of firms and was able to identify $1.6 million worth of investments in 2008 and $600,000 worth of investments in 2009 in the leather and apparel sectors. The firms surveyed indicated a dramatic drop in exports to the United States in 2009 after Bolivia lost its ATPA beneficiary status. Furthermore, none of these products were eligible for U.S. preferences under the GSP. Among the apparel firms surveyed, one indicated it was able to increase its sales to Europe, partially offsetting its lost sales to the United States, and another firm indicated it is focusing on the local market and made investments to open local stores in 2009. A third apparel firm indicated it had closed because of the loss of the U.S. market. The U.S. embassy also surveyed companies producing quinoa and found that investments remained fairly stable between 2008 and 2009; these companies were able to continue to export to the United States in 2009 under the GSP.[43]

Table 3.6. Foreign direct investment inflows, by host regions and by economies, 2005–09 (*Million dollars*)

Host region/economy	2005	2006	2007	2008	2009
World	958,697	1,461,074	1,978,838	1,697,353	1,040,000
Developing countries	316,444	433,764	529,344	620,733	406,000
Latin America and the Caribbean	76,412	74,794	111,844	131,938	76,681
Andean countries	13,033	10,672	15,096	19,016	12,691
Bolivia	-291	278	362	508	418
Colombia	10,252	6,656	9,049	10,583	7,201
Ecuador	493	271	194	1,001	312
Peru	2,579	3,467	5,491	6,924	4,760

Source: ECLAC, Foreign Direct Investment in Latin America and the Caribbean, 2009, table 1.2, table 1.3, and Annex table 1.A-2; United Nations' Conference on Trade and Development (UNCTAD), World Investment Report, 2009, Annex table B.1; and UNCTAD, World Investment Report, 2008, Annex table B.1.

The government of Bolivia estimated that before Bolivia's suspension, ATPA trade preferences created 19,300 jobs, mostly in the clothing sector. According to a submission from the Andean Community, the suspension of preferences for Bolivia affected thousands of these workers, particularly in the textiles and leather sectors. Also, the number of companies that exported to the United States declined from 57 to 49 following the suspension. The National Chamber of Exporters of Bolivia estimated that the level of employment in the sectors manufacturing textile made of cotton and other fibers has fallen by 30 percent.[44] According to the U.S. Embassy, the Bolivian government attempted to open markets in Venezuela, Brazil, and Argentina to offset losses in the U.S. market, but met only limited success. Other Bolivian products that formerly entered the United States under ATPA now enter under the GSP, such as jewelry, wooden furniture, hearts of palm, and onions.[45]

Bolivia: Textile and Apparel Sector

As noted above, Bolivia is only a small supplier of textiles and apparel to the United States, accounting for about 1 percent of total U.S. imports of textiles and apparel from the Andean region in 2009. The United States has been a major market for Bolivia's exports, and textile and apparel manufacturing is important to Bolivia's economy.[46] Most of Bolivia's production is in apparel and accessories, and access to high-quality raw materials, including cotton, alpaca, angora, and llama, has made Bolivia globally competitive in these niche markets.[47] Preferential tariff treatment under ATPA benefited Bolivia's textile and apparel sector for several years by increasing employment, improving facilities, and expanding training programs.[48]

Between 2008 and 2009, Bolivia's exports of textiles and apparel to the United States fell sharply (by 46 percent) to $8.3 million; exports of men's and boys' cotton knit shirts, a leading export category, declined by 40 percent to $3.3 million.[49] The drop in U.S. imports of textiles and apparel from Bolivia in 2009 can be attributed to the suspension of ATPA tariff benefits for Bolivia on December 15, 2008.[50] The suspension of ATPA benefits also reportedly led to thousands of job losses, apparel plant closures, and declines in revenues.[51] Ametex, a leading Bolivian textile and apparel manufacturer serving U.S. customers such as Polo Ralph Lauren, reportedly lost many U.S. customers and saw projected annual revenues reduced by half since the suspension of ATPA benefits for Bolivia; [52] it laid off 1,800 direct and indirect workers and sent almost 1,000 workers home on paid leave. Several other Bolivian apparel firms reported sharp declines in export sales to the U.S. market, and in response, some have shifted their focus to domestic or regional markets or to Europe.[53]

Colombia

Following a record high in 2008, overall FDI in Colombia declined in 2009 because of the global economic downturn. However, FDI was still significantly higher in 2009 than FDI levels a decade ago, largely because of the improved security situation, which has significantly improved Colombia's investment environment. Although the U.S. Embassy in Colombia said that specific investment information was not available for ATPArelated products, it indicated that FDI dropped dramatically in the manufacturing and agricultural/fishing sectors in 2009, which include the major ATPA-related industries in Colombia. In particular, the U.S. Embassy noted that both the cut flower and the textile and apparel industries "have suffered in recent years" for a variety of reasons, including a strong peso vis-à-vis the U.S. dollar, a Venezuelan ban on imports of Colombian goods since August 2009[54] that has hurt the apparel industry, competition with China in the case of apparel (see below), and unexpected freezing weather and depressed global demand (in the case of flowers).[55]

Although specific data are not available, one source indicated that Colombian flower growers have "invested heavily" over the last few years to increase their productivity, which also mitigated the adverse effects of three freezes during December 2009 and January 2010. However, the relatively strong peso has resulted in "razor-thin margins" for flower exporters, which has "prevented them from making the considerable investments needed to develop new varieties and continue providing a differentiated product in world markets." About 20 Colombian flower farms went out of business in 2009, and the number of workers in the industry declined slightly in 2009.[56]

According to the government of Colombia, "ATPA-ATPDEA has had a positive effect in promoting export-oriented production in Colombia, which in turn, has generated economic growth and employment in both Colombia and the United States." However, the government indicated that the short-term extensions of ATPA have acted as a strong disincentive to long-term investment, particularly in the flower and textile and apparel industries.[57] Industry representatives in these sectors said that the lack of long-term certainty prevents the robust investment necessary to "put these industries on a track toward long-term viability."[58] According to Colombian flower industry officials, the continued uncertainty surrounding ATPA renewal is "unsustainable and disruptive."[59]

Colombia: Textile and Apparel Sector

Colombia, the second largest Andean supplier of textiles and apparel to the United States, accounted for 28 percent of total U.S. imports of textiles and apparel from the ATPA countries in 2009. Colombia's textile and apparel sector has been a leading source of economic activity and employment for years. In 2009, with 129,434 workers, textile and apparel manufacturing accounted for 20 percent of Colombia's manufacturing jobs, 1.3 percent of Colombia's GDP, 10 percent of Colombia's manufacturing GDP, and 4 percent of total exports.[60] In 2009, Colombia's exports of textiles and apparel to the United States totaled just under $248 million, a 34 percent decline from the 2008 level.[61] Seventy-one percent of these exports ($209 million) entered the United States under ATPA; leading products included cotton trousers and pants, cotton underwear, cotton hosiery, cotton pile towels, and cotton knit shirts and blouses.

Colombian apparel producers contract with many well-known U.S. brands and retailers, including Abercrombie & Fitch, Adidas, Avon, Brooks Brothers, Charter Club, DKNY, Dockers, Eddie Bauer, the Gap, Hanes, Jockey, Land's End, Levi Strauss & Co., Oscar de la Renta, and many others.[62] Industry sources report that Inditex, the Benetton Group, Payless, and the Cherokee Group have been expanding their sourcing from Colombia. [63] Although wool suit-type coats had been a significant export from Colombia to the United States in earlier years, exports of these garments fell 70 percent to $7.1 million during 2008–09.

Industry sources in Colombia report that in recent years, Colombia's textile and apparel sector has experienced a 20 percent downturn in production and several factory closings, as well as a loss of 40,000 jobs, because of several competitive challenges.[64] Industry sources report that short-term extensions to ATPA and the absence of an implemented free trade agreement with the United States have created uncertainty and discouraged new foreign investment in Colombia's textile and apparel manufacturing sector. [65] Increased competition from contraband and legal apparel imports from China and the appreciation of the Colombian peso from 2,561 per dollar in March 2009 to 1,997 per dollar by year-end 2009 may have also reduced the price competitiveness of Colombia's textile and apparel exports.[66] Although security concerns related to Colombia's history of political and drug-related violence reportedly have eased in recent years, the possibility of the return of violence remains and may deter foreign investors.[67]

Colombia, with significant denim production, has supplied U.S. apparel firms such as Levi Strauss & Co with the cloth.[68] Although Colombia grows short and medium-staple cotton, it must import a significant amount of cotton to meet its production requirements.[69] The United States is the largest supplier of Colombia's imported cotton and accounted for 95 percent ($77 million) of Colombia's cotton imports in 2009.[70] Like the rest of the textile and apparel sector, Colombia's denim producers experienced reduced profits and downturns of sales during the recent global economic crisis.[71] Nevertheless, in early 2010, sources in Colombia began to report signs of recovery and a focus on high-end products for new customers like American Eagle and Abercrombie & Fitch.[72]

Chief among the priorities of Colombia's government and its textile and apparel sector is securing a longer-term extension of ATPA not only for Colombia, but also for Peru, which currently benefits under both ATPA and the U.S.-Peru TPA. Colombian government officials assert that "if the program is not extended for Peru, these products would be affected and that also has an impact for Colombian garments that use Peruvian inputs which are later exported duty-free to the United States."[73]

Ecuador

Overall FDI in Ecuador fell in 2009, particularly in mining. FDI in the petroleum and manufacturing sectors also declined, while FDI in the agriculture, hunting, and forestry sector increased slightly.[74] In addition to the global economic downturn, Ecuador's investment environment has become increasingly uncertain because of evolving and sometimes unpredictable government policies, which have discouraged private investment.[75] According to the U.S. Embassy in Ecuador, investments in the production of many ATPA-eligible products also declined in 2009, including flowers, frozen broccoli, and textiles and apparel.[76]

The U.S. Embassy conducted an informal survey of companies producing Ecuador's major exports under ATPA, including fresh cut flowers, frozen broccoli, pineapples, textiles and apparel, plywood, and mangoes. (Producers of pouched tuna, another major export under ATPA, did not respond to the survey.) Should ATPA preferences lapse, most of the industries surveyed claimed there would be a significant adverse impact on their exports. Ecuadorian exports of plywood and mangoes, however, are also eligible for GSP treatment.

According to the Embassy, the health of the Ecuadoran flower sector has suffered from the global economic downturn as well as government policies that have increased taxes and labor costs. In 2009, about 12 flower growers reportedly closed. Also, the flower sector suffered a 10 percent decline in the area under cultivation and a 16 percent loss of employment that year. Growers responding to the survey indicated stable or declining investments between 2008 and 2009.[77]

In the frozen broccoli sector, the survey indicated that investments fell between 2008 and 2009 and that no major investments have been made over the past several years because of the uncertainties stemming from the short-term extensions of ATPA, despite growth potential in the U.S. market. Two broccoli companies closed in 2009. Although data were not available in the pineapple sector, pineapple growers indicated that investments of about $50 million annually are required to maintain the crop until harvest. Cultivated area in this sector fell by about 20 percent in 2009 compared to 2008. Investment in the textile and apparel sector fell in 2009 (see below); the main policy concern among industry producers is that ATPA regional cumulation continue, because Ecuador exports fabric to Colombia, where it is used to produce apparel that is exported to the United States under ATPA.

There have been no new investments in the mango sector over the last few years, and the cultivated area destined for exports has contracted. Companies producing plywood reported varying trends in investment; one reported no investments in 2008 or 2009, while another reported an investment in 2009 that, while small, was higher than in 2008.

According to the government of Ecuador, ATPA has enabled Ecuador to diversify its exports, increasing the number of products from 250 in 2008 to 262 in 2009.[78] Examples of non-traditional agricultural products that are benefiting from ATPA or expected to take advantage of ATPA preferences are fresh papaya; canned fruits and vegetables; organic sugar;[79] gourmet products, including edible oils, macadamia nuts, and special chocolates; tropical fruit juices and concentrates; and crabmeat.[80]

Ecuador: Textile and Apparel Sector

Ecuador, the smallest Andean supplier of textiles and apparel to the United States, accounted for less than 1 percent of total U.S. imports in this sector from the region in 2009. Textile and apparel manufacturing has nevertheless been a historically significant component of the country's economy, an important contributor to employment, and one of Ecuador's principal export sectors.[81] Ecuador's textile industry reportedly has been growing in recent years, largely because of the duty preferences granted by ATPA.[82] The Textile Industry Association of Ecuador (AITE) reported that investment in Ecuador's textile and apparel sector totaled $53.9 million in 2008 and $45.0 million in 2009, of which an estimated 40 percent was related to the ATPA program.[83]

With an estimated 60,000 workers, Ecuador's textile and apparel sector primarily manufactures yarns and fabrics, but also produces materials for industrial production, finished clothing, and household products.[84] During 2008–09, Ecuador's textile and apparel exports to the United States fell by one-third to $7.4 million, which can likely be attributed to the downturn in the U.S. economy and uncertainty caused by the short-term extensions of ATPA.[85] Like those in other beneficiary countries, industry sources in Ecuador have stated that the recent short-term renewals of ATPA have been destabilizing and counterproductive. They assert that renewals for longer periods such as 3–5 years would allow companies to "make the appropriate investments" to further expand their success.[86]

Over 90 percent ($7.2 million) of U.S. imports of textiles and apparel from Ecuador entered under ATPA. In 2009, man-made fiber hosiery represented the bulk of Ecuador's apparel exports to the United States. Ecuador's demand for raw materials, particularly cotton, for textile and apparel production exceeds supply, and therefore its textile and apparel sector relies on imported inputs to meet its needs. In 2009, the United States was the leading supplier of cotton and cotton yarns and fabrics to Ecuador, accounting for just over one-fourth ($21.2 million) of Ecuador's imports of these items.[87]

A major issue for Ecuador's textiles and apparel sector is competition from China and other Asian suppliers, whose yarn and fabric can be priced 25 percent lower than Ecuador's. Although China has recently begun to lose its competitive edge because of rising labor rates, revaluation of the yuan, and elimination of export subsidies, its large-scale manufacturing operations enable it to remain a principal source of competition for Ecuador and other global textile and apparel suppliers.[88] Consequently, maintaining the existing rules of origin in the ATPA that allow cumulation of Andean content and permit the leveraging of the competitive advantages of each participating country (Ecuador, Peru, Colombia, and the United States) is considered vital for Ecuador and its Andean neighbors.[89] The government of Ecuador has been taking steps and implementing reforms to increase the competitiveness of its manufacturers and industry sources anticipate that by the end of 2010, U.S. firms will be moving some of their sourcing to the Andean region.[90]

Peru

Like other countries in the region, Peru saw its overall FDI inflows decline in 2009 because of the world economic downturn. However, the $4.76 billion level of FDI recorded in 2009 was still significantly higher than in any other year except 2007–08. The mining sector was the primary recipient of FDI in 2009. The U.S. Embassy in Peru reported that although investments are slowly turning to less traditional sectors, such as non-traditional agricultural and textile products, Peru's vast natural resource reserves will likely continue to drive investments towards the extractive industries.[91]

According to the U.S. Embassy, ATPA continued to have a positive impact on exports from and investment in Peru in 2008–09, and implementation of the U.S.-Peru TPA in February 2009 "has enabled investment and exports to become further entrenched while continuing to grow." The U.S. Embassy noted that Peru's most dynamic export sectors are textiles and apparel (see below), agribusiness, fisheries, wood products, and metal products. Peruvian agricultural exports reached a record high in 2008, in part reflecting important growth in non-traditional products, such as asparagus, grapes, mangoes, artichokes, avocados, and paprika. These products were important and growing Peruvian exports under ATPA, but now they can enter the United States under the TPA. Exports of organic products and biofuels are also expected to grow. According to the U.S. Embassy, the agricultural sector is expected to grow in coming years because of Peru's potential for agricultural land expansion as well as government incentives that improved the agricultural investment environment. Investment in the agriculture sector grew from $55 million in 2007 to $100 million in 2008, before dropping to $76 million in 2009. These figures include major investments in the biofuels (primarily sugarcane and ethanol) sector.[92]

Peru: Textile and Apparel Sector

Although a small sector of Peru's economy, textile and apparel manufacturing is an important export industry. As the leading Andean textile and apparel exporter to the United States since 2004, Peru accounted for 70 percent ($620 million) of U.S. sector imports from the region in 2009. Peru has a skilled labor force with competitive labor rates compared to neighboring Latin American countries and a vertically integrated textile and apparel industry, from the production of high-quality raw material inputs (indigenous supplies of pima cotton renowned worldwide for its fineness, sheen, and silky texture, as well as alpaca, llama, and vicuña) to the manufacture of intermediate products such as yarns and fabrics, and finally, to the production of high-quality, finished apparel.[93] Peru's leading textile companies include Topy Top, Textimax, Diseño y Color, Sudamerica de Fibras, and Industrias Nettalco.[94] Most of Peru's garment production is exported to the United States and to nearby Venezuela and Colombia.[95] U.S. buyers of Peru's apparel products include Land's End, which sells pima cotton knit shirts in its online and print catalogs, as well as Calvin Klein, Polo Ralph Lauren, Zara, and Saks Fifth Avenue.[96]

Although U.S. sector imports from Peru climbed steadily for the first few years following the implementation of ATPDEA in 2002, since 2006, U.S. imports have decreased annually and declined by 24 percent during 2008–09. The year 2009 was particularly challenging for Peru's textile and apparel sector, being marked not only by the dip in exports, but also by a 25 percent drop in industry revenues to about $2.6 billion.[97] The economic downturn in the global and U.S. markets, uncertainty concerning the short-term extensions of ATPA in 2008 and 2009, and competition from China contributed to these developments.[98] As a result, in

2009, there were no reports of any significant new foreign investments made in Peru's textile and apparel industry. However, industry sources reported that higher margins obtained in international markets for garment exports prompted fiber production companies to invest in knitting and apparel equipment and infrastructure.[99]

Currently, qualifying U.S. sector imports from Peru may enter free of duty under either ATPA or the TPA, which entered into force in February 2009. Whereas in 2008, 95 percent of total U.S. sector imports from Peru entered free of duty under ATPA, in 2009, the share of total U.S. imports entering free of duty under ATPA declined to two-thirds, as imports from Peru began entering under the TPA.[100] Industry representatives have expressed concern, however, that if Peru is graduated from ATPA, Peruvian garments made of inputs sourced from neighboring countries such as Colombia will likely no longer qualify for duty-free entry into the United States; the same will be true of sector products made of inputs from Peru that are later imported into the U.S. market from other Andean countries.[101]

Cotton knit shirts and blouses were the leading apparel products entering the United States from Peru in 2009. U.S. exports of cotton yarns and fabrics to Peru totaled $16.5 million in 2009, down 11 percent from 2008. Although Peru grows cotton, its textile and apparel sector must supplement a shortfall of domestic cotton production used in export garments with cotton imports, primarily from the United States, which supplied 99 percent ($68.8 million) of Peru's cotton imports in 2009.[102]

IMPACT OF ATPA ON DRUG-RELATED CROP ERADICATION AND CROP SUBSTITUTION IN 2008 AND 2009

A key aim of ATPA is to improve access to U.S. markets for certain imports from Bolivia, Colombia, Ecuador, and Peru in order to promote legal economic alternatives to illegal drug activity.[1] This chapter assesses the estimated effects of ATPA on drug-related crop eradication and crop substitution efforts for each of these countries during 2008 and 2009. Information in this chapter has been drawn from official U.S. and other national government sources, as well as testimony before, and submissions to, the Commission. Data presented in this chapter are official statistics published by the U.S. Department of State unless otherwise noted.

Overview

The importation of cocaine continues to be a major domestic concern for the United States despite the decline in the rate of U.S. cocaine consumption—in fact, of all illegal drug consumption—over the past decade.[2] Because essentially all cocaine originates in the Andean countries of Bolivia, Colombia, and Peru, the United States has channeled a significant portion of its international counternarcotics resources toward eliminating illegal coca cultivation, and it continues to provide assistance to these countries in an effort to reduce coca cultivation, the processing of coca into cocaine, cocaine abuse domestically in these countries, and the transport of cocaine to other countries.[3]

U.S. as well as international counternarcotics agencies have long stated that drug crop eradication alone only temporarily disrupts the flow of illegal drugs unless producers reliant on drug crop cultivation can successfully develop an alternative livelihood.[4] Alternative development (AD) programs offer farmers opportunities to abandon illegal activities and join the legitimate economy, [5] an objective supported by the ATPA provisions that help build an international export market for the legal alternative crops developed through these programs. In 2008 and 2009, ATPA continued to contribute to U.S. counternarcotics efforts in this way, indirectly helping to promote the eradication of illegal drug crops and the substitution of legal crops, as implemented through U.S. and multilateral economic assistance programs, even though these programs and ATPA duty-free provisions are not directly connected.

AD policies, initially conceived as simple crop substitution projects, have expanded their focus more recently to include not just legal crop substitution for illegal drug cultivation, but also broader social and economic development projects. The Alternative Development and Livelihoods programs operated by the U.S. Agency for International Development (USAID), as part of the U.S. Department of State, now look not only to generate sustainable, legal employment and income opportunities in regions vulnerable to drug production and conflict, but also to improve the capacity of municipal governments to plan and provide basic social services and infrastructure; foster citizen participation in local decisionmaking; strengthen social infrastructure; and promote transparency and accountability at the local level.[6]

These AD programs are now seeking to consolidate gains achieved to date as these legal crops begin to reach full-yielding maturity.[7] The programs are also starting to work more closely with national government AD and counternarcotics programs, increasingly integrating U.S. projects with national AD projects and objectives.[8] As a consequence, ATPA continues to contribute indirectly to U.S. counternarcotics efforts by operating in tandem with other U.S. economic programs that are not part of the ATPA provisions, the combination helping to establish an environment where local farmers have an incentive to abandon illegal crop production in favor of legal crop production that can in turn be exported to the U.S. market free of duty for products from eligible countries.[9]

Role of ATPA in Counternarcotics Efforts

A central goal of ATPA's trade-based incentives is to encourage legal crops and products, in particular those for export both to the United States and elsewhere, as an alternative to illegal crop production. Increased production of ATPA-eligible exports helps support job growth in the legitimate economy in a variety of economic sectors in the region. Mainstream export crops such as bananas, cacao, coffee, corn, cotton, and pineapples have prospered as a result of U.S. and other countries and organizations' AD projects; their success has led to an expansion in the types of additional agricultural and nonagricultural products available for export. These include exports of annatto seed (achiote), amaranth, broccoli, hearts of palm (palmito), herbs, honey, milk, palm fruit (pijuayo), palm oil, poultry, stevia (a natural sweetener), tea, and other fruits and vegetables and their preparations, as well as fish products.[10] Moreover, as a result of the 2002 ATPDEA, additional jobs have been created in the textile and apparel industries in the Andean countries eligible under ATPA, and to a lesser extent, in industries such as jewelry and wood products as well.

Regional Cultivation and Eradication Trends during 2008 and 2009

Illegal coca cultivation fell substantially in the Andean countries of Bolivia, Colombia, and Peru, from a 20-year peak of 232,500 hectares (ha) in 2007 to 192,000 ha in 2008, according to the U.S. Department of State—a decline of over 17 percent (see table 4.1 and Figure 4.1). [11] Using a different approach, the United Nations also recorded a reduction in coca cultivation in these countries, from 181,600 ha in 2007 to 167,600 ha in 2008, a decline of nearly 8 percent; the figure fell to 158,800 ha in 2009, a decline of over 5 percent from 2008.[12] Ecuador—also an ATPA beneficiary country—effectively eradicated its coca cultivation by 1992, although it remains a major transit country for illegal drugs trafficked from Colombia and Peru.[13]

Country Profiles on Eradication and Alternative Development during 2008 and 2009

Colombia

The U.S. Department of State reports that illegal coca cultivation in Colombia fell, from 167,000 ha in 2007 to 119,000 ha in 2008, a decline of nearly 29 percent.[14] The United Nations recorded a similar drop, from 99,000 ha in 2007 to 81,000 ha in 2008 and to 68,000 ha in 2009. This represents a decline of over 18 percent between 2007 and 2008, and a further 16 percent decline between 2008 and 2009.[15]

Since the start of Plan Colombia in 1999, eradication of illegal crops in Colombia has increasingly required manual eradication to supplement widespread aerial spraying, as narcotics traffickers move coca plantings to ever more remote and rugged areas in the country's interior—such as border areas, national parks, reserves for indigenous peoples, and forest management areas.[16] In particular, traffickers are moving coca cultivation to within the 10-kilometer zone along the border where Colombian authorities have suspended the aerial eradication program in response to objections from Ecuador and Venezuela to the drifting of the herbicide spray (glyphosate) into their territories.[17] Nonetheless, the aerial eradication program sprayed 104,771 ha in 2009.[18]

Table 4.1. Coca cultivation and eradication in the Andean countries, in hectares, 1991–2009

Year	Bolivia	Colombia	Ecuador[a]	Peru	Total[b]
	Total cultivation[c]				
1991	53,388	38,472	120	120,800	212,780
1992	48,652	38,059	0	129,100	215,811
1993	49,597	40,493	0	108,800	198,890
1994	49,158	49,610	0	108,600	207,368
1995	54,093	59,650	0	115,300	229,043
1996	55,612	72,800	0	95,659	224,071
1997	52,826	98,500	0	72,262	223,588
1998	49,621	168,166	0	58,825	276,612
1999	38,799	166,046	0	52,500	257,345
2000	22,253	183,571	0	40,200	246,024
2001	29,335	254,051	0	37,900	321,286

Table 4.1. (Continued)

Year	Bolivia	Colombia	Ecuador[a]	Peru	Total[b]
2002	33,439	267,145	0	42,000	342,584
2003	33,200	246,617	0	42,463	322,280
2004	33,037	261,646	0	35,105	329,788
2005	32,573	314,033	0	42,966	389,572
2006	30,870	370,924	0	52,137	453,931
2007	35,769	386,529	0	47,057	469,355
2008	37,484	348,228	0	51,143	436,855
2009	41,341	in process	0	in process	tbd
		Eradication			
1991	5,488	972	80	0	6,540
1992	3,152	959	0	0	4,111
1993	2,397	793	0	0	3,190
1994	1,058	4,910	0	0	5,968
1995	5,493	8,750	0	0	14,243
1996	7,512	5,600	0	1,259	14,371
1997	7,026	41,843	0	3,462	52,331
1998	11,621	66,366	0	7,825	85,812
1999	16,999	43,246	0	14,733	74,978
2000	7,953	47,371	0	6,206	61,530
2001	9,435	84,251	0	6,436	100,122
2002	11,839	122,695	0	7,134	141,668
2003	10,000	132,817	0	7,022	149,839
2004	8,437	147,546	0	7,605	163,588
2005	6,073	170,033	0	8,966	185,072
2006	5,070	213,724	0	10,137	228,931
2007	6,269	219,529	0	11,057	236,855
2008	5,484	229,228	0	10,143	244,855
2009	6,341	165,272	0	10,025	181,638
1991	47,900	37,500	40	120,800	206,240
1992	45,500	37,100	0	129,100	211,700
1993	47,200	39,700	0	108,800	195,700
1994	48,100	45,000	0	108,600	201,700
1995	48,600	50,900	0	115,300	214,800
1996	48,100	67,200	0	94,400	209,700
1997	45,800	79,500	0	68,800	194,100
1998	38,000	101,800	0	51,000	190,800
1999	21,800	122,800	0	34,700	179,300
2000	19,600	136,200	0	31,700	187,500
2001	19,900	169,800	0	32,100	221,800
2002	21,600	144,450	0	34,700	200,750
2003	23,200	113,800	0	29,250	166,250
2004	24,600	114,100	0	27,500	166,200
2005	26,500	144,000	0	34,000	204,500
2006	25,800	157,200	0	42,000	225,000
2007	29,500	167,000	0	36,000	232,500

Year	Bolivia	Colombia	Ecuador[a]	Peru	Total[b]
2008	32,000	119,000	0	41,000	192,000
2009	35,000	in process	0	in process	T.B.D.

Source: USDOS, INCSR 2010, and previous issues.

Note: T.B.D. indicates "to be determined." "In process" indicates most recent data available as of September 1, 2010.

a Ecuador eliminated its small area of coca cultivation by 1992. The United Nations estimates that Ecuador grew less than 25 ha of coca in 2008 and 2009.

b Total is the simple sum of the data shown for the four Andean countries.

c The USDOS discontinued publication of the data series "cultivation" (i.e., total cultivation) following INCSR 2005, but continued the data series "net cultivation." The figures for "net cultivation" plus "eradication" would typically sum to "total cultivation," the method used in this table. (The terms "estimated cultivation" and "potential harvest" were reported in earlier INCSR reports for Colombia, in place of the terms "cultivation" and "net cultivation.") Starting in 2004, two series for eradication were published for Colombia—"aerial eradication" and "manual eradication"—which are added together here in table 4.1 for a single total.

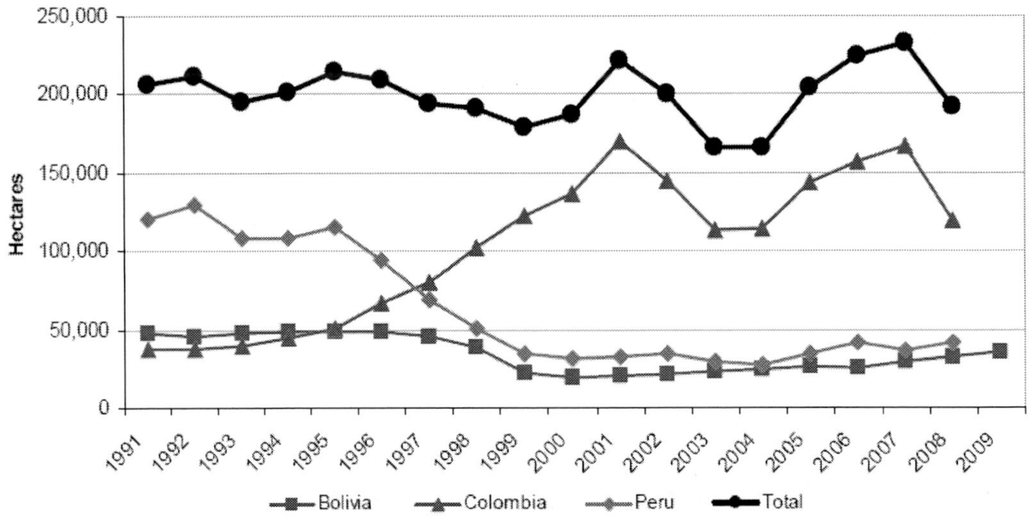

Source: USDOS, INCSR 2010, and previous issues. Table includes most recent data available.
Figure 4.1. Net coca cultivation in the Andean countries, 1991–2009.

Alternative Development

The U.S. Department of State reported that U.S. alternative development initiatives in Colombia have provided support for over 238,000 ha of legal crop cultivation by mid-2008.[19] Taken together with Colombian government AD programs, AD projects over the past seven years are reported by the U.S. Department of State to cover over 659,926 ha of agricultural cultivation, forestry plantation, and natural forest management activities by the end of September 2009, reaching or strengthening government presence in 18 administrative departments in Colombia.[20]

The United States continues to work closely with the government of Colombia to eradicate coca and opium poppies, as well as provide options to deter replanting of coca and encourage legal livelihoods.[21] U.S. imports from Colombia under ATPA include agricultural products—such as cut flowers, apparel, sugar, and vegetable and fruit preparations [22] —which can provide legal employment opportunities to communities renouncing illegal drug crop cultivation.

In January 2007, the Colombian government presented a new strategy to consolidate gains made under Plan Colombia, a strategy implemented in March 2009 as the National Consolidation Plan.[23] The plan seeks to integrate security, counternarcotics efforts, AD projects, and justice programs in targeted zones to reduce violence and consolidate security and state presence in priority areas.[24] Beginning in 2010, the USAID's AD program in Colombia is scheduled to be aligned in large part with the government's National Consolidation Plan.[25]

Ecuador

Coca cultivation in Ecuador is negligible, according to the United Nations Office of Drugs and Crime, although Ecuador is a major transit country for illegal drugs trafficked from Colombia and Peru.[26] The government has kept Ecuador virtually free of coca production since the mid-1980s.[27] The current government of Ecuador has adopted a tougher stance than previous administrations on combating narcotics trafficking by implementing new policies and programs, particularly along its northern border with Colombia,[28] with AD programs playing a role in preventing coca cultivation and other narcotics-related activities.

Alternative Development

USAID's AD program in Ecuador contributes to the economic and social development of both the northern and southern border regions, areas where poverty, lack of legitimate employment, and geographic isolation, as well as proximity to narcotics traffickers and insurgents in Colombia in particular, contribute to instability.[29] This program supports the government of Ecuador's efforts to improve livelihoods and infrastructure, strengthen local government, and open opportunities to expand legal economic activity, in particular as part of its northern border development master plan.[30]

In fiscal year (FY) 2008, USAID's AD program in Ecuador financed the construction of a number of infrastructure projects—such as roads, bridges, irrigation canals, and water and sanitation systems—in the northern border region.[31] USAID also provided assistance to 10 "anchor" firms that strengthened linkages between small farmers and production and marketing networks involving cacao, coffee, broccoli, and milk.[32] As a result, licit jobs were created in the northern border region, increasing participating farmers' income roughly 22 percent to approximately $1,200 on average and expanding legal crop coverage by 2,000 ha.[33] USAID also extended potable water and sanitation access to nearly 15,000 people, and helped establish local community water management boards that manage and maintain these new water works projects.[34]

USAID assistance has moved to help create new supply and value chains ("clusters") where small producers and businesses aim to become specialized suppliers to larger firms selling in both local and international markets. USAID investment in FY2008 was more than matched by private sector investment to create new cluster groups in Ecuador. These value-chain activities are primarily in the agroindustrial export sectors, producing items such as dairy products, hearts of palm, chili peppers, and medicinal herbs, as well as in the jewelry and hat industries. This AD investment has created jobs and increased revenues for nearly 2,000 small and medium-sized firms.[35] Future USAID projects are planned to implement the value-chain methodology in key areas in an effort to increase employment, raise incomes of participating families by 25 percent on average, and improve productivity on 3,400 new hectares of land.[36] USAID further provided technical training to several of Ecuador's largest banks in the financial analysis of these value-chain operations, designed to improve credit access for these new businesses. USAID reports over 1,700 loans to value-chain members, at an average of $5,900 per loan, with newly available credit, often provided due to USAID credit guarantees for such businesses.[37]

In collaborating on future projects, the U.S. and Ecuadorian governments are to select an executive branch agency in Ecuador that USAID will train and support with technical assistance to act as a centralized contracting agent for small-scale infrastructure activities and projects aimed at improving the economic environment along Ecuador's border communities, where illegal narcotics activity and drug cultivation are most evident.[38]

According to the U.S. Embassy in Ecuador, the Textile Industry Association of Ecuador (AITE) estimates that roughly 40 percent of the investments in the textile and apparel sector in 2008 and 2009 were related to the ATPA program. The AITE reported strong growth in both domestic and regional textile and apparel markets in 2008 and 2009, attracting nearly $50 million in investments per year. The sector benefits principally by ATPA's provision permitting cumulation of Andean content under its rules of origin, according to the AITE. Most of the fabric exported by Ecuador to Colombia is incorporated into clothing that is then exported free of duty to the United States under the ATPA program.[39]

The U.S. Embassy also reported that two other sectors in Ecuador—broccoli and plywood products—would be at risk without ATPA preferences. The reason is that Ecuadorians in these sectors must compete with other suppliers—notably producers in Mexico and Colombia—who also enjoy duty-free access to the U.S. market under the NAFTA and GSP program, respectively.[40]

Comments by the Embassy of Ecuador to the USITC in June 2010 noted that Ecuador's major nonpetroleum export products to the United States under ATPA are fresh cut flowers, tuna, broccoli, pineapples, and textiles and apparel.[41] Several of these represent industries, and related employment, initially supported under the U.S. alternative development program in Ecuador.

Peru

The U.S. Department of State reports that illegal coca cultivation in Peru expanded from roughly 36,000 ha in 2007 to roughly 41,000 ha in 2008, an increase of nearly 14 percent.[42] The United Nations recorded an increase as well, although smaller, from 53,700 ha in 2007 to 56,100 ha in 2008, and to 59,900 ha in 2009, an annual increase of roughly 4–5 percent in 2007–08 and 6–7 percent in 2008–09.[43] USTR notes that coca cultivation in Peru is expanding to new areas, while densities of coca cultivation are increasing in the traditional source zones.[44]

On the other hand, according to the U.S. Embassy in Peru, efforts to eradicate coca cultivation and to provide alternative development opportunities have achieved important results,[45] with ATPA providing support through its positive effect on exports. Between 2002 and 2007, USAID and the Peruvian National Commission for Development and Life without Drugs (DEVIDA)[46] helped reduce illegal coca cultivation by 15,000 ha in 800 communities in selected areas through promotion of a voluntary eradication plan.[47] DEVIDA continues to help implement the 2007–11 National Strategy against Drugs, with cooperation from USAID.[48]

Alternative Development

The AD program in Peru following voluntary eradication of local coca plantings has focused on developing legal crops, small-scale infrastructure, and improved social services.[49] The apparent success achieved through AD programs in the Department of San Martín in the Upper Huallaga valley has been widely reported in the media, despite the area's reputation as a historically notorious location for drugs as well as for the Shining Path rebel insurgency.[50]

More recently, USAID and DEVIDA have developed a National Program for Comprehensive and Sustainable Alternative Development as part of the government's 2007–11 National Strategy against Drugs. This national program aims to provide technical assistance to consolidate and expand production and increase the productivity of crops supported under the program—for example, cacao, coffee, and oil palm.[51] One focus has been strengthening producer associations and cooperatives so that members can reach local and international markets and command optimum prices for their products.[52] DEVIDA reports that 13 cooperative companies in the DEVIDA AD program have increased sales by 55 percent in 2008, compared to 2007, to roughly $92.3 million.[53]

In addition, as a result of banking alliances developed under the USAID AD program, private banking institutions have started to provide credit to pre-vetted clients to finance the production and marketing of legal crops. USAID reports that in the first six months of FY2010, over 1,000 families have accessed credit under this program, resulting in over $1 million in loans disbursed.[54]

The post-eradication assistance program also seeks to draw private sector investment, national and international, to the sectors and regions targeted by this economic assistance.[55] Moreover, the program's investments in community infrastructure work to draw additional public sector investment and support to areas that often lack a strong government presence and basic government services: for example, where a health center project may prompt upgraded public sector services from the Ministry of Health.[56]

In addition, the AD program in Peru, like others, increasingly works in cooperation with other aid providers. One example involves the joint alternative crop research and extension project—supported by the U.S. Department of State and the Organization for American States (OAS), in conjunction with the Peruvian Institute of Tropical Crops and Peru's DEVIDA—aimed at controlling diseases found in cacao plantings established in the Huallaga River basin as a result of past AD projects.[57]

Several U.S. imports under ATPA—such as grapes, mangoes, and asparagus, and their preparations—represent licit crops that provide alternative development and employment opportunities to communities renouncing illegal drug crop cultivation. With the entry into force of the U.S.-Peru TPA on February 1, 2009, however, the share of some imports from Peru—for example, asparagus—has shifted from entry under ATPA provisions to entry under TPA provisions.[58]

TEXTBOX 4.1 Bolivia

Coca cultivation in Bolivia rose from 32,000 ha in 2008 to 35,000 ha in 2009, an increase of nearly 9.4 percent, according to the U.S. Department of State. The United Nations recorded an increase as well, although smaller: from 30,500 ha in 2008 to 30,900 ha in 2009, an increase of 1.3 percent. Coca cultivation in Bolivia has been increasing fairly steadily since 2000, when a 20-year low of 19,600 ha was recorded. Since the election in December 2005 of Evo Morales—a coca grower and president of a local coca growers federation—as President of Bolivia, his administration has proposed an increase in legal coca cultivation, from 12,000 ha to 20,000 ha. In November 2008, the President of the United States determined for the first time that Bolivia had failed to adhere to its obligations under international counternarcotics agreements, and so suspended Bolivia's designation as an ATPA and ATPDEA beneficiary, effective December 15, 2008.

Earlier, in June 2008, USAID was forced to leave the Chapare region of Bolivia due to threats from the leaders of local coca grower federations, raising security concerns for USAID personnel. In September 2008, the government denied permission for aircraft from the U.S. Drug Enforcement Agency (DEA) to fly inside of Bolivia and, later in September 2008, President Morales declared the U.S. Ambassador to Bolivia persona non grata. On November 1, 2008, President Morales announced the immediate suspension of DEA activities in Bolivia, and he subsequently expelled all DEA personnel and dependents from the country.[1]

On June 30, 2009, the President of the United States continued the suspension following statutory review, after determining that Bolivia had failed to adhere to its counternarcotics obligations. As a result, Bolivia's trade preferences remaining suspended under ATPA and ATPDEA for the second consecutive year.

Despite meeting its minimum annual eradication target of 5,000 ha (5,484 ha in 2008, and 6,341 ha in 2009) under international counternarcotics agreements, Bolivian government efforts have not kept pace with increasing coca cultivation in the country. Nonetheless, regional changes in coca cultivation have taken place, with cultivation in the traditional growing region of the Yungas increasing from 21,000 ha in 2008 to 23,000 in 2009 (a 9.5 percent increase); increasing less rapidly among the Chapare's newer, nontraditional coca plantings, from 8,300 ha to 8,800 ha (a 6.0 percent increase); increasing in the Caranavi region from 1,600 ha to 2,200 ha (a 37.5 percent increase); but decreasing in the Apolo region, from 660 ha to 260 ha (a 60.6 percent decrease), as well as in the Vandiola region, from 315 ha to 255 ha (a 19.0 percent decrease).

Alternative development [5]

In 2009, USAID terminated most of its work in the Cochabamba (Chapare) region at the request of the Bolivian government, continuing its focus in the Yungas region—ongoing since FY2007—in cooperation with the Bolivian government's coca rationalization plans. The Bolivian government continues to work closely with USAID and other donors on AD in Bolivia, according to the USTR's fifth report to the Congress on ATPA. USAID estimates that the cultivation of alternative crops and pastures in the Cochabamba and Yungas areas increased steadily from 1986 to 2006, with high-value, licit crop exports—such as bananas, pineapple, canned hearts of palm, coffee, and cacao—increasing from $7.5 million in 2001 to $37.8 million in 2008.

In FY2008, the USAID AD program in Bolivia provided assistance to farm communities and businesses that helped generate new jobs and promote sales of AD products worth nearly $28 million. In FY2008, USAID also helped the Bolivian government register the last 51,400 ha of a total of 466,000 ha of land in the Cochabamba (Chapare) region, the step prior to deeding title to the land, in an effort intended to strengthen land ownership rights and thereby encourage farmer investments in raising AD products.

A relatively large number of new initiatives in the La Asunta area of the south Yungas—an underdeveloped region highly dependent on coca cultivation, where the government has started a voluntary eradication program—have been jointly approved by USAID and the Bolivian government over the past year. There has been significantly more demand from communities in this region for AD production than originally envisioned, according to the U.S. Department of State, and data over the last year indicate that USAID's AD program has helped introduce and establish thousands of hectares of legal crops—such as bananas, cacao, hearts of palm, and coffee—as well as place additional land under forest management plans.

USAID has continued its AD program in Bolivia elsewhere besides the Cochabamba region, focusing on coffee, cacao, bananas, hearts of palm, pineapples, amaranth, stevia, annatto seed (achiote), tea, poultry, and honey. Trade in products eligible under ATPA/ATPDEA accounted for 26 percent of overall U.S.-Bolivian trade in 2008. Of the $140 million in Bolivian products exported through the ATPA/ATPDEA program in 2008, 60 percent lost preferential treatment when the program was suspended. This change affected a number of sectors, including mineral fuels/oils, apparel, milled products, and leather articles. Other Bolivian ATPA/ATPDEA exports—such as jewelry, wood furniture, and agricultural products, including hearts of palm and onions—continued to receive benefits in the U.S. market under other preferential trade programs, such as the U.S. GSP program.

Sources: USDOS, INL, *INCSR 2010*, and previous reports; USDOS, INL, *Fiscal Year 2010: Program and Budget Guide*; USDOS, U.S. Embassy, La Paz, "2010 USITC Andean Investment and Drug Crop Survey"; UNODC, *Estado Plurinacional de Bolivia: Monitoreo de Cultivos de Coca 2009*.

1 Nevertheless, the U.S. Embassy in La Paz reports that the Bolivian government has continued its eradication program with support from the Embassy's Narcotics Affairs Section. The United States maintains a significant counternarcotics assistance program in Bolivia, according to the U.S. Department of State.

POSITIONS OF INTERESTED PARTIES

The Commission held a public hearing regarding the impact of ATPA on July 7, 2010, and also invited interested parties to file written submissions. This chapter first provides an overview of interested parties' major comments and then provides summaries of hearing testimony and written submissions for each interested party.[1]

Impact of ATPA: Overview of Hearing and Written Submissions

A wide range of interested parties testified at the Commission's public hearing and provided written submissions, including government officials from Andean countries, regional organizations, industry associations, U.S. producers and importers, and Andean producers and exporters.[2] Although most of the witnesses and providers of written comments cited ATPA's positive benefits, many also noted that uncertainties related to ATPA's extensions were adversely affecting, or threatening to adversely affect, trade and investment. Several of the main themes that emerged from this information are discussed below.

ATPA Has Had a Minimal Effect on the Overall U.S. Economy, but Mixed Effects on Specific U.S. Sectors

Several foreign governments and Andean regional organization officials stated that ATPA has never had a substantial adverse impact on U.S. industry.[3] Some also expressed the view that ATPA stimulated economic growth and demand for U.S. consumer and capital goods, which has benefited U.S. exports and employment.[4]

Many industry and government representatives cited positive effects on specific U.S. sectors that they attributed to ATPA. These effects include increased U.S. exports of capital equipment and inputs used in the production of ATPA-eligible products; direct benefits to U.S. goods and services industries; indirect benefits for firms handling ATPArelated imports; benefits to U.S. consumers, such as greater choice, broader product availability, and lower prices; and company-specific benefits. For example, the Secretary General of the Andean Community indicated that the United States is an important source of cotton and cotton yarns for the Andean countries' textile and apparel industries.[5]

Furthermore, representatives of the textile and apparel industry stated that ATPA has supported sourcing partnerships between U.S. and beneficiary country companies.[6] Under these partnerships, which do not exist with Chinese and other Asian companies, U.S. companies supply cotton, yarn, fabrics, dyes, chemicals, trims, packaging materials, and sometimes machinery to the region, where they are used to assemble finished apparel that is exported to the United States under ATPA.

Several companies and associations in agriculture and food-processing industries attributed several sector-specific benefits to ATPA. According to various organization officials, about 225,000 U.S. jobs in the transportation, distribution, processing, and retail industries depend on imports of cut flowers from Colombia and Ecuador.[7] The U.S. Chamber of Commerce asserted, however, that the imports provide U.S. consumers with more choices at better prices. The Association of Floral Importers of Florida said that U.S. companies have invested $250 million directly into the Colombian flower industry, own about 17 percent of Colombian flower production, and account for almost 20 percent of Colombia's flower exports to the United States.[8] Superior Foods, an importer of frozen broccoli from Ecuador, asserted that Ecuadorian broccoli is an important component in its vegetable blends and prepared meals, and that the year-round access helps the company lower its costs and remain competitive.[9]

A few interested parties stated that ATPA has had negative economic effects on specific industries. The California Cut Flower Commission said that the U.S. market share for California flowers has declined significantly because of ATPA, and expressed the view that California growers have been unable to obtain a range of incentives and subsidies that are available to Colombian growers through ATPA.[10] Bumble Bee Foods said that ATPA has had a negative impact on the U.S. tuna processing industry. Its submission stated that granting duty-free status to canned tuna from Ecuador will flood the United States with cheap imports, will result in the downsizing and closure of U.S. tuna processing and canning industries, and may lead to the demise of the U.S. tuna fishing fleet.[11]

ATPA Has Had a Positive Effect on Beneficiary Countries

According to testimony and written submissions, ATPA has promoted exports and investment, which have generated economic growth and employment in the beneficiary countries. The Ecuadoran-American Chamber of Commerce stated that ATPA has promoted investment, export-oriented production, and regional and intra-regional supply chain integration, all of which have stimulated the generation of employment in Ecuador.[12] The chamber also stated that economic growth stimulated by ATPA/ATPDEA beneficiary industries enabled Ecuador to generate jobs for more than 400,000 workers, corresponding to about 8 percent of the total working population. In addition, the majority of these jobs are held by women, who are the primary breadwinners in many Ecuadorian households. The Peruvian ambassador to the United States said that "ATPDEA has been instrumental in promoting growth, creating employment and reducing poverty in Peru."[13] The Association of Colombian Flower Exporters stated that the Colombian flower industry has grown from 20,000 employees in 1991 to nearly 220,000 in 2010 due to ATPA/ATPDEA.[14]

ATPA Has Had a Positive Effect on Drug Crop Eradication and Crop Substitution[15]

Foreign government and industry representatives observed that through increased exports and investment, ATPA has created employment opportunities for workers who might otherwise engage in drug crop production. The ambassador from Peru said that "rising Peruvian exports under ATPDEA have helped in creating thousands of jobs in Peru, while offering our people alternatives to illegal activities." [16] He also stated that "ATPDEA preferences have also helped in offering sustainable alternatives to farmers. Since 2001, more than 80,000 hectares of illegal crops have been eradicated in Peru, more than the area currently presumed to hold illegal crops."[17]

The Colombian Government Trade Bureau stated:

> The industries promoted by ATPA/ATPDEA in Colombia have provided employment alternatives to illegal drug cultivation and this has been a great contribution in the fight against drugs. . . . Colombia has made an enormous progress in terms of illegal crop eradication. The positive outcomes accomplished in the last years in terms of drug crop reduction not only represent a constructive national achievement but also a positive contribution to security issues for the U.S and for the Andean region, given the fact that the illegal drug industry has become one of the main sources for financial and social control for criminal networks, illegal groups and terrorism. Furthermore, the drug industry has weakened Colombian democratic institutions, increased violence levels, generated human rights violations and destroyed the environment. Fortunately, the drug control policy adopted by the Colombian Government over the past few years—combining security and development—has resulted in a historic reduction in cultivation of coca in the region.[18]

The General Secretary of the Andean Community stated in his submission that "the social impacts of [the ATPA] initiative are significant and illustrate the scope of alternative projects to the illicit production of drugs as well as possible mechanisms for the integration of small producers into domestic supply chains and export. The side effect, in terms of poverty reduction, or governance, should not be underestimated when evaluating the impact of measures such as the ATPDEA and the achievement of underlying objectives: the eradication of illegal crops."[19] The General Secretary also said that "the member countries of the Andean Community and beneficiaries of the ATPDEA, have made significant progress in reducing coca leaf plantations."

Uncertainties Regarding ATPA Expiration and Implementation of U.S. Bilateral FTAs with Colombia and Peru Have Adversely Affected Investment and Trade

Several who testified at the Commission's hearing asserted that the uncertainties related to the repeated expiration and short-term renewals of ATPA since 2006 have negatively affected the investment environment and bilateral trade. For example, a Colombian Government Trade Bureau representative stated that "the numerous short-term extensions that the Program has had over the years, plus the recent U.S. recession, has resulted in a disincentive to long-term investment and trade in sectors that are being benefited by the program."[20] The same representative also stated that, although the pending FTA "is a priority in the bilateral trade agenda," ATPA/ATPDEA continues to be essential to Colombia while it awaits approval of the FTA. If ATPA/ATPDEA were allowed to expire, the submission asserted that the loss of duty-free status would cause the Andean Region to lose its ability to compete globally on price. The trade bureau representative reported that the delay in making ATPA permanent and the possible loss of duty-free access would put at risk legitimate jobs in Colombia, particularly in the textile sector and flower industry.[21]

Summaries of Positions of Interested Parties

Colombian Government Trade Bureau [22]

In testimony at the Commission's hearing, Claudia Candela, director of the Colombian Government Trade Bureau, made the following points:

- ATPA/ATPDEA has been effective in developing business in Colombia, particularly in labor-intensive economic sectors such as flowers, and apparel and textiles. Industries promoted by ATPA/ATPDEA have provided employment alternatives to illegal drug cultivation.
- Businesses in the United States have also benefited from the program, through duty-free imports of inputs used in products manufactured in the United States. ATPA/ATPDEA has been a fundamental economic tool for trade diversification and job creation in Colombia, while supporting jobs in the United States.
- The success of U.S. trade policy toward Colombia is exemplified by the Colombian flower industry which, at the same time, provides clear evidence that Colombia also meets the eligibility criteria of ATPA. In 2009, approximately 75 percent of the total U.S. flower market consisted of imported flowers, 60 percent of which originated in

Colombia. Flower exports from Colombia support approximately 19.8 million U.S. floral retail businesses, and provide 225,000 jobs in the United States.

Ms. Candela expressed the view that the last four extensions of ATPA have discouraged investment in Colombia, saying that "faced with uncertainty of continued trade benefits, Colombian firms began to lose business in the U.S. market since production has shifted to other countries and regions."[23] She said that the trade bureau opposes the graduation of Peru from the ATPA/ATPDEA program and stated that such action would likely have an adverse impact on Colombian exports—apparel in particular—given that the program since its inception has offered cumulation provisions concerning rules of origin for the region. She stated that more than 70 percent of the apparel that Peru shipped to the United States in 2009 entered free of duty under the Andean program rather than under the free trade agreement [the U.S.-Peru Trade Promotion Agreement (TPA)]. She also noted that Colombia is using a significant amount of yarn and fabric from Peru in the apparel that it exports to the United States free of duty under ATPDEA. If Peru were to graduate from the Andean program, she noted, such Colombian garments using Peruvian inputs would no longer receive duty-free access to the U.S. market.

Government of Ecuador[24]

In a written submission, Ambassador Luis Gallegos stated that the government of Ecuador strongly supports ATPA/ATPDEA, asserting that the program has had a positive impact on the economies of both the United States and Ecuador while promoting drug-related crop eradication. He said that this growth has benefited both countries by:

- job creation in both countries;
- hundreds of thousands of Ecuadorians lifted out of poverty;
- successful counternarcotics operations in Ecuador, the United States, and the Western Hemisphere;
- political and economic stability in Ecuador; and
- long-standing commercial, political, and cultural ties between Ecuador and the United States.

The ambassador indicated that ATPA has contributed to the creation of a formal dialogue between Ecuador and the United States. He explained that the U.S.-Ecuador Bilateral Dialogue, headed by the U.S. Department of State and the Ecuadorian Ministry of Foreign Affairs, addresses issues including security, migration, trade and investment, and cooperation and technical assistance. Similarly, he noted that the U.S.-Ecuador Trade and Investment Council, headed by the U.S. Trade Representative, considers issues such as technical barriers to trade, sanitary and phytosanitary standards, nontariff measures, customs issues, investment policies, workers' rights, and intellectual property rights.

In his submission, the ambassador said that:

- ATPA has made a tremendous contribution to Ecuador's trade with the United States, with many of Ecuador's non-petroleum export products—including fresh cut flowers, tuna, broccoli, pineapples, and textiles and apparel—entering the United States free of duty as a result of the program. He pointed out that fresh cut flowers alone represent 39 percent of Ecuador's non-oil exports under ATPA, while pouched tuna products represent 11 percent and broccoli products approximately 7 percent.

- Eliminating ATPA would likely result in a 50 percent reduction in Ecuador's exports to the United States, affecting major industries that support Ecuador's economic growth and more than 400,000 jobs in the country.
- Some areas likely to be affected adversely if ATPA were not renewed included roses, broccoli, pouched tuna, artisan crafts, fresh cut flowers, fresh papaya, canned fruits and vegetables, organic sugar, crabmeat, and tropical fruit juices and concentrates.

Government of Peru[25]

In a written submission, Ambassador Luis Valdivieso said that ATPA/ATPDEA has been instrumental in promoting growth, creating employment, and reducing poverty in Peru. Through 2008, almost half of Peru's exports to the United States enjoyed benefits under U.S. trade preference programs. He indicated that although these preference programs have never posed "a substantial adverse impact on the U.S. industry, rising Peruvian exports under ATPDEA have helped in creating thousands of jobs in Peru, while offering our people alternatives to illegal activities."

ATPDEA Regional Impact

The ambassador said ATPDEA has supported considerable integration among industries located in Ecuador, Colombia, and Peru, by allowing the cumulation of materials among beneficiary countries to determine product origin. Such provisions, according to the ambassador, benefit Peruvian exports to the United States using inputs from other ATPDEA beneficiaries as well as Peruvian exports of materials to other Andean countries that are then used to produce goods exported to the United States under ATPDEA.

From ATPDEA to Bilateral Free Trade Agreements

The ambassador said that ATPDEA was supposed to pave the way to successful bilateral trade negotiations between the Andean countries, because most goods with preferential customs treatment get zero tariffs under the U.S.-Peru TPA. Peru, Colombia, and Ecuador were expected to reach bilateral trade agreements with the United States at about the same time, with most of their trade with the United States covered through bilateral agreements. He said that, if this had happened, the trade relationship featuring one-way preferences under ATPDEA would have shifted to a more reciprocal trade relation between the United States and Andean countries, extending equivalent trade preferences to the United States that would benefit U.S. producers, manufacturers, farmers, trademark holders, and investors. However, he continued, Peru became the only ATPA beneficiary country that reached a bilateral trade agreement with the United States, which entered into force in February 2009. The ambassador noted that by the rules of the agreement, Peru would be forbidden to cumulate origin with Colombia and Ecuador in its export products.

Extending ATPDEA Benefits

The ambassador said that the decision by the U.S. Congress to extend ATPDEA to all Andean beneficiaries helped address their concerns about losing an important export market that could affect Andean trade both bilaterally (with the United States) and regionally. He stated that if Peru ceased to be an ATPDEA beneficiary country, despite having the TPA in effect, a substantial part of the production of its small and medium-sized textile companies—which currently incorporate Colombian inputs—would no longer have access to the U.S. market. Peru, he noted, would no longer have access under ATPDEA rules, which allow for cumulation of product origin between Andean countries, nor would it have the possibility of cumulation of product origin under the TPA. The ambassador asserted that the "decision to remove Peru from ATPDEA would expose Peruvian workers and farmers, many already moving away from illegal crops, to the threat of populism and violence still present in Latin America." He also stated that ATPDEA "provides a platform to support further trade development between the U.S. and Peru and other Andean trade partners."

The Andean Community[26]

In a written submission, Adalid Contreras Baspineiro, general secretary of the Andean Community, made two main points:

- The United States is the main trading partner of the Andean Community, with the value of exports to the United States reaching a record $30.029 million in 2008, of which $13.778 million were sold under the ATPDEA program. U.S. floriculture activity has contributed to the creation of about 226,000 direct and indirect jobs in the United States, in areas such as transportation companies, flower shops, and supermarkets, as a result of importing fresh flowers from the Andean countries under this program. In the same way, the U.S. food industry has been able to create approximately 5,000 new jobs in the distribution chain alone because of imported asparagus from Peru under the ATPA program, according to the Association of Food Industries.
- ATPDEA is an instrument that gives the recipient countries a chance to produce value-added goods, enabling them to sustain and expand their participation in international markets. The program enables them to raise the standard of living of the people involved while also creating the possibility for positive impact in some U.S. consumer markets over time, particularly on agricultural goods and goods of agroindustrial origin.

American Apparel & Footwear Association[27]

In a written submission, the American Apparel and Footwear Association (AAFA) stated that it is a national trade association that represents U.S. apparel and footwear industries and their suppliers—members who produce and market sewn products throughout the United States and the world, including the Andean region. The submission said that AAFA strongly supports ATPA and has spoken out for its continuation in the face of numerous short-term extensions.

The AAFA addressed two issues it considered critical to the continued success of ATPA: (1) the association's view that Peru should not be graduated from the program, and (2) its opposition to Ecuador's use of balance-of-payments safeguard measures.

The AAFA recounted that the ATPA program was expanded through the Andean Trade Promotion and Drug Eradication Act (ATPDEA), which allowed beneficiary countries to produce apparel, under certain rules, for export to the United States free of duty. Given the near doubling of U.S. apparel imports from the Andean region between 2001 and 2004, the AAFA considered the program a success in its effort to promote integration between the

United States and the Andean countries, as well as among Andean countries. Since more than 70 percent of the apparel Peru shipped to the United States in 2009 entered under ATPA, rather than the U.S.-Peru TPA, the association stressed that it was critical to keep Peru in the program. If Peru were "graduated" from ATPA, AAFA said that Colombian garments using Peruvian inputs would likely no longer receive duty-free access to the U.S. market. The submission noted that Colombia presently uses significant quantities of Peruvian yarn and fabric in its apparel exports to the United States.

AAFA also said that it opposed Ecuador's decision to use balance-of-payments safeguard restrictions and surcharges on apparel and footwear, surcharges AAFA reported as $10 per pair on all footwear imports and $12 per kilogram on most apparel imports. These surcharges essentially closed the Ecuadorian market to U.S.-made and U.S.-branded apparel and footwear, according to AAFA's submission.

AAFA indicated that Ecuador has announced that it will replace the $10 per pair surcharge with a mixed ad valorem/specific duty of 10 percent plus $6 per pair. As most footwear imported into Ecuador has an average f.o.b. (free on board) value ranging from $3 to $18, and retails for the equivalent of from $9 to $48, footwear imports would be subject to an actual duty of anywhere from 43 percent to 210 percent at the new duty rate, according to the association.

Association of Colombian Flower Exporters[28]

In a written submission, the Association of Colombian Flower Exporters stated that it is a nonprofit trade association that represents and supports Colombian flower growers and exporters, companies that account for 75 percent of Colombia's total cut flower exports. According to its submission, the U.S. floral industry is dependent on Colombian flowers, since more than 60 percent of the 4.2 billion flowers imported into the United States come annually from Colombia. In its submission, the association suggested that Colombian flower imports support nearly 225,000 jobs in the United States in sectors such as transportation, import brokerage, wholesale operations, retail florist shops, Internet providers, supermarkets, and convenience stores. The association said that it strongly supports ATPA because it has enabled Colombia's cut flower industry to grow from 20,000 employees in 1991 to more than 220,000 in 2010. The association also said that the U.S. government has recognized the Colombian flower industry as an important ally in efforts to combat the illegal drug trade.

Association of Floral Importers of Florida[29]

In testimony before the Commission, the Association of Floral Importers of Florida (AFIF) explained that it was founded to give flower importers, located mainly in Miami, a united voice on issues affecting the flower importing industry. AFIF member companies now represent roughly 80 percent of the flowers imported into Florida, according to the association.

In her testimony, Christine Boldt, executive vice president of the AFIF, made the following points:

- Approximately 220,000 U.S. jobs in the floral industry depend on the free flow of Andean flowers into the United States. Jobholders include airline industry employees, U.S. Customs and Border Protection personnel, U.S. Department of Agriculture (USDA) personnel, custom brokers, flower importers, truck transporters, and people working in wholesale operations, retail flower shops, Internet providers, and supermarkets.

- The vast majority of the approximately 4.2 billion stems of flowers imported yearly into the United States are imported from Colombia and Ecuador (with 60 percent from Colombia, 30 percent from Ecuador, and 10 percent from the rest of the world).
- These flowers play a major role in supporting the $20 billion U.S. horticulture industry. Imported flowers make up approximately 75 percent of the total fresh flower supply in the United States.

Ms. Boldt stated that the U.S. flower industry is intensely competitive, with very thin margins and with operating profits for most flower importers of 2 to 4 percent. She went on to say that the short-term extensions of the ATPA over the last four years have created uncertainty in the flower industry, and that the expiration of the ATPA program slated for December—just prior to the flower industry's two major holidays—makes it difficult to "pre-sell to prepare pricing" and makes proper cost analysis and correct pricing almost impossible. The industry requires "set pricing" or "pre-books" months in advance and sometimes a year ahead, she explained. Ms. Boldt's testimony also pointed out that U.S. companies have invested more than $250 million directly into the Colombian flower industry and own approximately 17 percent of Colombian flower production, accounting for nearly 20 percent of total exports to the United States.

Atlas Flowers[30]

In testimony at the Commission's hearing, Gabriel Becerra, president of Atlas Flowers, doing business as Golden Flowers, stated that it imports and distributes fresh flowers throughout the United States. He said that Golden Flowers imports its flowers from more than 30 farms in Colombia that provide employment for several thousand workers, a high percentage being single females who are heads of households. He stated that the Colombian floral industry is located mainly in the regions of Bogotá and Rionegro, near Medellín, and provides more than 120,000 direct jobs and more than 90,000 indirect jobs. Mr. Becerra said that investment in flower farms is capital-intensive and requires well-trained labor in order to be competitive.

Mr. Becerra asserted that the floral industry is one of the most important job generators in South Florida, with more than 15,000 direct employees and many thousands of indirect jobs involving U.S. Customs, USDA, the airlines industry, freight forwarders, importers, trucking companies, and jobs located at Miami International Airport. He said that ATPA has been extremely important in preserving these jobs during the recent economic crisis as the industry is already highly competitive and very price-sensitive—operating at very low margins—and is totally dependent on the preferences provided under ATPA.

Bumble Bee Foods[31]

In a written submission, Bumble Bee Foods said that it is a U.S.-owned and -operated company that provides shelf-stable seafood products. Its submission made the points that:

- Current trade policies have allowed the Andean tuna industry to grow dramatically.
- The number of tuna factories, production capacity, employment in, and exports from, Andean countries have all risen considerably in the past 20 years, and Andean

nations currently have the largest fleet in the eastern tropical Pacific Ocean. Bumble Bee said that it operates two of the last three canned tuna production facilities in the United States in Santa Fe Springs, California, and Mayaguez, Puerto Rico.

- Bumble Bee opposes current trade preference benefits for Andean nations because reduced tariffs provided to Ecuador under ATPA threaten Bumble Bee's tuna processing operations. The company asserted that granting duty-free entry to canned tuna from Ecuador will flood the U.S. market with inexpensive imports and will result in the downsizing and closure of U.S. tuna processing and canning industries, possibly leading to the demise of the U.S. tuna fishing fleet due to excess capacity in the industry.

California Cut Flower Commission[32]

In testimony at the Commission's hearing and in a written submission, the California Cut Flower Commission (CCFC) stated that the Andean Trade Preferences and Drug Eradication Act has adversely affected California flower farmers. The CCFC said that it is a commission established by the state legislature, overseen by the California Department of Food and Agriculture, and funded by 225 farms growing flowers and foliage throughout the state. According to the CCFC, California's floral industry has a $10.3 billion annual impact on California and generates more than 121,000 jobs. The commission stated that California flower farms employ more than 7,500 people directly, but suggested that a ripple effect generates an additional 19,000 jobs for California.

In testimony before the Commission, Kasey Cronquist, executive director of the CCFC, remarked that California flower growers have extensively diversified their crop varieties to better compete with imports. Nonetheless, she said that, over the past 20 years, California has seen generations of flower farmers give up, close their doors, and sell their farms due to the import pressures generated by ATPDEA. Ms. Cronquist highlighted that, during 2003–07, the number of acres dedicated to cut flower production in the United States declined by 22.3 percent, whereas U.S. imports from Colombia increased by 75 percent. Currently, Colombia and other countries account for between 75 and 80 percent of all cut flowers sold in the United States, according to her testimony. The primary frustration with ATPA is not just the duty-free access, as the CCFC views the situation, but that the implementation of the policy does not ensure or safeguard a fair and competitive market, leaving California farms to compete with imports that are priced below the cost of production in California. In her testimony, Ms. Cronquist contended that, while California's farms have focused on diversifying away from products that are imported from other countries, they still face the day-to-day competition on price. CCFC said that when the natural advantages of sunlight, climate, cost of labor, and the price of land are combined with significant government support and subsidies, domestic farms cannot compete with foreign producers.

Ms. Cronquist stated that the U.S. State Department reported in 2009 that Colombian flower growers received support from the Colombian government in the form of incentives or subsidies, which amounted to roughly $210 million since 2005.[33] She cited four Colombian programs that her organization finds benefit Colombian flower growers: (1) the exchange-rate hedge incentive, (2) the sanitary measures incentive, (3) the salary protection program for producers of exportable agricultural goods, and (4) the special line of credit for exporters. In closing her testimony, she also said that the Colombian flower industry also receives substantial financial support from the U.S. government for economic development and trade capacity building.

Ecuadorian-American Chamber of Commerce[34]

In a written submission, the Ecuadorian-American Chamber of Commerce said that it had been asked by Ecuador's private sector to coordinate industry efforts to secure the renewal and continuation of ATPDEA benefits for Ecuador.

The Chamber made the following points in support of the ATPDEA program:

- ATPDEA is the cornerstone of Ecuador's export promotion policy among all the duty preference programs that Ecuador uses.
- The program has been used to help craft a major policy mechanism in terms of one of ATPA's fundamental objectives—to help curb the production, transportation, and sale of controlled narcotic substances.
- ATPA has promoted investment, export-oriented production, and the development of regional and interregional supply chain integration, all of which has stimulated the generation of employment in Ecuador as well as in the United States.
- Of the $4.6 billion in exports from Ecuador to the United States in 2009, most entered the United States free of duty under ATPDEA. In addition to traditional exports—such as petroleum, bananas, shrimp, coffee, and cocoa— more than $365 million in exports to the United States was generated in 2009 in newer, nontraditional industries dependent on ATPDEA, such as cut flowers, broccoli, wood articles, tropical fruits (e.g., mangoes, pineapples), tuna, and textiles.
- These new export industries that depend on the ATPDEA program generated more than 400,000 jobs in Ecuador. Many of these jobs are located in the country's northern provinces, near the border with Colombia, a region known for both its poverty and its susceptibility to drug cultivation.

Superior Foods Companies[35]

In a written submission, Superior Foods Companies said that it is a U.S. company that imports frozen broccoli from Ecuador. Over the last 25 years, U.S. producers have increasingly emphasized fresh broccoli over frozen production, with Mexico becoming the primary source for frozen broccoli. Nonetheless, Ecuador has carved out a niche in U.S. and European broccoli markets due to the high quality and year-round availability of Ecuadorian broccoli. Broccoli is also the principal ingredient in many value-added blends and prepared meals currently produced by U.S. companies and distributed in the United States and Europe. In its submission, Superior said that although imports of Ecuadorian broccoli account for only a minor percentage of its total revenue, it depends on these imports to compete with broccoli from Mexico, Europe, and China. Superior reported that frozen broccoli from Ecuador was a "linchpin component" in its overall competitiveness and revenue base. Superior Foods' submission also stated that the "discontinuation of economic access to frozen broccoli from Ecuador would cause, at the very least, a crippling disadvantage to Superior Foods and U.S. companies like ours, and, in turn, to our employees and the numerous American producers who depend on us."

Textiles La Escala[36]

In his testimony, Jeff Sheedy, chief executive officer of Textiles La Escala, said that Textiles La Escala is a yarn-spinning mill and fabric operation located in Quito, Ecuador, and is part of the 230-member Ecuadoran Textile Association. Concerning job creation and its benefits resulting from ATPA/ATPDEA trade provisions, he said that "the great thing about ATPDEA is it's a two-way street. We're generating jobs both here and in the United States." Mr. Sheedy said in his testimony that approximately 93 percent of the cotton consumed in Ecuador comes from the United States, with most such cotton imported free of duty from the southern states, Arizona, and California. In addition to the direct benefits to the U.S. cotton and textile industries, Mr. Sheedy said that apparel imports from Ecuador under ATPA have generated benefits to the U.S. economy across the entire transportation, distribution, and retail chain. He pointed out in this testimony that the United States has consistently maintained a textile trade surplus with Ecuador, reporting that this surplus reached $44.3 million in 2008 before declining to $36.7 million in 2009. Nonetheless, he reported that in the first three months of 2010, the United States again enjoyed a surplus estimated at $9.2 million. The most important aspect of ATPA is the rules of origin. Mr. Sheedy stressed the importance of maintaining cumulation among the four countries—Ecuador, Peru, Colombia, and the United States. The four countries are able to leverage off each other's competitive advantage, he stated in his testimony, enabling them to compete against mainly Asian imports.

U.S. Chamber of Commerce[37]

In testimony at the Commission's hearing, Patrick Kilbride of the U.S. Chamber of Commerce (Chamber) stated that it has been a consistent supporter of ATPA because of the economic and foreign policy benefits that accrue both to the United States and to its Andean neighbors:

- The Andean beneficiary countries gain ATPA-related jobs that tend to pay above-average wages and that often serve as a gateway for workers to enter the formal economy, which is a big priority for the Chamber and the region.
- U.S. businesses benefit by being allowed to import components and materials, as well as labor-intensive consumer goods, on a duty-free basis, which enhances the global competitiveness of U.S. businesses and their ability to create and maintain jobs.

Mr. Kilbride said that U.S. imports from the Andean countries frequently contain a high percentage of U.S. content, supporting this view with a citation from the American Apparel and Footwear Association's Web site:

> The Andean region is a growing and important market for U.S. textile and cotton exports as about $250 million worth of U.S. cotton and textiles were exported last year to the Andean region. Most of these products are incorporated into finished garments. Those finished products made with U.S. yarns, fabrics, fibers, cotton and other textile inputs—the whole gamut of the supply chain—are then brought back to the U.S. duty-free.[38]

Mr. Kilbride said that the Chamber considers that ATPA has played a useful role in U.S. efforts to promote sustained economic growth in Colombia by helping create jobs, isolate violent extremist groups in the Andean countries, restore economic growth, and provide citizens with long-term alternatives to narcotics trafficking and out-migration. He said that the Chamber urges that ATPA benefits for Colombia be continued until the U.S.- Colombia FTA takes effect, to help avoid trade disruption and job losses in both countries.

REFERENCES

American Apparel and Footwear Association. Written submission to the United States International Trade Commission in connection with inv. no. 332-352, *Andean Trade Preference Act: Impact on U.S. Industries and on Consumers and on Drug Crop Eradication and Crop Substitution, 2009*, July 14, 2010.

Ametex. Written submission to the House Committee on Foreign Affairs, Subcommittee on the Western Hemisphere, March 3, 2009.

Andean Community. Written submission to the United States International Trade Commission in connection with inv. no. 332-352, *Andean Trade Preference Act: Impact on U.S. Industries and on Consumers and on Drug Crop Eradication and Crop Substitution, 2009*, July 13, 2010.

Andina. "France, England & Germany Become Biggest Consumers of Peruvian Fashion," April 14, 2010. http://www.andina.com.pe/ingles/NoticiaImprimir.aspx?id=227891.

_____. "Hand-harvested Pima Cotton from Peru Reduces Waste," September 18, 2008. http://www.andina.com.pe/ingles/NoticiaImprimir.aspx?id=194688.

_____. "Peru's Textiles and Apparel Exports to Jump 15% This Year Totaling US $1.7 Billion," April 29, 2010. http://www.andina.com.pe/ingles/ NoticiaImprimir. aspx?id= 293120.

_____. "Tommy Hilfiger Eyes Peruvian Organic Cotton," May 2, 2010. http://www.andina. com.pe/ingles/NoticiaImprimir.aspx?id=293483.

Association of Colombian Flower Exporters (ASCOLFLORES). Statement to the United States Committee on Ways and Means, Subcommittee on Trade. Hearing on the Operation, Impact, and Future of U.S. Preference Programs, November 17, 2009.

_____. Written submission to the United States International Trade Commission in connection with inv. no. 332-352, *Andean Trade Preference Act: Impact on U.S. Industries and on Consumers and on Drug Crop Eradication and Crop Substitution, 2009*, July 8, 2010.

Association of Floral Imports of Florida. South Florida Industry Statistics. http://www.afifnet.org/south_floridia_stats.html (accessed August 25, 2010).

Bolivia Investment Gateway. "Bolivia–FAQ Textil Environmental," n.d. http://bolivia. investway.org/en/environment (accessed November 18, 2009).

Bolivia-American Chamber of Commerce. "Strategic Sectors for Investing in Bolivia," n.d. http://www.bolivia-us.org/invest4.htm (accessed July 26, 2010).

Bumble Bee Foods, Inc. Written submission to the United States International Trade Commission in connection with inv. no. 332-352, *Andean Trade Preference Act: Impact on U.S. Industries and on Consumers and on Drug Crop Eradication and Crop Substitution, 2009*, June 25, 2010.

Business Monitor Online. "BMI Industry View: Colombia; Q4–2009; Colombia; Textiles and Clothing," October 14, 2009. Available for a fee at http://www.businessmonitor.com.

_____. "Industry Forecast: Peru; Q4–2009; Textiles and Clothing; Textile and Clothing Market Outlook," October 14, 2009. Available for a fee at http://www.businessmonitor.com

_____. "Industry Trends and Developments: Colombia; Industry Trends and Developments," October 14, 2010. Available for a fee at http://www.businessmonitor.com.

California Cut Flower Commission. Written submission to the United States International Trade Commission in connection with inv. no. 332-352, *Andean Trade Preference Act: Impact on U.S. Industries and on Consumers and on Drug Crop Eradication and Crop Substitution, 2009*, July 14, 2010.

Colombian Government Trade Bureau. Written submission to the United States International Trade Commission in connection with inv. no. 332-352, *Andean Trade Preference Act: Impact on U.S. Industries and on Consumers and on Drug Crop Eradication and Crop Substitution, 2009*, July 14, 2010.

_____. Written submission to the United States International Trade Commission in connection with inv. no. 332-352, *Andean Trade Preference Act: Impact on U.S. Industries and on Consumers and on Drug Crop Eradication and Crop Substitution, 2009*, June 30, 2010.

Cotton Council International. "Cotton USA Licensee in Colombia Improves Production Process with U.S. Cotton," April 1, 2009.

_____. "CCI Leverages Colombiamoda to Pursue Business Opportunities for U.S. Cotton Yarns and Fabrics in Colombia, n.d.
http://www.cottonusa.org/events/SouthAmerica.cfm?navItemNumber=2565
(accessed February 22, 2010).

Economic Commission for Latin America and the Caribbean (ECLAC). *Foreign Direct Investment in Latin America and the Caribbean*. Santiago, Chile: United Nations, May 2010.

Economist Intelligence Unit (EIU). ViewsWire. "Colombia: Country Report; Main report, June 15th 2010; Economic performance; Trade surplus soars on oil exports," June 21, 2010. http://www.eiu.com/article247220009.html?pubtypeId=50000205&text=.

_____. "Ecuador: Business Environment Ranking Summary," July 1, 2010. http://viewswire.eiu.com/index.asp?layout=VWArticleVW3&article id=1887320573.

Ecuadorian-American Chamber of Commerce. Written submission to the United States International Trade Commission in connection with inv. no. 332-352, *Andean Trade Preference Act: Impact on U.S. Industries and on Consumers and on Drug Crop Eradication and Crop Substitution, 2009*, July 14, 2010.

Embassy of Ecuador in the United States. Posthearing submission to the United States International Trade Commission in connection with inv. no. 332-352, *Andean Trade Preference Act: Impact on U.S. Industries and on Consumers and on Drug Crop Eradication and Crop Substitution, 2009*, August 19, 2010.

_____. Posthearing submission to the United States International Trade Commission in connection with inv. no. 332-352, *Andean Trade Preference Act: Impact on U.S. Industries and on Consumers and on Drug Crop Eradication and Crop Substitution, 2009*, July 14, 2010.

_____. Written submission to the United States International Trade Commission in connection with inv. no. 332-352, *Andean Trade Preference Act: Impact on U.S.*

Industries and on Consumers and on Drug Crop Eradication and Crop Substitution, 2009, June 30, 2010.

Embassy of Peru in the United States. Written submission to the United States International Trade Commission in connection with inv. no. 332-352, *Andean Trade Preference Act: Impact on U.S. Industries and on Consumers and on Drug Crop Eradication and Crop Substitution, 2009*, July 12, 2010.

Gallaway, Michael P., Christine A. McDaniel, and Sandra A. Rivera. "Short-Run and Long-Run Estimates of U.S. Armington Elasticities." *North American Journal of Economics and Finance* 14 (2003), 49–68.

Global Trade Atlas database. Global Trade Information Services. http://www.gtis.com (accessed various dates).

Inexmoda. "Colombiatex de las Americas 2009," n.d. http://www.inexmoda.org.co/Default.aspx?alias=www.inexmoda.org.co/colombiatex2009 (accessed February 2, 2009).

International Monetary Fund. *International Financial Statistics: Colombia.* January 2010, 358–59.

Just-style. "Colombia's Clothing and Textile Industry Has Growth Potential," June 24, 2010. http://www.just-style.com/management- (accessed July 29, 2010).

_____. "Colombia's Clothing Industry in Crisis?" February 23, 2010. Available for a fee at http://www.just-style (accessed May 28, 2010).

_____. "Colombia's Denim Cluster on Road to Recovery," February 22, 2010. Available for a fee at http://www.just-style. (accessed May 28, 2010).

_____. "June 2010 Management Briefing: Latin American Textile Sector Weathers Economic Storm." Available for a fee at http://www.just-style. (accessed July 13, 2010).

Library of Congress. Federal Research Division. "Country Profile: Bolivia," January 2006. Washington, DC: Library of Congress, 2006. http://memory

_____. "Country Profile: Colombia," February 2007. Washington, DC: Library of Congress, 2007. http://memory

Namihas, Sandra. "Se puede derrotar al narcotráfico con una estrategia integral y sostenida." *Boletín Electrónico del IDEI*, Año 3, No. 27 (December 2009). Pontificia Universidad Católica del Perú. Instituto de Estudios Internacionales. Narcotráfico y Gobernabilidad. http://200.16.1.206/idei/narcotrafico-gobernabilidad-articulos-detalle.php?id=60&boletin=16.

Organization of American States (OAS). Inter-American Drug Abuse Control Commission (CICAD). "Alternative Development: Projects: Tropical Crops Research; Biological Control of Cacao Diseases in Peru," n.d. http://www.cicad.oas.org/Desarrollo_Alternativo/ENG/Projects%20By%20Country/Peru/ (accessed June 21, 2010).

Proexport Colombia. "Colombia's Apparel Industry: Fabric and Clothing Production for Iconic U.S. Brands," May 4, 2010. http://www.proexport.com.co/vbecontent/NewsDetail.asp?Source=ExpiredNews&ID=10950&ID Company=16.

República de Colombia. Presidencia. "Normas: Directivas; 2009; Directiva Presidencial No. 01, Asunto:

Coordinación del Gobierno Nacional para llevar a cabo el Plan Nacional de Consolidación Territorial." March 1, 2009. http://web (accessed June 21, 2010).

_____. "Territorios libres de ilícitos, retos del Plan Nacional de Consolidación." Sala de Prensa; Noticias [press releases], March 13, 2010. http://web.presidencia.gov.co/sp/2010/marzo/13/21132010.html (accessed June 21, 2010).

Superior Foods International LLC. Written submission to the United States International Trade Commission in connection with inv. no. 332-352, *Andean Trade Preference Act: Impact on U.S. Industries and on Consumers and on Drug Crop Eradication and Crop Substitution, 2009*, July 8, 2010.

Textiles La Escala. Written submission to the United States International Trade Commission in connection with inv. no. 332-352, *Andean Trade Preference Act: Impact on U.S. Industries and on Consumers and on Drug Crop Eradication and Crop Substitution, 2009*, July 14, 2010.

U.S. Department of Agriculture (USDA). Agriculture Marketing Service (AMS). *Ornamental Crops Report*, January 2010.

_____. Economic Research Service (ERS). *Floriculture and Nursery Crops*, May 2002.

_____. National Agricultural Statistics Service (NASS). *Floriculture Crops, 2006 Summary*, April 2007.

_____. NASS. *Floriculture Crops, 2009 Summary*, April 2010.

U.S. Department of Commerce (USDOC) and U.S. Agency for International Development (USAID). *Guidebook to the Andean Trade Preference Act.* Washington DC: Government Printing Office, 1992.

U.S. Department of Labor (USDOL). Wage and Hour Division. "The Tuna Processing Industry." http://www.dol.gov/whd/as/sec3.htm (accessed May 12, 2010).

U.S. Department of State (USDOS). *Congressional Budget Justification: Foreign Operations; Annex; Regional Perspectives, Fiscal Year 2011*, released March 10, 2010. http://www.state

_____. Bureau for International Narcotics and Law Enforcement Affairs (INL). "Counternarcotics and Law Enforcement Country Program: Colombia." Fact sheet, May 7, 2010. http://www.state

_____. INL. *Fiscal Year 2010: Program and Budget Guide*, n.d. http://www.state (accessed June 9, 2010).

_____. INL. *International Narcotics Control Strategy Report (INCSR 2000)*, March 2001.

_____. INL. *International Narcotics Control Strategy Report (INCSR 2008), Volume I, Drug and Chemical Control*, March 2008.

_____. INL. *International Narcotics Control Strategy Report (INCSR 2009), Volume I, Drug and Chemical Control*, March 2009.

_____. INL. *International Narcotics Control Strategy Report (INCSR 2010), Volume I, Drug and Chemical Control*, March 2010.

_____. Bureau of Economic, Energy and Business Affairs. "2010 Investment Climate Statement: Ecuador," March 2010.

_____. Bureau of Western Hemisphere Affairs (WHA). "Background Note: Bolivia; U.S.-Bolivian Relations," May 13, 2010. http://www.state

_____. WHA. "Background Note: Colombia; Defense; Narcotics and Rule of Law," June 2, 2010. http://www.state

_____. WHA. "Background Note: Ecuador; U.S.-Ecuadorian Relations," May 24, 2010. http://www.state

_____. WHA. "Background Note: Peru; U.S.-Peruvian Relations," January 25, 2010. http://www.state

_____. U.S. Embassy, Bogota. "Colombian Flower Industry Surviving Adversity (BOGOTA 001110)," March 25, 2010.

_____. U.S. Embassy, Bogota. "Colombian Textile Industry: Dying or Just Downsizing? (BOGOTA 000103)," January 28, 2010.

_____. U.S. Embassy, Bogota. "Input for USITC Andean Investment and Drug Crop Survey for Report on ATPA.docx." Attachment "Input for USITC Andean Investment and Drug Crop Survey for Report on ATPA.docx." E-mail message to USITC staff, July 2, 2010.

_____. U.S. Embassy, Bogota. "News: Bilateral Topics; U.S. Assistance to Colombia," n.d. http://bogota.usembassy.gov/plancolombia.html (accessed July 26, 2010).

_____. U.S. Embassy, Bogota. USAID. Colombia. "Acerca del Usaid: Perfil," n.d. https://colombia.usaid.gov/Default.aspx?id=2 (accessed July 22, 2010).

_____. U.S. Embassy, La Paz. "2010 USITC Andean Investment and Drug Crop Survey Report on ATPA (LA PAZ 001230)," July 6, 2010.

_____. U.S. Embassy, La Paz. "Bolivia Continues to Trade Mainly Primary Products (LA PAZ 000045)," February 10, 2010.

_____. U.S. Embassy, La Paz. "The U.S.-Bolivia Trade Relationship (LA PAZ 000934)," June 24, 2009.

_____. U.S. Embassy, La Paz. "The United States Remains Bolivia's 4th Largest Trading Partner (LA PAZ 000057)," February 23, 2010.

_____. U.S. Embassy, La Paz. USAID. Bolivia. "Integrated Development Program: Economic Diversification of Coca Growing and Associated Areas Is Increasingly Sustainable," June 2010. http://bolivia.usaid.gov/US/5Id.htm.

_____. U.S. Embassy, Lima. "Peru Response to Request for Information on Andean Investment and Drug Crop Survey (LIMA 001412)," July 15, 2010.

_____. U.S. Embassy, Lima. USAID. "Alternative Development," November 2009. http://www.usaid.gov/pe/downloads/alternative-development-english-november2009.pdf (accessed July 29, 2010).

_____. U.S. Embassy, Lima. USAID. "Desarrollo alternativo," November 2008. http://www.usaid.gov/pe/downloads/alternative-development-spanish.pdf (accessed July 29, 2010).

_____. U.S. Embassy, Lima. USAID. Peru. "Alternative Development," February 2008. http://peru.usaid.gov/.

_____. U.S. Embassy, Quito. "Input for the USITC Report to Congress on the Andean Trade Preference Act-Ecuador." E-mail message to USITC staff, July 8, 2010.

_____. U.S. Embassy, Quito. "Input for the USITC Report to Congress." E-mail message to USITC staff, June 18, 2010.

_____. U.S. Embassy, Quito. "Preliminary Input for the USITC Andean Investment and Drug Crop Survey." Attachment "06-18-10 Input for the USITC Report to Congress.docx: Input for the USITC Report to Congress on the Andean Trade Preference Act; Ecuador." E-mail message to USITC staff, June 18, 2010.

_____. U.S. Embassy, Quito. "Preliminary Input for the USITC Andean Investment and Drug Crop Survey." Attachment "07-01-10 Additional Input for the USITC Report to

Congress.doc: Additional Input for the USITC Report to Congress on the Andean Trade Preference Act; Ecuador." E-mail message to USITC staff, July 8, 2010.

_____. U.S. Embassy, Quito. "Preliminary Input for the USITC Andean Investment and Drug Crop Survey." Attachment "USAID Input for USITC (2).doc: FY 2009 Performance Plan and Report (excerpt)." E-mail message to USITC staff, June 18, 2010.

_____. U.S. Embassy, Quito. "Preliminary Input for the USITC Andean Investment and Drug Crop Survey." E-mail message to USITC staff, June 18, 2010.

_____. U.S. Embassy, Quito. USAID. "Results Report 2008," June 2009. http://ecuador.usembassy.gov/root (accessed July 29, 2010).

_____. U.S. Embassy, Quito. USAID. Ecuador. "Integrated Municipal Development," n.d. http://ecuador.usaid.gov/portal/content/view/200/175/ (accessed July 22, 2010).

_____. USAID. Bureau for Latin America and the Caribbean (LAC). "Bolivia," July 13, 2010. http://www.usaid.gov/locations/latin america caribbean/country/bolivia/.

_____. USAID. LAC. "Colombia," June 15, 2010. http://www.usaid.gov/locations/latin america caribbean/country/colombia/.

_____. USAID. LAC. "Ecuador," June 15, 2010. http://www.usaid.gov/locations/latin america caribbean/country/ecuador/.

_____. USAID. LAC. "Peru," May 27, 2010. http://www.usaid.gov/locations/latin america caribbean/country/peru/.

_____. USAID. Policy. "FY 2009 Foreign Operations Performance Report and FY 2011 Performance Plan," n.d. http://www.usaid.gov/policy (accessed July 29, 2010). U.S. International Trade Commission (USITC). *Andean Trade Preference Act: Impact on the United States. Fourth Report 1996*. Publication No. 3058. Washington, DC: USITC, 1997.

_____. *Andean Trade Preference Act: Impact on U.S. Industries and Consumers, and on Drug Crop Eradication and Crop Substitution, 2007. Thirteenth Report*. Publication No. 4037. Washington, DC: USITC, 2008.

_____. *Andean Trade Preference Act: Impact on U.S. Industries and Consumers. Fifth Report 1997*. Publication No. 3132. Washington, DC: USITC, 1998.

_____. *Caribbean Basin Economic Recovery Act, Impact on U.S. Industries and Consumers, Annual Report*, Publication No. 1897. Washington, DC: USITC, September 1986.

_____. Hearing transcript in connection with inv. no. 332-352, *Andean Trade Preference Act: Impact on U.S. Industries and on Consumers and on Drug Crop Eradication and Crop Substitution, 2009*, July 7, 2010.

_____. Interactive Tariff and Trade Data Web (Dataweb). http://dataweb.usitc.gov (accessed various dates).

U.S. Trade Representative (USTR). *Fifth Report to the Congress on the Operation of the Andean Trade Preference Act as Amended.* Washington, DC: USTR, June 30, 2010.

_____. *First Report to the Congress on the Operation of the Andean Trade Preference Act As Amended.* Washington, DC: USTR, April 30, 2003.

United Nations Office on Drugs and Crime (UNODC). *Colombia: Coca Cultivation Survey 2009*. "Table 4. Coca cultivation in the Andean Region 2001–2009 (in hectares)," 2010.

_____. *Ecuador: Monitoreo de Cultivos de Coca 2009*. "Tabla 1: Cultivos de coca en la Región Andina, 1997–2009 (ha)," 2010.

_____. *Estado Plurinacional de Bolivia: Monitoreo de Cultivos de Coca 2009*. "Tabla 1. Cultivo de hoja de coca en Bolivia 1999–2009 (ha)," 2010.

_____. *Perú: Monitoreo de Cultivos de Coca 2009*. "Figura 1. Cultivos de coca en el Perú, 1996–2009 (ha)," 2010.

White House. Office of the Press Secretary. "Statement by Press Secretary Dana Perino." News release, November 26, 2008. http://www.whitehouse.gov/news/releases/2008/11/20081126-10.html.

_____. "Text of a Letter from the President to the Chairmen and Ranking Members of the House Committee on Ways and Means, and the Senate Committee on Finance: Determinations and Report of the President Concerning the Review of Ecuador and Bolivia Under the Andean Trade Preference Act, As Amended," June 30, 2009.

Wyler, Liana Sun. *International Drug Control Policy*. Congressional Research Service. RL34543, August 24, 2009.

Yarns and Fibers Exchange. "Peruvian Textiles See Recovery after 2009 Collapse," June 25, 2010. http://www.yarnsandfibers.com/news/index fullstory.php3?id=22347& section= 33&country=Per u&p_type=General# (accessed July 13, 2010).

Appendix A: Federal Register Notice

Federal Register / Vol. 75, No. 87 / Thursday, May 6, 2010 / Notices 24967

endangered species. With some exceptions, the Endangered Species Act (Act) prohibits activities with endangered and threatened species unless a Federal permit allows such activity. The Act requires that we invite public comment before issuing these permits.

DATES: We must receive any written comments on or before June 7, 2010.

ADDRESSES: Send written comments by U.S. mail to the Regional Director, Attn: Peter Fasbender, U.S. Fish and Wildlife Service, Ecological Services, 1 Federal Drive, Fort Snelling, MN 55111–4056; or by electronic mail to *permitsR3ES@fws.gov*.

FOR FURTHER INFORMATION CONTACT: Peter Fasbender, (612) 713–5343.

SUPPLEMENTARY INFORMATION:

Background

We invite public comment on the following permit applications for certain activities with endangered species authorized by section 10(a)(1)(A) of the Act (16 U.S.C. 1531 *et seq.*) and our regulations governing the taking of endangered species in the Code of Federal Regulations (CFR) at 50 CFR part 17. Submit your written data, comments, or request for a copy of the complete application to the address shown in **ADDRESSES.**

Permit Applications

The applicant requests a permit to take (capture, rear and release) Karner blue butterflies (*Lycaeides melissa samuelis*) throughout the range of the species in New York, Indiana, Michigan, and Wisconsin. Proposed activities involve capture of adult butterflies for captive rearing, experimental treatments on captive-reared larvae, and nonlethal tissue sampling in the wild. Population studies are designed to answer questions posed in the Karner blue butterfly recovery plan and are aimed at enhancement of survival of the species in the wild.

Permit Application Number: TE10891A.
Applicant: Illinois State Museum, Department of Natural Resources, Springfield, Illinois.

The applicant requests a permit renewal to take (capture and release, collect) Hine's emerald dragonfly (*Somatochlora hineana*) throughout the range of the species in the States of Alabama, Arkansas, Connecticut, Delaware, District of Columbia, Georgia, Illinois, Indiana, Iowa, Kentucky, Maine, Maryland, Massachusetts, Michigan, Minnesota, Missouri, New Hampshire, New Jersey, New York, North Carolina, Ohio, Oklahoma, Pennsylvania, Rhode Island, South Carolina, Tennessee, Vermont, Virginia, West Virginia, and Wisconsin. Proposed activities are for the recovery and enhancement of survival of the species in the wild.

Permit Application Number: TE212427.

Public Comments

We seek public review and comments on these permit applications. Please refer to the permit number when you submit comments. Comments and materials we receive are available for public inspection, by appointment, during normal business hours at the address shown in the **ADDRESSES** section. Before including your address, phone number, e-mail address, or other personal identifying information in your comment, you should be aware that your entire comment—including your personal identifying information—may be made publicly available at any time. While you can ask us in your comment to withhold your personal identifying information from public review, we cannot guarantee that we will be able to do so.

National Environmental Policy Act (NEPA)

In compliance with NEPA (42 U.S.C. 4321 *et seq.*), we have made an initial determination that the proposed activities in these permits are categorically excluded from the requirement to prepare an environmental assessment or environmental impact statement (516 DM 6 Appendix 1, 1.4C(1)).

Dated: April 30, 2010.

Lynn M. Lewis, *Assistant Regional*

Permit Application Number: TE09357A.
Applicant: Ecological Specialties LLC, Symsonia, Kentucky.

The applicant requests a permit renewal/amendment to take (capture, radio-tag, and release) Indiana bats (*Myotis sodalis*), gray bats (*Myotis grisescens*), Ozark big-eared bats (*Corynorhinus townsendii ingens*), Virginia big-eared bats (*Corynorhinus townsendii virginianus*), Mexican longnosed bats (*Leptonycteris nivalis*), and Sanborn's long-nosed bats (*Leptonycteris sanborni (=yerbabuenae)*) throughout the States of Arkansas, Alabama, California, Illinois, Indiana, Iowa, Michigan, Minnesota, Missouri, New Jersey, New Mexico, New York, Ohio, Pennsylvania, Tennessee, Texas, Virginia, and West Virginia to document presence/absence and distribution of the species and to conduct habitat use assessments. Proposed activities are aimed at enhancement of survival of the species in the wild.

Permit Application Number: TE010887A.
Applicant: U.S. Geological Survey, Great Lakes Science Center, Porter, Indiana.
Applicant: Ecology & Environment, Inc., Lancaster, New York. The applicant requests an amendment to permit number TE212427 for the Indiana bat, Ozark big-eared bat, and gray bat. The applicant's request includes addition of qualified personnel and addition of the States of Iowa, Michigan, and Pennsylvania to their area of jurisdiction for conducting survey and assessment work. Activities are for the enhancement of survival of the species in the wild.

Permit Application Number: TE11035A.
Applicant: Robert J. Vande Kopple, University of Michigan, Pellston, Michigan.
The applicant requests a permit renewal to take (capture and release, collect) Hungerford's crawling water beetle (*Brychius hungerfordi*) throughout the States of Michigan and Wisconsin. Proposed activities include surveys to document presence of the species, habitat use, and scientific study related to recovery and enhancement of the survival of the species in the wild.

Director, Ecological Services, Region 3.

[FR Doc. 2010–10659 Filed 5–5–10; 8:45 am]

BILLING CODE 4310–55–P

INTERNATIONAL TRADE COMMISSION

[Investigation No. 332–352]

Andean Trade Preference Act: Impact on the U.S. Economy and on Andean Drug Crop Eradication

AGENCY: United States International Trade Commission.

ACTION: Notice of public hearing and opportunity to submit comments in connection with the 14th report on the Andean Trade Preference Act (ATPA).

SUMMARY: Section 206 of the ATPA (19 U.S.C. 3204) requires the Commission to report biennially to the Congress by September 30 of each reporting year on the economic impact of the Act on U.S. industries and U.S. consumers, as well as on the effectiveness of the Act in promoting drug related crop eradication and crop substitution efforts by beneficiary countries. The Commission prepares these reports under investigation No. 332–352, *Andean*

Trade Preference Act: Impact on the U.S. Economy and on Andean Drug Crop Eradication.

DATES: *June 24, 2010:* Deadline for filing requests to appear at the public hearing.

June 30, 2010: Deadline for filing prehearing briefs and statements.

July 7, 2010: Public hearing.

July 14, 2010: Deadline for filing posthearing briefs and statements and all other written submissions.

September 30, 2010: Transmittal of Commission report to Congress.

ADDRESSES: All Commission offices, including the Commission's hearing rooms, are located in the United States International Trade Commission Building, 500 E Street SW., Washington, DC. All written submissions should be addressed to the Secretary, United States International Trade Commission, 500 E Street SW., Washington, DC 20436. The public record for this investigation may be viewed on the Commission's electronic docket (EDIS) at *http://www.usitc.gov/secretary/edis.htm.*

FOR FURTHER INFORMATION CONTACT: Walker Pollard (202–205–3228, or *walker.pollard@usitc.gov*), Country and Regional Analysis Division, Office of Economics, U.S. International Trade Commission, Washington, DC 20436.

For information on the legal aspects of this investigation, contact William Gearhart of the Commission's Office of the General Counsel (202–205–3091 or *william.gearhart@usitc.gov*). The media should contact Peg O'Laughlin, Public Affairs Officer (202–205–1819 or *margaret.olaughlin@usitc.gov*).

(3) The estimated effect that ATPA has had on drug-related crop eradication and crop substitution efforts of beneficiary countries.

Notice of institution of this investigation for preparing these reports was published in the **Federal Register** of March 10, 1994 (59 FR 11308). This 14th report, covering the period since the previous report and focusing on calendar year 2009, is to be submitted by September 30, 2010.

Public Hearing: A public hearing in connection with this investigation will be held at the U.S. International Trade Commission Building, 500 E Street SW., Washington, DC, beginning at 9:30 a.m. on July 7, 2010. Requests to appear at the public hearing should be filed with the Secretary, no later than 5:15 p.m., June 24, 2010, in accordance with the requirements in the ''Submissions'' section below. All pre-hearing briefs and statements should be filed not later than 5:15 p.m., June 30, 2010, and all post-hearing briefs and statements should be filed not later than 5:15 p.m., July 14, 2010. In the event that, as of the close of business on June 24, 2010, no witnesses are scheduled to appear at the hearing, the hearing will be canceled.

Any person interested in attending the hearing as an observer or nonparticipant may call the Secretary to the Commission (202–205–2000) after June 24, 2010, for information concerning whether the hearing will be held.

Written Submissions: In lieu of or in addition to participating in the hearing, interested parties are invited to submit written statements concerning this investigation. All written submissions should be addressed to the Secretary, and should be received not later than 5:15 p.m., July 14, 2008. electronic filing should contact the Secretary (202–205–2000).

Any submissions that contain confidential business information must also conform with the requirements of section 201.6 of the *Commission's Rules of Practice and Procedure* (19 CFR 201.6). Section 201.6 of the rules requires that the cover of the document and the individual pages be clearly marked as to whether they are the ''confidential'' or ''non-confidential'' version, and that the confidential business information be clearly identified by means of brackets. All written submissions, except for confidential business information, will be made available for inspection by interested parties.

Congressional committee staff has indicated that the receiving committees intend to make the Commission's report available to the public in its entirety, and has asked that the Commission not include any confidential business information or national security classified information in the report that the Commission sends to the Congress.

Any confidential business information received by the Commission in this investigation and used in preparing this report will not be published in a manner that would reveal the operations of the firm supplying the information.

Issued: May 3, 2010.

By order of the Commission.

General information concerning the Commission may be obtained by accessing its internet server (*http://www.usitc.gov*).

Background: Section 206 of the Andean Trade Preference Act (ATPA) (19 U.S.C. 3204) requires that the Commission submit biennial reports to the Congress regarding the economic impact of the Act on U.S. industries and consumers and, in conjunction with other agencies, the effectiveness of the Act in promoting drug-related crop eradication and crop substitution efforts of the beneficiary countries. Section 206(b) of the Act requires that each report include:

(1) The actual effect of ATPA on the U.S. economy generally as well as on specific domestic industries which produce articles that are like, or directly competitive with, articles being imported under the Act from beneficiary countries;

(2) The probable future effect that ATPA will have on the U.S. economy generally and on such domestic industries; and

All written submissions must conform with the provisions of section 201.8 of the Commission's *Rules of Practice and Procedure* (19 CFR 201.8). Section 201.8 requires that a signed original (or a copy so designated) and fourteen (14) copies of each document be filed. In the event that confidential treatment of a document is requested, at least four (4) additional copies must be filed, in which the confidential information must be deleted (see the following paragraph for further information regarding confidential business information). The Commission's rules authorize filing submissions with the Secretary by facsimile or electronic means only to the extent permitted by section 201.8 of the rules (*see* Handbook for Electronic Filing Procedures, *http://www.usitc.gov/secretary/fed□reg□notices/rules/handbook□on□electronic□filing.pdf*). Persons with questions regarding

Marilyn R. Abbott, *Secretary.*

[FR Doc. 2010–10688 Filed 5–5–10; 8:45 am]

BILLING CODE 7020–02–P

INTERNATIONAL TRADE COMMISSION

[Investigation No. 731–TA–1070A (Review)]

Crepe Paper Products From China

Determination On the basis of the record [1] developed in the subject five-year review, the United States International Trade Commission (Commission) determines, pursuant to section 751(c) of the Tariff Act of 1930 (19 U.S.C. 1675(c)), that revocation of the antidumping duty order on crepe paper from China would be likely to lead to continuation or recurrence of material injury to an industry in the United States within a reasonably foreseeable time.

Background

The Commission instituted this review on December 1, 2009 (74 FR

[1] The record is defined in sec. 207.2(f) of the Commission's Rules of Practice and Procedure (19 CFR 207.2(f)).

APPENDIX B: HEARING CALENDAR

Calendar of Public Hearing

Those listed below appeared as witnesses at the United States International Trade Commission's hearing:

Subject: Andean Trade Preference Act: Impact on the U.S. Economy and on Andean Drug Crop Eradication
Inv. No.: 332-352
Date and Time: July 7, 2010 - 9:30 a.m.

A sessions was held in connection with this investigation in the Main Hearing Room (room 101), 500 E Street, S.W., Washington, D.C.

EMBASSY WITNESS:

Embassy of Peru Washington, D.C.
His Excellency Luis M. Valdivieso, Ambassador of Peru to the United States of America

ORGANIZATION AND WITNESS:
Colombian Government Trade Bureau Washington, D.C.
on behalf of
Embassy of Colombia
Claudia Candela, Director
Carolina Acosta, Counselor
American Chamber of Commerce Washington, D.C.
Patrick Kilbride, Director of the Americas Office; and Executive Vice President, Association of American Chambers of Commerce (AACCLA)

ORGANIZATION AND WITNESS:

Association of Floral Importers of Florida Miami, FL
Christine Boldt, Executive Vice President
Gabriel Becerra, Board Director
California Cut Flower Commission Sacramento, CA
Kasey Cronquist, Executive Director/Ambassador
Textiles La Escala Quito, Ecuador
Jeff S. Sheedy, Chief Executive Officer

-END-

APPENDIX C: TECHNICAL NOTES TO CHAPTER 3

Technical Notes to Chapter 3: Partial Equilibrium Analysis

This section presents the methodology used to estimate the impact of ATPA on the U.S. economy in 2009.[1] The economic effects of ATPA duty reductions[2] were evaluated with a comparative static analysis. Since ATPA tariff preferences were already in effect in 2009, the impact of the program was measured by comparing the market conditions currently present (duty-free entry for eligible products entered under ATPA provisions) with those that might have existed under full tariffs (i.e., no ATPA tariff preferences). Thus, the analysis provides an estimate of what the potential costs and benefits to the U.S. economy would have been if ATPA had not been in place during 2009. However, the material on welfare and displacement effects, in the section titled "Analytical Approach" in chapter 1 and in this appendix, discusses the impact of ATPA in terms of duty reductions, rather than the "removal" of duty eliminations already in place.[3] The effects of a duty reduction and a duty imposition are symmetrical and lead to results that are equivalent in magnitude but opposite in sign.[4] Thus, the discussion is framed with respect to the implementation of duty reductions simply for clarity.

A partial equilibrium framework was used to model three different markets in the United States, namely, the markets for ATPA products, competing non-ATPA (foreign) products, and competing domestic products. These three markets are depicted in panels *a, b,*and c of figure C.1. In the model, imports from ATPA beneficiaries, imports from non-ATPA countries, and competing domestic output are assumed to be imperfect substitutes for each other, and each is characterized by a separate market where different equilibrium prices exist.

The ATPA and non-ATPA import demand curves, D_a *and* D_n, and the demand curve for domestic output, D_d, are all assumed to be downward sloping with a constant elasticity of demand.[5] It is assumed that the ATPA import supply curve to the U.S. market, the non-ATPA import supply curve, and the domestic industry supply curve, S_a S_n , and S_d , are all horizontal, that is, perfectly elastic. The assumption of perfectly elastic supply curves greatly simplifies computation although it leads to an upward bias in the estimates of the welfare and domestic displacement effects on the U.S. economy.[6]

The change from full tariffs to duty-free treatment for ATPA imports causes the import supply curve, S_a, in panel *a* to shift down to S'_a by the amount of the ad valorem tariff, t. Thus, the equilibrium price in the U.S. market for ATPA imports decreases from P_a to P'_a , whereas the quantity imported increases from Q_a to Q'_a..The relationship between the price with the tariff (P_a) and the tariff-free price P'_a is $P_a = P'_a(1+t)$.

The decrease in the price of ATPA imports leads to a decrease in demand for similar goods from other countries and domestic U.S. producers. Thus, the demand curves for both non-ATPA imports and domestic output, D_n and D_d, shift back to D'_n and D_d, respectively. Since the supply curves in both of these markets are assumed to be perfectly elastic, the equilibrium prices do not change. The equilibrium quantity supplied in each market decreases from Q_n and Q_d to Q'_n and Q'_d respectively.

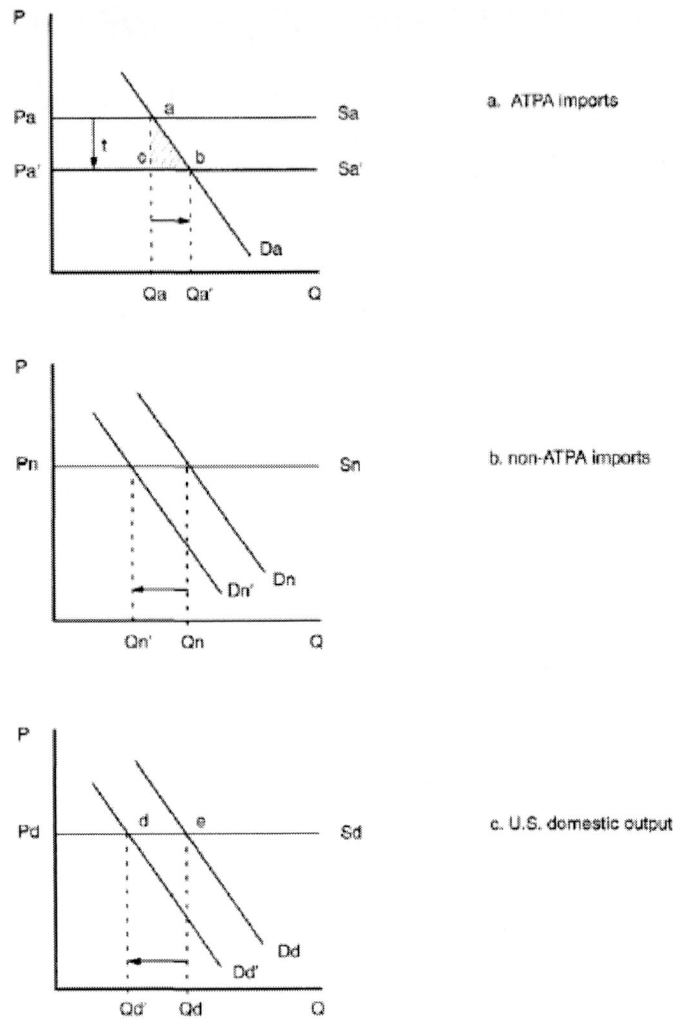

Figure C-1. Partial equilibrium analysis of the effects of ATPA duty provisions on U.S. Imports.

The impact of ATPA on the U.S. economy was measured by examining the welfare effects of the tariff reduction in the market for ATPA imports and the domestic displacement effects of a decrease in demand in the competing U.S. market. The displacement of non-ATPA country imports because of ATPA tariff preferences was not estimated because the focus of the analysis was on the direct effects of ATPA provisions on the United States.

The decrease in the tariff for ATPA imports leads to an increase in consumer surplus for these products. This is measured by the trapezoid $P_a abP'_a$ in panel *a* . There is also an accompanying decrease in the tariff revenue collected from ATPA imports. This is measured by the area of the rectangle $P_a acP'_a$ in panel *a*.

The net welfare effect of ATPA is equal to the increase in consumer surplus plus the decrease in tariff revenue—the trapezoid $P_a abP'_a$ minus the rectangle $P_a acP'_a$ in panel *a* , that is, triangle abc.[7] The dollar amount by which ATPA imports displace U.S. output is measured by the rectangle $Q'_d deQ_d$ in panel *c* .

Given the above assumptions and the additional assumption of constant elasticity demand curves, the markets for the three goods are described by the following three equations:

$$(Q_a/Q'_a) = (P_a/P'_a)^{\varepsilon_{aa}} \quad (1)$$

$$(Q_n/Q'_n) = (P_a/P'_a)^{\varepsilon_{na}} \quad (2)$$

$$(Q_d/Q'_d) = (P_a/P'_a)^{\varepsilon_{da}} \quad (3)$$

Given that $P_a = P'_a(1+t)$, these can be restated as

$$(Q_a/Q'_a) = (1+t)^{\varepsilon_{aa}} \quad (1)$$

$$(Q_n/Q'_n) = (1+t)^{\varepsilon_{na}} \quad (2)$$

$$(Q_d/Q'_d) = (1+t)^{\varepsilon_{da}} \quad (3)$$

where ε_{ij} is the uncompensated elasticity of demand for good *i* with respect to price *j*.

The values for the elasticities ε_{aa}, ε_{na}, and ε_{da} are derived from the following relations:

$$\varepsilon_{aa} = V_a\eta - V_n\sigma_{ca} - V_d\sigma_{da} \quad (4)$$

$$\varepsilon_{na} = V_a(\sigma_{na} + \eta) \quad (5)$$

$$\varepsilon_{da} = V_a(\sigma_{da} + \eta) \quad (6)$$

where the V_i's are market shares for ATPA imports, non-ATPA imports, and domestic output, respectively, η is the aggregate demand elasticity, and the σ_{ij} 's are the elasticities of substitution between the *i* th and *j* th products.[8] Estimates of the aggregate demand elasticities were taken from the literature.[9] Ranges of potential net welfare and industry displacement estimates are reported. The reported ranges reflect a range of assumed substitutabilities between ATPA products and competing U.S. output. The upper estimates reflect the assumption of high substitution elasticities. The lower estimates reflect the assumption of low substitution elasticities.[10]

Since the implementation of ATPDEA in October 2002, apparel assembled in ATPA countries from U.S.-made fabric and components has come to dominate the list of leading imports benefiting exclusively from ATPA. U.S. producers of such fabric and components benefit from ATPA duty preferences. Where the U.S. value of components can be identified (for example, the U.S. value of components assembled abroad under HTS heading 9802.00.80 is recorded and data are readily available), it is possible to estimate the effect of ATPA tariff preferences on U.S. producers of the components. In the case of cut apparel parts used in the assembly of apparel in ATPA countries, the U.S.- produced cut parts are recorded as apparel production in the United States and the effect of ATPA tariff preferences can be added to the (negative) displacement effects for that industry.

Given equations (1)' through (3)' , one can derive the following equations for calculating the changes in consumer surplus, tariff revenue, and domestic output:

Consumer surplus (where k is a constant)
area of
trapezoid

$$P_a ab P'_a = \int_{P'_a}^{P_a} k P_a^{\varepsilon_{aa}} dP_a$$

$$= [1/(1+\varepsilon_{aa})][(1+t)^{(1+\varepsilon_{aa})} - 1] P'_a Q'_a \quad \text{if } \varepsilon_{aa} \neq -1$$

$$k \ln(1+t) \quad \text{if } \varepsilon_{aa} = -1$$

Tariff revenue from U.S. imports from ATPA partners
area of rectangle

$$P_a ac P'_a = (P_a - P'_a) Q_a$$

$$= P'_a t Q_a \quad \text{given } P_a = P'_a(1+t)$$

$$= t P'_a Q'_a (1+t)^{\varepsilon_{aa}} \quad \text{given } Q_a = Q'_a (1+t)^{\varepsilon_{aa}}$$

Domestic output
area of rectangle

$$Q'_d de Q_d = P_d (Q_d - Q'_d)$$

$$= P_d Q'_d [(1+t)^{\varepsilon_{da}} - 1]$$

The change in the value of U.S. cut apparel parts $= uP'_a Q'_a[(1+t')^{\varepsilon_{aa}} - 1]$, where u is the ratio of the value of U.S. cut apparel parts to total imports under ATPA, and t' is the ad valorem equivalent of duties paid on imports under HTS 9802.00.80 under ATPA; t is opposite in sign to the displacement effect shown above. The net effect of ATPA tariff preferences on domestic output is estimated as

$$P_d Q'_d [(1+t)^{\varepsilon_{da}} - 1] + uP'_a Q'_a [(1+t')^{\varepsilon_{aa}} - 1].$$

APPENDIX D: STATISTICAL TABLES

Table D.1. U.S. imports for consumption from ATPA countries, by duty treatment, by country, 2005–09

Duty treatment	2005	2006	2007	2008	2009
	Millions of $				
Bolivia					
Dutiable imports	10.9	33.4	6.1	69.2	97.5
Duty-free value:					
NTR duty-free	98.2	141.1	138.7	252.5	282.6
ATPA:					
Exclusive	81.3	76.8	76.8	83.7	0.0
Non-exclusive	76.0	89.4	71.3	56.2	0.0
Total ATPA	157.4	166.2	148.1	140.0	0.0
GSP	26.8	21.7	40.7	47.6	123.9
Other duty-free	0.0	0.1	([a])	0.1	0.0
Total duty-free value	282.4	329.0	327.6	440.2	406.5
U.S. Virgin Islands[b]	0.0	0.0	0.0	31.0	0.0
Total imports	293.3	362.4	333.6	540.4	504.0
Colombia					
Dutiable imports	895.7	721.3	817.5	1,057.6	1,250.8
Duty-free value:					
NTR duty-free	2,865.6	3,290.0	3,492.3	4,315.1	4,178.7
ATPA:					
Exclusive	4,259.7	4,365.2	4,146.4	6,928.8	5,205.7
Non-exclusive	393.3	426.0	381.3	410.4	383.8
Total ATPA	4,653.1	4,791.2	4,527.7	7,339.2	5,589.5
GSP	188.9	181.6	236.4	235.8	188.7
Other duty-free	([a])	0.1	0.4	0.4	1.2
Total duty-free value	7,707.5	8,262.9	8,256.8	11,890.6	9,958.0
U.S. Virgin Islands[b]	167.0	255.6	176.9	110.7	0.5
Total imports	8,770.3	9,239.8	9,251.2	13,058.8	11,209.4
Ecuador					
Dutiable imports	527.5	486.5	318.1	1,128.4	989.8
Duty-free value:					
NTR duty-free	918.0	1,128.2	1,104.1	1,263.0	1,445.5
ATPA:					
Exclusive	4,221.8	5,138.5	4,460.9	6,433.4	2,586.5
Non-exclusive	148.8	186.7	152.9	161.3	162.0
Total ATPA	4,370.7	5,325.2	4,613.8	6,594.8	2,748.4
GSP	57.7	71.2	76.6	57.1	52.3

Table D.1. (Continued)

Duty treatment	2005	2006	2007	2008	2009
Other duty-free	([a])	0.1	0.2	0.1	0.4
Total duty-free value	5,346.4	6,524.7	5,794.6	7,914.9	4,246.6
U.S. Virgin Islands[b]	0.1	0.2	18.2	0.5	9.5
Total imports	5,873.9	7,011.4	6,131.0	9,043.8	5,245.9
Peru					
Dutiable imports	127.7	103.3	151.1	332.1	274.4
Duty-free value:					
NTR duty-free	2,498.0	2,399.5	1,727.8	1,988.2	1,611.7
ATPA:					
Exclusive	2,085.5	2,951.0	2,804.5	2,915.2	1,019.8
Non-exclusive	197.1	250.8	212.7	253.5	356.5
Total ATPA	2,282.6	3,201.8	3,017.2	3,168.7	1,376.3
GSP	174.8	179.4	245.5	271.0	30.7
Peru FTA	0.0	0.0	0.0	0.0	898.1
Other duty-free	([a])	([a])	0.1	0.2	0.0
Total duty-free value	4,955.4	5,780.7	4,990.6	5,428.1	3,916.8
U.S. Virgin Islands[b]	39.5	12.9	65.3	79.7	43.4
Total imports	4,994.9	5,793.6	5,056.0	5,507.9	3,960.3

[a] Value is less than $50,000.

[b] The U.S. Virgin Islands has its own tariff schedule and laws separate from the rest of the United States and is outside the U.S. customs territory; therefore, imports that enter the U.S. Virgin Islands are not identified as either dutiable or free of duty. [c]Value is less than 0.05 percent.

Table D.2. Leading U.S. imports for consumption from Andean countries, HS chapter, in value and share of non-oil imports for consumption, 2005–09

HS chapter	Description	2005	2006	2007	2008	2009	Change 2008–09
			Value (millions of $)				*Percent*
27	Mineral fuels, mineral oils and products of their distillation; bituminous substances; mineral waxes	7,951.8	9,138.4	8,224.9	13,353.4	7,363.8	-44.9
06	Live trees and other plants; bulbs, roots and the like; cut flowers and ornamental foliage	549.7	594.2	652.7	635.3	626.8	-1.3
61	Articles of apparel and clothing accessories, knitted or crocheted	953.6	1,000.0	922.0	889.2	490.3	-44.9
74	Copper and articles thereof	587.5	1,038.1	1,032.0	905.4	245.6	-72.9

HS chapter	Description	2005	2006	2007	2008	2009	Change 2008–09
20	Preparations of vegetables, fruit, nuts, or other parts of plants	80.4	115.4	118.9	174.8	146.6	-16.1
62	Articles of apparel and clothing accessories, not knitted or crocheted	364.7	321.3	243.7	219.5	134.3	-38.8
07	Edible vegetables and certain roots and tubers	179.9	204.1	245.7	248.8	115.3	-53.7
08	Edible fruit and nuts; peel of citrus fruit or melons	62.7	77.8	87.8	99.2	92.7	-6.5
16	Edible preparations of meat, fish, crustaceans, molluscs or other aquatic						
	invertebrates	70.7	84.2	78.5	86.8	68.4	-21.2
39	Plastics and articles thereof	93.3	93.2	111.0	82.7	60.4	-26.9
	Subtotal	10,894.3	12,666.6	11,717.4	16,695.1	9,344.1	-44.0
	All other	569.6	817.8	589.5	547.6	370.1	-32.4
	Total	11,463.9	13,484.4	12,306.8	17,242.7	9,714.2	-43.7
Percent of total imports							*In percentage points*
27	Mineral fuels, mineral oils and products of their distillation; bituminous substances; mineral waxes	69.4	67.8	66.8	77.4	75.8	-1.6
			Percent of non-oil total				
06	Live trees and other plants; bulbs, roots and the like; cut flowers and ornamental foliage	15.7	13.7	16.0	16.3	26.7	10.3
61	Articles of apparel and clothing accessories, knitted or crocheted	27.2	23.0	22.6	22.9	20.9	-2.0
74	Copper and articles thereof	16.7	23.9	25.3	23.3	10.4	-12.8
20	Preparations of vegetables, fruit, nuts, or other parts of plants	2.3	2.7	2.9	4.5	6.2	1.7
62	Articles of apparel and clothing accessories, not knitted or crocheted	10.4	7.4	6.0	5.6	5.7	0.1
07	Edible vegetables and certain roots and tubers	5.1	4.7	6.0	6.4	4.9	-1.5
08	Edible fruit and nuts; peel of citrus fruit or melons	1.8	1.8	2.2	2.6	3.9	1.4

Table D.2. (Continued)

HS chapter	Description	2005	2006	2007	2008	2009	Change 2008–09
16	Edible preparations of meat, fish, crustaceans, molluscs or other	2.0	1.9	1.9	2.2	2.9	0.7
39	Plastics and articles thereof	2.7	2.1	2.7	2.1	2.6	0.4
	Subtotal	83.8	81.2	85.6	85.9	84.3	-1.7
	All other	16.2	18.8	14.4	14.1	15.7	1.7
	Total	100.0	100.0	100.0	100.0	100.0	

Source: Compiled from official statistics of the U.S. Department of Commerce.

Table D.3. Leading U.S. imports for consumption from ATPA countries, by 8-digit HTS number, 2005–09

HTS number	Description	2005	2006	2007	2008	2009	Change 2008–09
		Millions of $					*Percent*
2709.00.10	Petroleum oils and oils from bituminous minerals, crude, testing under 25 degrees A.P.I.	5,182.1	5,873.0	5,840.3	10,128.1	6,036.1	-40.4
2709.00.20	Petroleum oils and oils from bituminous minerals, crude, testing 25 degrees A.P.I. or more	1,770.3	2,165.9	1,644.9	2,078.5	920.6	-55.7
0603.11.00[a]	Sweetheart, spray and other roses, fresh cut	263.1	288.4	327.2	310.3	304.9	-1.7
2710.19.05	Distillate and residual fuel oil (including blends) derived from petroleum or oils from bituminous minerals, testing under 25 degrees A.P.I.	541.5	458.8	408.7	628.7	244.7	-61.1
7403.11.00	Refined copper cathodes and sections of cathodes	556.4	993.0	989.1	844.4	218.4	-74.1
0603.19.00[b]	Fresh cut, anthuriums,alstroemeria,gypsophilia,lilies, snapdragons and flowers, n.e.s.o.i.	159.4	172.2	187.8	192.5	187.8	-2.5
6110.20.20	Sweaters, pullovers and similar articles, knitted or crocheted, of cotton, n.e.s.o.i.	295.2	318.2	297.4	239.9	126.7	-47.2
2710.11.25	Naphthas (exc. motor fuel/mtr fuel blend. stock) fr petroleum oils & bitumin minerals (o/than crude) or preps 70%+ by wt. fr petroleum oils	406.2	613.0	294.1	377.1	126.6	-66.4
6109.10.00	T-shirts, singlets, tank tops and similar garments, knitted or crocheted, of cotton	164.2	168.8	155.5	162.5	95.3	-41.4
6105.10.00	Men's or boys' shirts, knitted or crocheted, of cotton	193.8	190.7	165.4	176.2	85.4	-51.5
0603.14.00[c]	Chrysanthemums, fresh cut	63.5	63.4	65.5	66.9	75.3	12.5
6203.42.40	Men's or boys' trousers and shorts, not bibs, not knitted or crocheted, of cotton, not containing 15% or more by weight of down, etc.	156.4	140.8	98.6	85.8	48.7	-43.2
0709.20.90	Asparagus, n.e.s.o.i., fresh or chilled	87.1	126.6	159.3	145.2	45.7	-68.5
1604.14.30	Tunas and skipjack, not in oil, in airtight containers, n/o 7 kg, not of u.s. possessions, over quota	47.8	64.9	67.9	70.1	43.4	-38.1
0603.12.70[d]	Other carnations, fresh cut	33.2	37.4	42.2	37.8	33.9	-10.3
2710.11.45	Light oil mixt. of hydrocarbons fr petro oils & bitum min(o/than crude) or prep 70%+ wt. fr petro oils, n.e.s.o.i., n/o 50% any single hydrocarbon	0.0	0.0	0.0	36.1	31.5	-12.6
0804.50.40	Guavas, mangoes, and mangosteens, fresh, if entered during the period September 1 through May 31, inclusive	27.3	31.5	30.0	32.6	31.4	-3.8

Table D.3. (Continued)

HTS number	Description	2005	2006	2007	2008	2009	Change 2008–09
2005.99.80[e]	Artichokes, prepared or preserved otherwise than by vinegar or acetic acid, not frozen	16.6	35.9	39.1	46.5	30.8	-33.6
0806.10.60	Grapes, fresh, if entered during the period July 1 through the following February 14, inclusive	9.8	15.2	17.9	24.4	27.4	12.5
0710.80.97	Vegetables n.e.s.o.i., uncooked or cooked by steaming or boiling in water, frozen, reduced in size	19.1	27.5	34.8	36.0	27.3	-24.1
	Subtotal	9,992.9	11,784.8	10,865.8	15,719.6	8,742.0	-44.4
	All other	1,471.0	1,699.6	1,441.0	1,523.1	972.3	-36.2
	Total	11,463.9	13,484.4	12,306.8	17,242.7	9,714.2	-43.7

Source: Compiled from official statistics of the U.S. Department of Commerce.

Note: The abbreviation "n.e.s.o.i." stands for "not elsewhere specified or otherwise included."

a Imports of HTS 0603.11.00 were reported under 0603.10.60 during 2005–06.

b Imports of HTS 0603.19.00 were reported under 0603.10.7040 and 0603.10.80 during 2005–06.

c Imports of HTS 0603.14.00 were reported under 0603.10.7010 and 0603.10.7020 during 2005–06.

d Imports of HTS 0603.12.70 were reported under 0603.10.7030 during 2005–06.

e Imports of HTS 2005.99.80 were reported under 2005.90.80 during 2005–06.

Table D.4. Leading imports that benefited exclusively from ATPA, 2008 and 2009, customs value

HTS number Description		2008	2009[a]	Change	
		Thousands of $			Percent
2709.00.10	Petroleum oils and oils from bituminous minerals, crude, testing under 25 degrees A.P.I.	10,128,077	5,744,680	-4,383,397	-43.3
2709.00.20	Petroleum oils and oils from bituminous minerals, crude, testing 25 degrees A.P.I. or more	2,078,530	914,001	-1,164,529	-56.0
0603.11.00	Sweetheart, Spray and other Roses, fresh cut	310,291	304,906	-5,385	-1.7
2710.19.05	Distillate and residual fuel oil (including blends) derived from petroleum or oils from bituminous minerals, testing under 25 degrees A.P.I.	628,662	244,655	-384,007	-61.1
0603.14.00[b]	Chrysanthemums, fresh cut	66,346	75,121	8,775	13.2
2710.11.25	Naphthas (exc. motor fuel/mtr fuel blend. stock) fr petroleum oils & bitumin minerals (o/than crude) or preps 70+ by wt. fr petroleum oils	377,141	85,998	-291,143	-77.2
6203.42.40	Men's or boys' trousers and shorts, not bibs, not knitted or crocheted, of cotton, not containing 15% or more by weight of down, etc	85,841	44,205	-41,636	-48.5
1604.14.30	Tunas and skipjack, not in oil, in airtight containers, n/o 7 kg, not of U.S. possessions, over quota	70,067	43,400	-26,667	-38.1
0603.12.70[b]	Other carnations, fresh cut	37,239	33,621	-3,618	-9.7
7403.11.00[c]	Refined copper cathodes and sections of cathodes	844,388	39,442	-804,947	-95.3
6908.90.00	Glazed ceramic flags and paving, hearth or wall tiles; glazed ceramic mosaic cubes and the like, n.e.s.o.i.	27,406	20,414	-6,992	-25.5
0710.80.97	Vegetables n.e.s.o.i., uncooked or cooked by steaming or boiling in water, frozen, reduced in size	35,970	23,801	-12,169	-33.8
6109.10.00	T-shirts, singlets, tank tops and similar garments, knitted or crocheted, of cotton	162,482	24,480	-138,002	-84.9
2710.11.45	Light oil mixt. of hydrocarbons fr petro oils & bitum min (o/than crude) or prep 70%+ wt. fr petro oils, n.e.s.o.i., n/o 50% any single hydrocarbon	36,107	22,472	-13,635	-37.8
0709.20.90	Asparagus, n.e.s.o.i., fresh or chilled	145,196	14,166	-131,030	-90.2
6110.20.20	Sweaters, pullovers and similar articles, knitted or crocheted, of cotton, n.e.s.o.i.	239,925	18,457	-221,468	-92.3
0804.30.40	Pineapples, fresh or dried, not reduced in size, in crates or other packages	12,144	15,411	3,267	26.9
6105.10.00	Men's or boys' shirts, knitted or crocheted, of cotton	176,191	15,712	-160,480	-91.1

Table D.4. (Continued)

HTS number Description		2008	2009[a]	Change	
		Thousands of $			Percent
6204.62.40	Women's or girls' trousers, breeches and shorts, not knitted or crocheted, of cotton, n.e.s.o.i.	21,347	14,547	-6,800	-31.9
6110.30.30	Sweaters, pullovers and similar articles, knitted or crocheted, of manmade fibers, n.e.s.o.i.	26,265	13,779	-12,487	-47.5
	Total of above	15,509,615	7,713,268	-7,798,348	-50.3
	Other Total	850,229	249,797	-598,421	-70.6
		16,359,841	7,963,064	-8,396,777	-51.3

Source: Estimated by the U.S. International Trade Commission from official statistics of the U.S. Department of Commerce.

Note: The abbreviation n.e.s.o.i. stands for "not elsewhere specified or otherwise included."

a Includes imports entered under ATPA from Peru only for Jan. 2009.

b Includes only imports from Colombia. Item is GSP-eligible, but imports from Colombia exceeded the competitive need limit and thus were eligible for duty-free entry only under ATPA.

c Includes only imports from Peru. Item is GSP-eligible, but imports from Peru exceeded the competitive need limit and thus were eligible for duty-free entry only under ATPA.

End Notes

Executive Summary

[1] Coca leaves are the raw material used in the production of cocaine. Essentially all cocaine worldwide originates in Bolivia, Colombia, and Peru. Ecuador has no significant coca cultivation, but serves as a major transit country for illegal drugs.

[2] Throughout this report, the term "ATPA" refers to ATPA as amended by subsequent legislation. Also for the purpose of this report, the term "Andean" refers only to the countries Bolivia, Colombia, Ecuador, and Peru.

[3] The analysis in this report covers developments since the previous ATPA report, generally focusing on developments during 2009 (or the most recent year for which data are available), or on changes during the 2005–09 period.

[4] App. A reproduces the *Federal Register* notice by which the Commission provided notice of a public hearing and solicited public comment, and chap. 5 contains summaries of submissions received by the Commission in response to *the Federal Register* notice.

Introduction

[1] Pub. L. 102-182, 105 Stat. 1236. ATPA as amended is codified at 19 U.S.C. 3201 et seq. ATPA became effective July 22, 1992, for Colombia and Bolivia (Presidential Proclamation 6455, 57 Fed. Reg. 30069, and Presidential Proclamation 6456, 57 Fed. Reg. 30087, respectively); Apr. 30, 1993, for Ecuador (Presidential Proclamation 6544, 58 Fed. Reg. 19547); and Aug. 31, 1993, for Peru (Presidential Proclamation 6585, 58 Fed. Reg. 43239).

[2] Pub. L. 107-210. ATPDEA duty-free treatment became effective for all four beneficiary countries on Oct. 31, 2002 (Presidential Proclamation 7616, 67 Fed. Reg. 67283).

[3] 19 U.S.C. 3206.

[4] On May 18–19, 2004, Colombia, Ecuador, and Peru launched FTA negotiations with the United States. See U.S. Trade Representative (USTR), "Peru and Ecuador to Join with Colombia in May 18-19 Launch of FTA Negotiations with the United States," press release, May 3, 2004.

[5] USTR, "United States and Peru Sign Trade Promotion Agreement," Apr. 12, 2006. See also USITC, *U.S.-Peru Trade Promotion Agreement: Potential Economy-wide and Selected Sectoral Effects*, June 2006, Proclamation No. 8341 of Jan. 16, 2009, 74 Fed. Reg. 4105 (Jan. 22, 2009).

[6] USTR, "United States and Colombia Conclude Free Trade Agreement," Feb. 27, 2006. Consistent with statutory requirements, the President notified Congress of his intention to enter into a free trade agreement with Colombia on Aug. 24, 2006. FTA negotiations between the United States and Ecuador were suspended after Ecuador canceled its contract with Occidental Petroleum in May 2006.

[7] The Colombian legislature ratified the FTA in 2007. USTR, *Fifth ATPA Report*, June 30, 2010, 28. The agreement was submitted to Congress by President Bush on Apr. 8, 2008, but it has yet to be considered.

[8] 19 U.S.C. 3204.

[9] Presidential Proclamation 7616 of Oct. 31, 2002, 67 Fed. Reg. 67283 (Nov. 5, 2002). See a later section in this chapter, "Trade Benefits under ATPA," for more specific information on the exception for import-sensitive products.

[10] These factors are set out in 19 U.S.C. 3202(c)–(d).

[11] 19 U.S.C. 3203(b)(6)(B).

[12] Proclamation 7616 of Oct. 31, 2002, 67 Fed. Reg. 67283 (Nov. 5, 2002).

[13] "Memorandum of Sept. 25, 2008, Assignment of Function Under Section 203(e)(2)(A) of the Andean Trade Preference Act, as Amended," 73 Fed. Reg. 56701 (Sept. 29, 2008).

[14] Presidential Determination No. 2008-28 of Sept. 15, 2008, "Major Drug Transit or Major Illicit Drug Producing Countries for Fiscal Year 2009: Memorandum for the Secretary of State," 73 Fed. Reg. 54927 (Sept. 24, 2008).

[15] Proclamation No. 8323 of November 25, 2008, 73 Fed. Reg. 72677 (November 28, 2008). USTR, "U.S. Trade Representative Schwab Announces Proposed Suspension of Bolivia's Tariff Benefits," Sept. 26, 2008; and 73 Fed. Reg. 57158 (Oct. 1, 2008).

[16] Pub. L. 110-436.

[17] Preferential treatment for Ecuador was to continue unless the President found that Ecuador did not satisfy the eligibility requirements, and would end for Bolivia unless the President found that Bolivia did satisfy the eligibility requirements. Pub. L. 110-436, section 1.

[18] "Determinations and Report of the President Concerning the Review of Ecuador and Bolivia Under the Andean Trade Preference Act, As Amended," June 30, 2009.

[19] Pub. L. 110-138.

[20] Proclamation No. 8341 of Jan. 16, 2009, 74 Fed. Reg. 4105 (Jan. 22, 2009).

[21] 74 Fed. Reg. 6441 (Feb. 9, 2009). The retention of ATPA beneficiary status by Peru is different from the usual practice when a beneficiary of a U.S. unilateral preference program has entered into an FTA with the United States. When the U.S.-Dominican Republic-Central America Free Trade Agreement entered into force for each country, each country's Caribbean Basin Economic Recovery Act (CBERA) beneficiary status was ended.

[22] General Note 3(c) to the Harmonized Tariff Schedule (HTS) summarizes the special tariff treatment for eligible products of designated countries under various U.S. trade programs, including ATPA. General Note 11 sets out product eligibility rules and country designations under ATPA and ATPDEA. ATPA does not cover trade in services.

[23] These U.S. measures include TRQs on imports of sugar, dairy products, beef, certain food preparations, and cotton fibers established pursuant to sections 401 and 404 of the Uruguay Round Agreements Act (URAA), with the exception of quotas on sugar, which had already been converted to TRQs in 1990 as a result of a General Agreement on Tariffs and Trade (GATT) ruling. The TRQs replaced absolute quotas on imports of certain agricultural products; U.S. quotas had been imposed under section 22 of the Agricultural Adjustment Act of 1933 (7 U.S.C. 624) and under the Meat Import Act of 1979 (Pub. L. 88- 482). The URAA also amended ATPA by excluding from tariff preferences any imports from beneficiary countries in quantities exceeding the new TRQ global trigger levels. Imports of agricultural products from beneficiary countries remain subject to sanitary and phytosanitary restrictions, such as those administered by the U.S. Animal and Plant Health Inspection Service.

[24] This provision applied to certain articles that were not designated for GSP duty-free entry as of Aug. 5, 1983 (the date of enactment of CBERA. Under the provisions of the original ATPA, beginning in 1992, duties on those goods were reduced by a total of 20 percent, not to exceed 2.5 percent ad valorem, in five equal annual stages (19 U.S.C. 3203(c)(repealed 2002)). ATPDEA eliminated this provision and allowed the President to determine if duty-free entry is appropriate.

[25] The original ATPA excluded watches and watch parts containing components produced in countries subject to column 2 duty rates—effectively, Communist countries. Since 1989, the number of countries subject to column 2 rates of duty has diminished to two—Cuba and North Korea.

[26] 19 U.S.C. 3203(b)(repealed 2002). Tafia is a type of cheap rum.

[27] As mentioned above, ATPDEA repealed 19 U.S.C. 3203(c), which had previously provided duty reductions for certain handbags, luggage, flat goods, work gloves, and leather wearing apparel.

[28] 19 U.S.C. 3203(b)(1).

[29] Presidential Proclamation 7616 of Oct. 31, 2002, 67 Fed. Reg. 67283 (Nov. 5, 2002); USTR, *First Report to the Congress on the Operation of the Andean Trade Preference Act As Amended*, Apr. 30, 2003, 6.

[30] USTR, "New Andean Trade Benefits," Sept. 25, 2002. Accordingly, about 90 percent of rate lines provide duty-free treatment to U.S. imports from the ATPA region (60 percent fall under ATPA and 30 percent have normal trade relations (NTR) rates of free). U.S. imports under the rate lines remaining (about 10 percent) are dutiable.

[31] 19 U.S.C. 3203(b)(2).

[32] Products undergoing the following operations do not qualify: simple combining or packaging operations, dilution with water, or dilution with another substance that does not materially alter the characteristics of the article (19 U.S.C. 3203(a)(2)).

[33] Since Jan. 1, 2009, the CBERA countries are Antigua, Aruba, The Bahamas, Barbados, Belize, British Virgin Islands, Dominica, Grenada, Guatemala, Guyana, Haiti, Jamaica, Montserrat, Netherlands Antilles, Panama, St. Kitts and Nevis, St. Lucia, St. Vincent and the Grenadines, and Trinidad and Tobago.

[34] 19 U.S.C. 3203(a).

[35] Double substantial transformation involves transforming foreign material into a new or different product that, in turn, becomes the constituent material used to produce a second new or different article in the beneficiary country. Thus, ATPA countries can import inputs from non-ATPA countries, transform the inputs into intermediate material, and transform the intermediate material into ATPA-eligible articles. The cost or value of the constituent intermediate material can be counted toward the 35 percent ATPA content requirement. For additional information, see U.S. DOC and U.S. Agency for International Development, *Guidebook to the Andean Trade Preference Act*, 1992, 5.

[36] The dyeing, printing, and finishing requirement does not refer to post-assembly and other operations such as garment dyeing and stone washing.

[37] This provision is one of the most important for apparel in ATPDEA. The cap on U.S. imports of apparel made in the ATPA countries from regionally knit or woven fabrics was set at 2 percent of the aggregate square meter equivalents (SMEs) of total U.S. imports of apparel from the world for the one-year period beginning on Oct. 1, 2002, increasing in each of the four succeeding one-year periods by equal increments up to its current maximum of 5 percent. For the period from Oct. 1, 2008, through Dec. 31, 2009, the fill rate was just 7.96 percent or 97.4 million SME. USDOC, Office of Textiles and Apparel (OTEXA), "Trade Data."

[38] Sec. 3103(d) of ATPDEA (19 U.S.C. 3202 note).

[39] 74 Fed. Reg. 43213–14 (Aug. 26, 2009). USTR has initiated the seventh ATPA review. 75 Fed. Reg. 47633 (Aug. 9, 2010).

[40] USTR, *Fifth ATPA Report*, June 30, 2010, 54.

[41] 19 U.S.C. 3202(f). The due date for the *Fifth Report* was moved to June 30, 2010, by sec. 2(c) of Pub. L. 111-124, Dec. 28, 2009.

[42] USTR, *Fifth ATPA Report*, June 30, 2010.

[43] Ibid.

[44] The U.S. GSP program originally was enacted for 10 years pursuant to title V of the Trade Act of 1974 (Pub. L. 93-618, 88 Stat. 2066 et seq.) and was renewed for an additional 10 years pursuant to title V of the Trade and Tariff Act of 1984 (Pub. L. 98-573, 98 Stat. 3018 et seq.), as amended (19 U.S.C. 2461 et seq.). Since that time, the GSP program has expired and been renewed several times. GSP preferences are currently effective through Dec. 31, 2010. Pub. L. 111-124.

[45] That is, those that are not excluded or do not receive unconditional column 1-general duty-free treatment or duty-free treatment under other preference programs such as GSP.

[46] A copy of the notice appears in app. A.

[47] This is nondiscriminatory tariff treatment, which is commonly and historically called "most-favorednation" (MFN) status but is officially called "normal trade relations" (NTR) status in the United States.

[48] A more detailed explanation of the approach can be found in app. C of this report.

[49] Consumer surplus is defined as the difference between the total value consumers receive from the consumption of a particular good and the total amount they pay for the good. The change in consumer surplus is a dollar measure of the total net gain to U.S. consumers from lower prices. Producer surplus is defined as the return to entrepreneurs and owners of capital that exceeds earnings for their next-best opportunities. The change in producer surplus is a dollar measure of the total net loss to competing U.S. producers from increased competition with imports. The welfare effects do not include adjustment costs to the economy from reallocating resources among different industries. These topics are discussed in more detail in app. C of this report.

[50] Commission industry analysts provided evaluations of the substitutability of ATPA products and competing U.S. products, which were translated into a range of substitution elasticities. A more detailed discussion of the elasticities used in the model is provided in app. C of this report.

[51] See table 3.2 in chap. 3 of this report. Commission industry analysts provided estimates of U.S. production and exports for the 20 leading items that benefited exclusively from ATPA, as well as evaluations of the substitutability of ATPA-exclusive imports and competing U.S. products. Items were ranked at the 8- digit level of HTS tariff classification.

[52] As discussed elsewhere in this report, ATPA imports include some articles that are also eligible for GSP duty-free entry. Imports that benefit exclusively from ATPA are discussed in chap. 3 of this report.

[53] A copy of the notice appears in app. A of this report.

U.S. Trade with the ATPA Countries

[1] All trade discussed in the report is merchandise trade.

[2] In this chapter, data on Bolivia's trade with the United States are included only for the years that Bolivia was eligible for ATPA—that is, 1991 through 2008. Bolivia is still eligible for GSP.

[3] Excludes imports from Bolivia in 2009, when it was not a beneficiary.

[4] Global Trade Atlas database.

[5] For country-specific duty treatment, see table D.1.

[6] Less than one percent of imports from ATPA countries entered the U.S. Virgin Islands. The U.S. Virgin Islands has its own tariff schedule and laws separate from the rest of the United States and is outside the U.S. customs territory; therefore, imports that enter the U.S. Virgin Islands are not identified as either dutiable or free of duty.

[7] According to public testimony by industry participants, uncertainty concerning renewal of ATPA, along with the short renewal periods, may have discouraged cut flower import growth (see chapter 3 section on cut flowers).

[8] See chap. 3 for additional analysis of the cut flower industry.

[9] This includes anthuriums, alstroemeria, gypsophilia, lilies, snapdragons, and other flowers.

[10] U.S. Department of Labor, Wage and Hour Division, "The tuna processing industry" (accessed May 13, 2010).

[11] See chap. 3 for additional analysis of the cut flower industry.

[12] This includes anthuriums, alstroemeria, gypsophilia, lilies, snapdragons and other flowers.

[13] See chap. 3 for additional analysis of the effects of ATPA legislation and uncertainties about pending FTAs on U.S. imports from the ATPA countries.

[14] Excludes imports from Bolivia in 2009, when it was not a beneficiary.

[15] In the United States, export data are reported under either the HTS or Schedule B, a separate U.S. export schedule based on the HS nomenclature, except for goods listed in the HTS Notice to Exporters (Schedule B only). For purposes of this report, and for ease of comparison with the analysis on imports, Schedule B numbers are referred to here as HS numbers. All Schedule B provisions either mirror the HS or aggregate to HS provisions at the 6-digit level. For goods noted in the HS Notice to Exporters, which enumerates unique Schedule B categories that must be used for reporting covered exports, the reporting categories provide different data (compared to the HTS) for goods of particular export interest.

Economic Impact of ATPA on the United States and Probable Future Effects

[1] As discussed in chap. 1 of this report, "ATPA" refers to ATPA as amended by subsequent legislation, and "original ATPA" is used to identify the original ATPA program that expired in Dec. 2001.

[2] For most intents and purposes, ATPA countries were not subject to apparel quotas. For a more detailed analysis of the erosion of the margin of preference, see USITC, *ATPA, Fifth Report, 1997*, 1998, 132.

[3] As mentioned in chap. 1, reduced-duty preferences under the original ATPA were terminated by ATPDEA, and those products previously eligible for reduced duties are now eligible for duty-free treatment.

[4] Because ATPDEA amended ATPA, imports under ATPA and imports benefiting exclusively from ATPA include imports made eligible for preferential treatment by ATPDEA.

[5] Thus, eligible products that are excluded from duty-free entry under GSP because their competitive need limits have been exceeded can still receive duty-free entry under ATPA. For additional information, see "ATPA and GSP" in chap. 1 of this report.

[6] The exclusively benefiting shares were markedly higher in 1995 and 1996, mainly because of the lapse in the GSP program from Aug. 1, 1995, through Sept. 30, 1996, and subsequent increased use of ATPA provisions to ensure duty-free entry. See USITC, *ATPA, Fourth Report, 1996*, 1997, 71–72, for further explanation of the assumptions and analysis used to address the lapse in GSP. Because of the assumptions about GSP made in the 1995 and 1996 ATPA reports, the findings derived from the analysis in those reports are not strictly comparable to the findings in subsequent reports in this series or in reports previous to the 1995 report, despite the similar analytical approach used.

[7] The share of imports benefiting exclusively from ATPA accounted for by copper cathodes dropped to 23 percent in 2002, and fell as low as 5 percent in 2005 before recovering to 8 percent in 2006 and 9 percent in 2007 and 2008. The share dropped to 0.5 percent in 2009, as they became eligible for entry under the FTA starting in Feb. 2009. The total quantity entered under both ATPA and the FTA actually increased.

[8] Cotton T-shirts (HTS 6109.10.00), down 85 percent; knitted cotton tops (HTS 6110.20.20), down 92 percent; and men's or boys' knitted cotton shirts (HTS 6105.10.00), down 91 percent.

[9] USITC industry analysts provided estimates of U.S. production and exports for the 20 leading items that benefited exclusively from ATPA, as well as evaluations of the substitutability of ATPA-exclusive imports and competing U.S. products.

[10] To estimate the impact of ATPA on U.S. textile producers, it would be necessary to separate imports of apparel made with U.S. fabric from imports made from regional fabric. Data available to the Commission do not allow this distinction to be made.

[11] Based on Standard International Trade Classification code 65.

[12] In the analysis, U.S. market expenditure shares were used to compute estimates of welfare and domestic production displacement effects. Because U.S. expenditures on imports necessarily include freight and insurance charges and duties, when applicable, the analysis used c.i.f. values for duty-free products benefiting exclusively from ATPA, and landed, duty-paid values for the remaining imports. Landed, duty-paid values are equal to c.i.f. values for products entering free of duty.

[13] The import values reported in tables 3.2 and 3.3 reflect only that portion of imports under each HTS number that entered free of duty under ATPA. Even though all of these items were eligible for ATPA tariff preferences, full duties were paid on a certain portion of imports under each HTS provision for a variety of reasons, such as failure to claim preferences, insufficient documentation, and indirect shipment patterns.

[14] For the list of items benefiting exclusively from ATPA in 2008, see table D.4.

[15] Other factors include the ad valorem equivalent tariff rate; the substitutability among beneficiary imports, nonbeneficiary imports, and domestic production; and the overall demand elasticity for the product category.

[16] The methodology used is described in app. C.

[17] All of the tuna benefiting exclusively from ATPA under HTS 1604.14.30 was entered in flexible foil containers under HTS 1604.14.3051 and HTS 1604.14.3091. For more information, see chap. 2.

[18] As noted in chap. 1 and app. C, the Commission's analysis assumes that the domestic supply is perfectly elastic. This assumption means that any change in the demand for domestic production (such as that resulting from a drop in the price of imports from ATPA country suppliers) results in quantity changes and not price changes.

[19] U.S. market share, ad valorem equivalent tariff rate, and elasticity of substitution between beneficiary imports and competing U.S. production share are the main factors that affect the estimated displacement of U.S. domestic shipments. In general, the larger the ATPA share of the U.S. market, ad valorem equivalent tariff rate, and substitution elasticity, the larger the displacement of domestic shipments.

[20] See USITC, *ATPA, Thirteenth Report, 2007*, 2008, 3-11.

[21] These rankings do not account for intra-European Union trade. Global Trade Atlas database, Global Trade Information Services.

[22] Global Trade Atlas database, Global Trade Information Services.

[23] Christine Boldt, Executive Vice President, Association of Floral Importers of Florida, USITC hearing transcript, July 7, 2010, 13.

[24] USDA, NASS, *Floriculture Crops, 2009 Summary*, Apr. 2010.

[25] USDA, NASS, *Floriculture Crops, 2009 Summary*, Apr. 2010. The number of growers includes only those with more than $100,000 in annual sales.

[26] U.S. Department of Agriculture, Agriculture Marketing Service, *Ornamental Crops Report,* Jan. 2010.

[27] USDA, NASS, *Floriculture Crops, 2009 Summary*, Apr. 2010.

[28] Christine Boldt, Executive Vice President, Association of Floral Importers of Florida, USITC hearing transcript, July 7, 2010, 11.

[29] South Florida Industry Statistics, Association of Floral Imports of Florida, http://www.afifnet.org/sflstats.htm.

[30] Association of Colombian Flower Exporters. Statement to the United States Committee on Ways and Means, Subcommittee on Trade, Nov. 17, 2009, 2; Christine Boldt, Executive Vice President, Association of Floral Importers of Florida, USITC hearing transcript, July 7, 2010, 12.

[31] Solano, written submission to the USITC, July 8, 2010, 2.

[32] During 1981–91, before ATPA was implemented, U.S. imports of cut flowers accounted for 34-45 percent of U.S. cut flower sales annually. USDA, NASS, *Floriculture Crops, 2006 Summary*, Apr. 2007; USDA, ERS, *Floriculture and Nursery Crops*, May 2002.

[33] ATPA beneficiary cut flower producers/exporters have the natural advantages of ideal year-round sunlight and climate, as well as low costs of labor and land. Kasey Cronquist, California Cut Flower Commission, USITC hearing transcript, July 7, 2010, 22.

[34] Imports of fresh cut chrysanthemums were eligible for duty-free treatment under the GSP (excluding those from Colombia, which exceeded the competitive-need limit), ATPA, CBERA, CAFTA-DR, NAFTA, and FTAs with Australia, Bahrain, Chile, Israel, Jordan, Morocco, and Singapore.

[35] USDA, NASS, *Floriculture Crops, 2009 Summary*, Apr. 2010.

[36] It is assumed that increased investment expands the capital stock and therefore the production base used to produce goods for export, extending the probable future effects of ATPA beyond the direct effects of tariff reductions. The practice of using investment to assess probable future economic effects on the United States was developed as part of the Commission's reporting requirement on the Caribbean Basin Economic Recovery Act, where similar analysis is provided for Caribbean countries. For a more detailed discussion of the methodology, see USITC, *Impact of the Caribbean Basin Economic Recovery Act, First Report, 1984–85*, 1986, 4-1.

[37] Bolivia was not eligible for ATPA trade preferences during 2009. For more information, see chap. 1.

[38] For example, see USITC, hearing transcript, July 7, 2010, 8, 12, 43–44, 46, 71.

[39] Ecuadorian-American Chamber of Commerce, written submission to the USITC, July 14, 2010, 11.

[40] For more complete information about qualifying rules of origin under ATPA, see chap. 1.

[41] For example, see Colombian Government Trade Bureau, written submission to the USITC, June 30, 2010; American Apparel and Footwear Association, written submission to the USITC, July 14, 2010; Ecuadorian-American Chamber of Commerce, written submission to the USITC, July 14, 2010, 3; and USITC, hearing transcript, July 7, 2010, 80–83.

[42] ECLAC, *Foreign Direct Investment in Latin America and the Caribbean*, May 2010, 29–33.

[43] U.S. Department of State, U.S. Embassy, La Paz, "2010 USITC Andean Investment and Drug Crop Survey Report on ATPA," July 6, 2010.

[44] Andean Community, written submission to the USITC, July 12, 2010, 8–9.

[45] U.S. Department of State, U.S. Embassy, La Paz, "The United States Remains Bolivia's 4th Largest Trading Partner," Feb. 23, 2010.

[46] Bolivian-American Chamber of Commerce, Inc., "Invest in Bolivia," n.d. (accessed July 26, 2010).

[47] Bolivia Investment Gateway, "Bolivia–FAQ Textile Environmental," n.d. (accessed July 26, 2010), and Bolivian-American Chamber of Commerce, Inc., "Invest in Bolivia," n.d. (accessed July 26, 2010).

[48] Iberkleid, statement to the House Committee on Foreign Affairs, Subcommittee on the Western Hemisphere, Mar. 3, 2009. Iberkleid also stated that the short-term extensions of the ATPA have had a negative impact on the textile and apparel sector by creating an uncertain business climate.

[49] The NTR duty rate of men's and boys' cotton knit shirts is 19.7 percent ad valorem.

[50] Lori J. Michaelson, (commercial officer, U.S. Embassy, La Paz), e-mail message to USITC, July 6, 2010.

[51] Iberkleid, statement to the House Committee on Foreign Affairs, Subcommittee on the Western Hemisphere, Mar. 3, 2009.

[52] Iberkleid, statement to the House Committee on Foreign Affairs, Subcommittee on the Western Hemisphere, Mar. 3, 2009.

[53] Lori J. Michaelson (commercial officer, U.S. Embassy, La Paz), e-mail message to USITC, July 6, 2010; Iberkleid, statement the House Committee on Foreign Affairs, Subcommittee on the Western Hemisphere, Mar. 3, 2009; and U.S. Department of State, Embassy, La Paz, "Bolivia Continues to Trade Mainly Primary Products," Feb. 11, 2010.

[54] Economist Intelligence Unit (EIU), "Colombia Economy: Trade Surplus Soars on Oil Exports," June 21, 2010.
[55] U.S. Department of State, U.S. Embassy, Bogota, "Input for USITC Andean Investment and Drug Crop Survey for Report on ATPA," July 2010.
[56] U.S. Department of State, U.S. Embassy, Bogota, "Colombian Flower Industry Surviving Adversity," Mar. 25, 2010.
[57] Colombian Government Trade Bureau, written submission to the USITC, June 30, 2010.
[58] U.S. Department of State, U.S. Embassy, Bogota, "Input for USITC Andean Investment and Drug Crop Survey for Report on ATPA," July 2010.
[59] Association of Colombian Flower Exporters, written submission to the USITC, July 8, 2010. Also see Christine Boldt, Executive Vice President, Association of Floral Importers of Florida, USITC hearing transcript, July 7, 2010, 12.
[60] Export data are from statistics reported in the Global Trade Atlas database.
[61] Based on U.S. Department of Commerce Major Shippers Report data.
[62] Inexmoda, "Colombiatex de las Américas 2009," n.d. (accessed Feb. 2, 2009); Just-style, "Colombia's Clothing and Textile Industry Has Growth Potential," June 24, 2010.
[63] Just-style, "Colombia's Clothing and Textile Industry Has Growth Potential," June 24, 2010.
[64] U.S. Department of State, U.S. Embassy, Bogota, "Colombian Textile Industry: Dying or Just Downsizing?" Jan. 28, 2010.
[65] Stephen Lamar (senior vice president, American Apparel and Footwear Association), e-mail message to USITC, June 30, 2010. One U.S. apparel company representative also stated that business was down in Colombia for their firm in 2009 because of the ongoing uncertainty caused by the short-term extensions of the ATPA. Apparel industry representative, telephone interview with USITC staff, July 2, 2010.
[66] U.S. Department of State, U.S. Embassy, Bogota, "Colombian Textile Industry: Dying or Just Downsizing?" Jan. 28, 2010; and Business Monitor Online, "Industry Trends and Developments: Colombia," Oct. 14, 2009; Exchange rate information is from International Monetary Fund, *International Financial Statistics*: *Colombia,* Jan. 2010, 358–359.
[67] Business Monitor Online, "BMI Industry View: Colombia," Oct. 14, 2009; Stephen Lamar (senior vice president, American Apparel and Footwear Association), e-mail message to USITC, June 30, 2010.
[68] Just-style, "Insight: Colombia's Denim Cluster on Road to Recovery," Feb. 22, 2010.
[69] Just-style, "Colombia's Clothing and Textile Industry Has Growth Potential," June 24, 2010; Inexmoda, "Textile Apparel Design and Fashion Sector in Colombia," undated, http://www.inexmoda.org.
[70] Global Trade Atlas database.
[71] Just-style, "Insight: Colombia's Denim Cluster on Road to Recovery," Feb. 22, 2010.
[72] Just-style, "Insight: Colombia's Denim Cluster on Road to Recovery," Feb. 22, 2010.
[73] Colombian Government Trade Bureau, written statement to the USITC, June 30, 2010.
[74] ECLAC, *Foreign Direct Investment in Latin America and the Caribbean*, May 2010, 32–33, 68.
[75] U.S. Department of State, "2010 Investment Climate Statement—Ecuador," Mar. 2010, 1, 3; EIU, ViewsWire, "Ecuador: Business Environment Ranking Summary," July 1, 2010.
[76] U.S. Department of State, U.S. Embassy, Ecuador, "Input for the USITC Report to Congress," e-mail message to USITC staff, June 18, 2010; "Additional Input for the USITC Report to Congress," e-mail message to USITC staff, July 8, 2010.
[77] U.S. Department of State, U.S. Embassy, Ecuador, "Additional Input for the USITC Report to Congress," e-mail message to USITC staff, July 8, 2010.
[78] Embassy of Ecuador, Washington, DC, written submission to the USITC, June 30, 2010, 5.
[79] Organic sugar is considered a specialty sugar that enters the United States under the smaller TRQ for refined sugar. As discussed above in chap. 1, ATPA affords duty-free entry for sugar imported from beneficiary countries that enters within the TRQ, but no preference is provided for sugar that would enter over quota.
[80] Embassy of Ecuador, Washington, DC, post-hearing comments, July 14, 2010.
[81] Embassy of Ecuador, Washington, DC, written submission to the USITC, June 30, 2010.
[82] Textiles La Escala, written submission to the USITC, June 3, 2010.
[83] Information provided by the economic section of the U.S. Embassy, Quito, in an e-mail message to Commission staff, June 24, 2010.
[84] Textiles La Escala, written submission to the USITC, June 3, 2010; Ecuadorexports.com, n.d., http://www.ecuadorexports.com/textiles (accessed June 10, 2010).
[85] Textiles La Escala, written submission to the USITC, July 7, 2010.
[86] Textiles La Escala, written submission to the USITC, July 7, 2010.

[87] Global Trade Atlas database. Industry sources in Ecuador report that 93 percent of the cotton consumed in Ecuador comes from the United States, especially the southern states, Texas, and California. U.S. cotton is valued for its consistent, high grade quality. Textiles La Escala, written submission to the USITC, July 7, 2010, and USITC hearing transcript, July 7, 2010, 28–29.

[88] USITC hearing transcript, July 7, 2010, 84–88, Jeff Sheedy (CEO, Textiles La Escala).

[89] Textiles La Escala, written submission to the USITC, July 7, 2010, and USITC hearing transcript, July 7, 2010, 29; and Jeff Sheedy (CEO, Textiles La Escala), e-mail message to Commission staff, July 13, 2010.

[90] USITC hearing transcript, July 7, 2010, 61. Jeff Sheedy (CEO, Textiles La Escala), e-mail message to USITC, July 13, 2010.

[91] U.S. Department of State, U.S. Embassy, Peru, "Peru Response to Request for Information on Andean Investment and Drug Crop Survey," July 15, 2010.

[92] U.S. Department of State, U.S. Embassy, Peru, "Peru Response to Request for Information on Andean Investment and Drug Crop Survey," July 15, 2010.

[93] Business Monitor Online, "Industry Forecast: Peru; Q4 2009; Textiles and Clothing," Oct. 14, 2009; Cotton Council International, "Peruvian Spinning Company Adjusts Sourcing to Include More U.S. Cotton," 2008; Andina, "Hand-harvested Pima Cotton from Peru Reduces Waste," Sept. 18, 2008; Perumoda.com, "Clothes Industry: Cotton," n.d.; and Andina, "France, England & Germany Become Biggest Consumers of Peruvian Fashion," Apr. 14, 2009.

[94] Just-style, "June 2010 Management Briefing: Latin American Textile Sector Weathers Economic Storm," June 16, 2010.

[95] Business Monitor International, "Industry Forecast: Peru; Q4 2009; Textiles and Clothing," Oct. 14, 2009. http://www.businessmonitor.com.

[96] Just-style, "June 2010 Management Briefing: Latin American Textile Sector Weathers Economic Storm," June 16, 2010. Tommy Hilfiger recently expressed interest in using organic Peruvian cotton to manufacture its clothes. Andina, "Tommy Hilfiger Eyes Peruvian Organic Cotton," May 2, 2010.

[97] Just-style, "Analysis: Peruvian Textiles See Recovery After 2009 Collapse," June 25, 2010.

[98] Just-style, "Analysis: Peruvian Textiles See Recovery After 2009 Collapse," June 25, 2010; Andina, "Peru's Textile and Apparel Exports to Jump 15% This Year Total U.S. $1.7 Billion," Apr. 29, 2010; and U.S. Department of State, U.S. Embassy, Lima, "Peru Response to Request for Information on Andean Investment and Drug Crop Survey," July 15, 2010.

[99] U.S. Department of State, U.S. Embassy, Lima, "Peru Response to Request for Information on Andean Investment and Drug Crop Survey," July 15, 2010.

[100] Although U.S. sector imports declined substantially in 2009, apparel was still the leading Peruvian export under ATPA that year, accounting for 30 percent of total ATPA entries. U.S. Department of State, U.S. Embassy, Lima, "Peru Response to Request for Information on Andean Investment and Drug Crop Survey," July 15, 2010.

[101] USITC hearing transcript, July 7, 2010, 8–9, 51, 81; American Apparel and Footwear Association, written submission to the USITC, July 14, 2010. The current rules of origin under the TPA do not allow cumulation—that is, the duty-free entry of textile or apparel imports from Peru made using inputs from any of the ATPA beneficiary countries. To enter free of duty, U.S. sector imports from Peru under the TPA must be made solely from Peruvian and U.S. inputs.

[102] Peru's import data are from the Global Trade Atlas database.

Impact of ATPA on Drug-Related Crop Eradication and Crop Substitution in 2008 and 2009

[1] The United States suspended Bolivia's designation as a beneficiary country under ATPA and ATPDEA, effective Dec. 15, 2008, citing its failure to cooperate with U.S. counternarcotics efforts in the region, as required for eligibility under these programs. Proclamation No. 8323, 73 Fed. Reg. 72677 (Nov. 28, 2008). Bolivia nonetheless continues to participate in U.S. and UN efforts to measure illegal coca cultivation in the Andes.

[2] USDOS, Bureau for International Narcotics and Law Enforcement Affairs (INL), *International Narcotics Control Strategy Report (INCSR) 2009*, Mar. 2009, 19.

[3] USDOS, INL, *INCSR 2009*, Mar. 2009, 19; USDOS, INL, *INCSR 2008*, Mar. 2008, 18. Ecuador has no significant coca cultivation, having eliminated its minor cultivation of coca by 1992. USTR, *Fifth ATPA Report*, June 30, 2010, 40; *INCSR 1999*, Mar. 1, 2000, "V. Statistical Tables, 1991–99." Nonetheless, Ecuador is a major transit country for illegal drugs as well as precursor chemicals involved in the manufacture of narcotics. USDOS,

INL, *INCSR 2010*, Mar. 2010, 261. Both Bolivia and Peru permit some legal coca cultivation for traditional and commercial use, but illegal coca cultivation far exceeds the legal limits in these countries. *INCSR 2010*, Mar. 2010, 155.

[4] USDOS, INL, *INCSR 2009*, Mar. 2009, 18; USDOS, INL, *INCSR 2008*, Mar. 2008, 18.

[5] USDOS, INL, *INCSR 2009*, Mar. 2009, 19.

[6] USDOS, "FY 2009 Foreign Operations Performance Report and FY 2011 Performance Plan," 271– 347, released Mar. 10, 2010, 284–85; USDOS, INL, *INCSR 2008*, Mar. 2008, 18; Wyler, "International Drug Control Policy," Aug. 24, 2009, 13–14.

[7] USDOS, INL, *INCSR 2010*, Mar. 2010, 207; USDOS, INL, *INCSR 2009*, Mar. 2009, 19, 433; USDOS, INL, *INCSR 2008*, Mar. 2008, 109, 127.

[8] USDOS, INL, *INCSR 2010*, Mar. 2010, 14, 214–15.

[9] USDOS, INL, *INCSR 2009*, Mar. 2009, 19.

[10] USTR, *Fifth ATPA Report*, June 30, 2010, 21; USDOS, U.S. Embassy, La Paz, "2010 USITC Andean Investment and Drug Crop Survey Report on ATPA," July 6, 2010, par. 7; USDOS, USAID, Bolivia, "Integrated Development Program," June 2010, 2; USDOS, USAID, Peru, "Alternative Development," Nov. 2009, 2; USDOS, USAID, Bureau for Latin America and the Caribbean, "Ecuador," June 15, 2010, 2.

[11] USDOS, INL, *INCSR 2010*, Mar. 2010, and previous reports.

[12] United Nations Office on Drugs and Crime (UNODC), *Colombia: Coca Cultivation Survey 2009*, "Table 4," June 2010; UNODC, *Ecuador: Monitoreo de Cultivos de Coca 2009*, "Tabla 1," June 2010; UNODC, *Estado Plurinacional de Bolivia: Monitoreo de Cultivos de Coca 2009*, "Tabla 1," June 2010; UNODC, *Perú: Monitoreo de Cultivos de Coca 2009*, "Figura 1," June 2010; and previous reports.

[13] USDOS, INL, *INCSR 2010*, Mar. 2010, 261; USDOS, INL, *INCSR 2006*, Mar. 2006, 24.

[14] USDOS, INL, *INCSR 2010*, Mar. 2010, 217.

[15] UNODC, *Colombia: Coca Cultivation Survey 2009*, "Table 4," June 2010; UNODC, *Ecuador: Monitoreo de Cultivos de Coca 2009*, "Tabla 1," June 2010, 7.

[16] USDOS, INL, *INCSR 2010*, Mar. 2010, 214; USDOS, INL, *INCSR 2009*, Mar. 2009, 204; USDOS, INL, *INCSR 2008*, Mar. 2008, 124. Plan Colombia was launched in Sept. 1999 by the Colombian government as a six-year strategy to address the country's long-running conflict with several armed insurgent groups, eliminate drug trafficking, and promote economic and social development. To support Plan Colombia's goals, the U.S. Congress approved in 2000 a $1.3 billion foreign assistance package, focused on the eradication of coca and opium poppy crops; alternative economic development programs to provide other income sources for coca and poppy farmers; narcotics interdiction; and the training and equipment of Colombian security forces to help in interdiction efforts as well as to extend democratic governance more broadly in the country. Wyler, "International Drug Control Policy," Aug. 24, 2009, 22–23; USDOS, INL, *INCSR 2000*, Mar. 2001, 36–37; USDOS, Western Hemisphere Affairs (WHA), "Background Note: Colombia; Defense; Narcotics," June 2, 2010.

[17] USDOS, INL, *INCSR 2010*, Mar. 2010, 211, 214; USDOS, INL, *INCSR 2009*, Mar. 2009, 25, 204. Since 2004, when manual eradication was first used to supplement aerial spraying, manual eradication has increased from less than 10 percent to over 35 percent of total coca eradication in Colombia. USDOS, INL, *INCSR 2010*, Mar. 2010, 211–12, and previous issues; USDOS, WHA, "Background Note: Colombia; Defense; Narcotics," June 2, 2010.

[18] USDOS, INL, *INCSR 2010*, Mar. 2010, 212.

[19] USDOS, INL, *INCSR 2009*, Mar. 2009, 206.

[20] USDOS, INL, *INCSR 2010*, Mar. 2010, 215.

[21] USTR, *Fifth ATPA Report*, June 30, 2010, 29.

[22] Ibid., 23. See discussion in chap. 1 concerning TRQs for agricultural producst such as sugar. APTA provides duty-free entry of in-quota imports from beneficiary countries, but does not reduce over-quota duties.

[23] USDOS, U.S. Embassy, Bogota, "News: Bilateral Topics; U.S. Assistance to Colombia," n.d. (accessed July 26, 2010). See also, República de Colombia, "Normas: Directivas; 2009; Directiva Presidencial No. 01," Mar. 1, 2010.

[24] USDOS, INL, *INCSR 2010*, Mar. 2010, 206. The plan includes regional government councils to strengthen governance, return and restore rights to people displaced by internal violence, a strategy of voluntary substitution of legal for illegal crop cultivation, social development and administration, rural electrification, and improvement of road and communications infrastructure. See República de Colombia, "Sala de Prensa: Noticias; Territorios libres de ilícitos," Mar. 13, 2010.

[25] ibid, 215.

[26] ibid, 261, 264.
[27] USDOS, WHA, "Background Note: Ecuador; U.S.-Ecuadorian Relations," May 24, 2010.
[28] USDOS, INL, *Fiscal Year 2010: Program and Budget Guide*, n.d. (accessed June 9, 2010), 282.
[29] USDOS, INL, *INCSR 2010*, Mar. 2010, 264–65; USDOS, USAID, "Ecuador: Country Profile," June 15, 2010.
[30] USDOS, INL, *INCSR 2010*, Mar. 2010, 264–65.
[31] USDOS, USAID, Ecuador, "Results Report 2008," June 2009, 1.
[32] Ibid.
[33] Ibid.
[34] Ibid.
[35] Ibid.
[36] USDOS, U.S. Embassy, Quito, "FY 2009 Performance Plan and Report (excerpt)," June 18, 2010.
[37] USDOS, USAID, Ecuador, "Results Report 2008," June 2009, 2–3.
[38] USDOS, U.S. Embassy, Quito, "FY 2009 Performance Plan and Report (excerpt)," June 18, 2010.
[39] USDOS, U.S. Embassy, Quito, "Preliminary Input for the USITC Survey," June 18, 2010.
[40] Ibid.
[41] Embassy of Ecuador in the United States, written submission to the USITC, June 30, 2010, 5–7.
[42] USDOS, INL, *INCSR 2010*, Mar. 2010, 512, "V. Statistical Tables."
[43] UNODC, *Perú: Monitoreo de Cultivos de Coca 2009*, "Figura 1," June 2010, 11.
[44] USTR, *Fifth ATPA Report*, June 30, 2010, 49.
[45] USDOS, U.S. Embassy, Lima, "Peru Response to Request for Information on Survey," July 15, 2010, par. 1.
[46] DEVIDA (La Comisión Nacional para el Desarrollo y Vida sin Drogas) is the Peruvian government agency created in June 2003 to conduct Peru's National Strategy against Drugs.
[47] USDOS, U.S. Embassy, Lima, "Peru Response to Request for Information on Survey," July 15, 2010, par. 21–22.
[48] USDOS, U.S. Embassy, Lima, "Peru Response to Request for Information on Survey," July 15, 2010, par. 22–23; USDOS, INL, *INCSR 2010*, Mar. 2010, 505.
[49] USDOS, U.S. Embassy, Lima, "Peru Response to Request for Information on Survey," July 15, 2010, par. 21; USDOS, USAID, Latin America and Caribbean Bureau, "Peru," May 27, 2010.
[50] USDOS, INL, *Fiscal Year 2010: Program and Budget Guide*, n.d. (accessed June 9, 2010), 328–29. By 2006, voluntary eradication evolved to forced eradication in remaining areas highly dependent on coca cultivation. USAID and DEVIDA also played a post-eradication role in these situations, in preventing recultivation of illegal coca due to a community's lost income source. USDOS, "Peru Response to Request for Information on Survey," July 10, 2010, par. 22. A Dec. 2009 university study highlighted some Peruvian provinces as more successful in converting over to legal alternative development crops—for example, the Department of San Martín—and others as less successful—for example, the Departments of Ayacucho, Cusco, and Huánuco. See Namihas, "Se puede derrotar al narcotráfico," Dec. 2009.
[51] USDOS, U.S. Embassy, Lima, "Peru Response to Request for Information on Survey," July 15, 2010, par. 22.
[52] USDOS, INL, *INCSR 2009*, Mar. 2009, 19, 476.
[53] USDOS, U.S. Embassy, Lima, "Peru Response to Request for Information on Survey," July 15, 2010, par. 24.
[54] USDOS, U.S. Embassy, Lima, USAID, Peru, "Alternative Development," Nov. 2009.
[55] Ibid.
[56] Ibid.
[57] OAS, Inter-American Drug Abuse Control Commission, "Alternative Development: Projects: Tropical Crops Research; Biological Control of Cacao Diseases in Peru," n.d. (accessed June 21, 2010).
[58] USTR, *Fifth ATPA Report*, June 30, 2010, 43.

Positions of Interested Parties

[1] In many instances, the chapter reflects only the principal points made by the particular party. The views expressed in the summarized materials should be considered to be those of the submitting parties and not the Commission. In preparing this summary, Commission staff did not undertake to confirm the accuracy of, or otherwise correct, the information summarized. For the full text of hearing testimony and written submissions, see entries associated with investigation 332-352 (2009) at the Commission's Electronic Docket Information System, http://searchapp.usitc.gov/edis3.app.
[2] For a list of hearing participants, see app. B.
[3] For example, see Luis M. Valdivieso, ambassador to the United States from Peru, written submission, July 20, 2010.
[4] For example, see USITC, hearing transcript, July 8, 2010, 30 (testimony of Textiles La Escala).

[5] Adalid Contreras Baspineiro, general secretary, General Secretariat of the Andean Community, written submission, July 13, 2010; USITC, hearing transcript, July 8, 2010, 29 (testimony of Textiles La Escala).

[6] For example, see American Apparel & Footwear Association, written submission, July 14, 2010.

[7] For example, see USITC, hearing transcript, July 8, 2010, 11 (testimony of the Association of Floral Importers of Florida).

[8] USITC, hearing transcript, July 8, 2010, 13 (testimony of the Association of Floral Importers of Florida).

[9] Mateo Lettunich, chairman, Superior Foods International LLC, written submission July 9, 2010.

[10] USITC, hearing transcript, July 8, 2010, 23 (testimony of the California Cut Flower Commission), and written submission, July 14, 2010.

[11] Christopher D. Lischewski, president and chief executive officer, Bumble Bee Foods, Inc., written submission, June 25, 2010. In hearing testimony, other participants noted that the American tuna industry is nearly 100 percent canned tuna, whereas the only product that comes in under ATPDEA is pouched tuna. USITC, hearing transcript, July 8, 2010, 90 (testimony of Textiles La Escala).

[12] Bernardo Traversari, executive director, Ecuadorian-American Chamber of Commerce, written submission, July 14, 2010.

[13] Luis M. Valdivieso, ambassador to the United States from Peru, written submission, July 20, 2010.

[14] Augusto Solano, executive president, Association of Colombian Flower Exporters, written submission, July 8, 2010.

[15] For more information on the Commission's analysis regarding ATPA's effect on drug crop eradication and crop substitution, see chap. 4 of this report.

[16] Luis M. Valdivieso, ambassador to the United States from Peru, written submission, July 20, 2010.

[17] Luis M. Valdivieso, ambassador to the United States from Peru, written submission, July 20, 2010.

[18] Claudia Candela, director, Colombian Government Trade Bureau, written submission, July 1, 2010.

[19] Adalid Contreras Baspineiro, general secretary, General Secretariat of the Andean Community, written submission, July 13, 2010.

[20] Claudia Candela, director, Colombian Government Trade Bureau, written submission, July 1, 2010.

[21] Claudia Candela, director, Colombian Government Trade Bureau, written submission, July 1, 2010.

[22] USITC, hearing transcript, July 8, 2010, 6–10 (testimony of the Colombian Government Trade Bureau).

[23] USITC, hearing transcript, July 8, 2010, 8 (testimony of the Colombian Government Trade Bureau).

[24] Luis Gallegos, ambassador to the United States from Ecuador, written submission, June 30, 2010.

[25] Luis M. Valdivieso, ambassador to the United States from Peru, written submission, July 20, 2010.

[26] Adalid Contreras Baspineiro, general secretary, General Secretariat of the Andean Community, written submission, July 13, 2010. The Andean Community is an organization that promotes surbregional integration whose member states are Bolivia, Colombia, Ecuador, and Peru.

[27] Kevin M. Burke, president and CEO, American Apparel and Footwear Association, written submission, July 14, 2010.

[28] Augusto Solano, executive president, Association of Colombian Flower Exporters, written submission, July 8, 2010.

[29] USITC, hearing transcript, July 8, 2010, 10–14 (testimony of the Association of Floral Importers of Florida).

[30] USITC, hearing transcript, July 8, 2010, 14–17 (testimony of the Association of Floral Importers of Florida).

[31] Christopher D. Lischewski, president and chief executive officer, Bumble Bee Foods, Inc., written submission, June 25, 2010.

[32] USITC, hearing transcript, July 8, 2010, 17–26 (testimony of the California Cut Flower Commission), and written submission, July 14, 2010.

[33] USITC, hearing transcript, July 8, 2010, 23 (testimony of the California Cut Flower Commission).

[34] Bernardo Traversari, executive director, Ecuadorian-American Chamber of Commerce, written submission, July 14, 2010.

[35] Mateo Lettunich, chairman, Superior Foods International LLC, written submission, July 9, 2010.

[36] USITC, hearing transcript, July 8, 2010, 27–34 (testimony of Textiles La Escala), written submission July 14, 2010.

[37] USITC, hearing transcript, July 8, 2010, 35–41 (testimony of the U.S. Chamber of Commerce).

[38] USITC, hearing transcript, July 8, 2010, 36 (testimony of the U.S. Chamber of Commerce).

Appendix C

[1] As discussed in chap. 1, the term "ATPA" refers to ATPA as amended by ATPDEA.

[2] Although the term *duty reduction* is used, the methodology employed in the analysis for this report applies equally to a duty elimination (which is a duty reduction in the full amount of the duty).

[3] Most comparative static analyses are used to evaluate the effects of an event that has not already happened— such as a proposed tariff elimination. This comparative analysis evaluates the effects of an event that has already happened—ATPA duty elimination has been in effect since 1992. The method described in this section can be used in either situation.

[4] This is technically true only if income effects are negligible. Given the small U.S. expenditure on goods from ATPA countries, income effects are likely to be negligible for the products under consideration. See R. Willig, "Consumer's Surplus Without Apology," *American Economic Review*, 66 (1976), 589-597.

[5] The subscripts a, n, and d refer to ATPA imports, non-ATPA imports, and U.S. domestic output, respectively.

[6] Since ATPA imports account for a very small share of U.S. domestic consumption in most sectors, even the upper estimates were very small. Assuming upward-sloping supply curves would have resulted in even lower estimates.

[7] Welfare effects typically include a measure of the change in producer surplus. The change in producer surplus for ATPA producers was not considered in this analysis because the focus of the analysis was on the direct effects of ATPA provisions on the United States.

[8] Equations (4) through (6) are derived from P.R.G. Layard and A.A. Walters, *Microeconomic Theory* (New York: McGraw-Hill, 1978).

[9] The aggregate elasticities were taken from sources referenced in USITC, *Potential Impact on the U.S. Economy and Selected Industries of the North American Free-Trade Agreement*, USITC publication 2596, January 1993.

[10] Commission industry analysts provided evaluations of the substitutability of ATPA products and competing U.S. products, which were translated into a range of substitution elasticities—3 to 5 for high substitutability, 2 to 4 for medium, and 1 to 3 for low. Although there is no theoretical upper limit to elasticities of substitution, a substitution elasticity of 5 is consistent with the upper range of estimates in the economics literature. Estimates in the literature tend to be predominantly lower. See, for example, Clinton R. Shiells, Robert M. Stern, and Alan V. Deardorff, "Estimates of the Elasticities of Substitution Between Imports and Home Goods for the United States," *Weltwirtschaftliches Archiv*, 122 (1986), 497–519; and Michael P. Gallaway, Christine A. McDaniel, and Sandra A. Rivera, "Short-Run and Long-Run Estimates of U.S. Armington Elasticities," *North American Journal of Economics and Finance*, 14 (2003), 49–68.

COMMISSIONERS
Deanna Tanner Okun, Chairman
Charlotte R. Lane
Daniel R. Pearson
Shara L. Aranoff
Irving A. Williamson
Dean A. Pinkert

Karen Laney
Acting Director of Operations

Robert B. Koopman
Director, Office of Economics

This report was principally prepared by
Project Leader
Walker A. Pollard

Deputy Project Leader
Nicholas Grossman

Primary Reviewer
Cathy Jabara

Contributing Authors

Office of Economics
Eric Cardenas, William Greene, Joanne Guth, Andrew Martinez, Edward C. Wilson

Office of Industries
Joanna Bonarriva, Laura Rodriguez
Assistance was provided by
Tabitha Scallan, *Office of Economics*
Under the direction of
Arona M. Butcher
Chief, Country and Regional Analysis Division

In: The Andean Trade Preference Act (ATPA)
Editor: Aaron J. Dohrnmann

ISBN: 978-1-61324-386-2

Chapter 3

FIFTH REPORT TO THE CONGRESS ON THE OPERATION OF THE ANDEAN TRADE PREFERENCE ACT AS AMENDED*

Ambassador Ron Kirk

EXECUTIVE SUMMARY

The Andean Trade Preference Act (ATPA), as amended by the Andean Trade Promotion and Drug Eradication Act (ATPDEA) (jointly referred to as ATPA/ATPDEA), requires the U.S. Trade Representative (USTR) to submit a report to Congress on the operation of the program no later than June 30, 2010,[1] and every two years thereafter during the period that the program is in effect. Congress directed that these reports include a general review of the ATPA/ATPDEA beneficiary countries based on the eligibility criteria and considerations described in the statute. This is the fifth USTR report to Congress on the ATPA/ATPDEA, and covers the year 2009, unless otherwise indicated.

The ATPDEA renewed and expanded the ATPA, which had expired on December 4, 2001, providing beneficiary countries duty-free access to the U.S. market for any product not specifically excluded. Sections 203(c) and 203(d) and Section 204 (b)(6)(B) of ATPA, as amended by the ATPDEA, require that countries meet certain criteria in order to be designated as an ATPDEA beneficiary country and to maintain such beneficiary status. In Presidential Proclamation 7616 of October 31, 2002, the President designated all four ATPA beneficiary countries – Bolivia, Colombia, Ecuador, and Peru – as ATPDEA beneficiary countries.[2] Originally, the ATPA, as amended, was set to expire on December 31, 2006, but Congress has enacted several extensions. In 2009, Congress extended the program through December 31, 2010.

In its previous extension of the program, Congress stipulated that Bolivia would not receive ATPA/ATPDEA benefits after June 30, 2009, unless by that date the President determined that Bolivia was satisfying the program's eligibility criteria. In a June 30, 2009 report to Congress, President Obama did not determine that Bolivia satisfied the

---

* This is an edited, reformatted and augmented version of the United States Trade Representative's publication, dated June 30, 2010.

program's eligibility requirements. As a result, no ATPA/ATPDEA benefits remained in effect for Bolivia after that date.

The objectives of the ATPA/ATPDEA are to promote broad-based economic development, diversification of exports, consolidation of democracy, and to help defeat the scourge of drug trafficking by providing sustainable economic alternatives to drug-crop production in beneficiary countries. This report shows that the ATPA/ATPDEA continues to make progress in achieving these goals.

The United States is the leading source of imports and the leading export market for the ATPA/ATPDEA beneficiary countries. The three current beneficiary countries collectively represented a market of about $16.7 billion for U.S. exports in 2009, and were home to about $16.1 billion in U.S. foreign direct investment in 2008. Thus, the ATPA/ATPDEA has benefited the trade of both the Andean region and the United States.

In furtherance of the ATPA/ATPDEA's objectives, in May 2004, the United States initiated free trade agreement (FTA) negotiations with Peru, Colombia, and Ecuador, with Bolivia participating as an observer. On December 7, 2005, the United States and Peru concluded negotiations on the United States-Peru Trade Promotion Agreement (PTPA) and signed the agreement on April 12, 2006. The PTPA entered into force on February 1, 2009. The United States and Colombia concluded negotiations on the United States-Colombia Trade Promotion Agreement (CTPA) on February 27, 2006, and signed the agreement on November 22, 2006. Negotiations with Ecuador took place through March 2006, but did not conclude. The United States did not initiate negotiations on an FTA with Bolivia.

The report is organized as follows. Chapter 1 briefly describes the key sections of the ATPA/ATPDEA, including the ATPDEA requirements and the designation of ATPDEA beneficiary countries. Chapter 2 highlights trade between the United States and the ATPA/ATPDEA beneficiary countries. Chapter 3 evaluates the beneficiary countries' compliance with the eligibility criteria of the statute and discusses the ATPA/ATPDEA's effect on trade with the beneficiary countries. Chapter 4 summarizes responses by interested parties to the Administration's notice in the *Federal Register* inviting comments on the program, as mandated by Section 203(f) of the ATPA/ATPDEA. Finally, Chapter 5 describes the operation of the ATPA/ATPDEA beneficiary review process.

Ambassador Ron Kirk
United States Trade Representative

DESCRIPTION OF THE ATPA/ATPDEA

Key Provisions

The ATPA was enacted in December 1991, to help four Andean countries (Bolivia, Colombia, Ecuador, and Peru) in their fight against drug production and trafficking by expanding their economic alternatives. To this end, the ATPA provided reduced-duty or duty-free treatment to most of these countries' exports to the United States.

The ATPDEA, which renewed and amended the ATPA, was enacted on August 6, 2002, as part of the Trade Act of 2002. The renewal of the ATPA applied as of December 4, 2001, the date on which the ATPA had expired. The ATPDEA program provides for the possibility of enhanced trade benefits for the four ATPA beneficiary countries. The ATPDEA amended the ATPA to provide duty-free treatment for certain products previously excluded under the

ATPA. In Presidential Proclamation 7616 of October 31, 2002, the President designated all four ATPA beneficiary countries – Bolivia, Colombia, Ecuador, and Peru – as ATPDEA beneficiary countries.

In response to the requirement in Section 3103(d) of the Trade Act of 2002, USTR published final regulations establishing a petition process relating to the eligibility of the countries for the benefits of the program. (These regulations may be found at 15 CFR 2016.) Pursuant to these regulations, USTR has conducted annual reviews of petitions submitted. The President has the authority to withdraw or suspend ATPA/ATPDEA designation, or withdraw, suspend, or limit benefits, if a country's performance under the eligibility criteria has been found to be no longer satisfactory.

The ATPA/ATPDEA was initially set to expire on December 31, 2006. Congress has enacted legislation extending the program five times. Currently, the ATPA/ATPDEA is scheduled to expire on December 31, 2010.

These four Andean countries are also beneficiaries of the U.S. Generalized System of Preferences (GSP) program. The ATPA/ATPDEA offers broader product coverage than the GSP, thus augmenting the benefits of the GSP for the four countries. In addition, U.S. imports under the ATPA/ATPDEA are not subject to the GSP's competitive need limitations or its country graduation requirements.

Country Eligibility

The ATPA/ATPDEA listed Bolivia, Colombia, Ecuador, and Peru as the only countries eligible to be designated by the President as ATPA/ATPDEA beneficiary countries and in 2002 the President designated all four countries as ATPA/ATPDEA beneficiary countries. Each ATPA/ATPDEA beneficiary country is eligible for the enhanced trade benefits of the ATPDEA if the President designates it as an ATPDEA beneficiary country, taking into account: (1) the criteria contained in sections 203(c) and 203(d) of the ATPA/ATPDEA; and (2) additional eligibility criteria provided for in section 204(b)(6)(B) of the ATPA/ATPDEA. These criteria are discussed in detail in Chapter 3, which also contains a discussion of each country's compliance with the criteria since being designated. Section 204(b)(5)(A)(ii)(I) of the ATPA/ATPDEA also includes criteria related to customs cooperation.

Bolivia's eligibility for benefits was suspended effective December 2008. Further, in accordance with the statute, since the President did not determine that Bolivia satisfied the program's eligibility requirements in his June 30, 2009 report to Congress, no benefits remain in effect under the program for Bolivia. This report covers all four countries listed in the statute as potentially eligible for designation as an ATPA/ATPDEA beneficiary country, although an act of Congress would be required to restore the President's authority to extend benefits to Bolivia.

Product Eligibility

Section 204 of the ATPA/ATPDEA identifies the articles eligible for preferential treatment. Duty-free treatment applies only to articles that meet the program's rules of origin, including a requirement that the sum of the cost or value of the inputs produced in the beneficiary country and the cost of processing operations performed in the country must not be less than 35 percent of the value of the article. Inputs from other ATPA/ATPDEA beneficiary countries, Puerto Rico, the U.S. Virgin Islands, and beneficiaries of the Caribbean Basin Economic Recovery Act (CBERA) may be counted toward the 35 percent requirement.

As noted, the ATPDEA renewed the ATPA and amended it to provide preferential treatment for certain previously excluded products, including: certain textile and apparel articles, footwear, tuna packaged in foil or other flexible packages, petroleum and petroleum derivatives, watches and watch parts, and certain leather goods. Inclusion of all of the new benefits, except textiles and apparel articles, was subject to a Presidential determination that they are not import sensitive in the context of imports from ATPDEA beneficiary countries. The President did determine that certain footwear articles were import sensitive, as reflected in Presidential Proclamation 7616 of October 31, 2002. In addition, the following products continue to be excluded by statute from receiving preferential treatment: textile and apparel articles not otherwise eligible for preferential treatment under the ATPDEA; rum and tafia; above-quota imports of certain agricultural products subject to tariff rate quotas (TRQs), including sugars, syrups, and sugar-containing products; and tuna in cans.

Petition Process

Pursuant to Section 3103(d) of the ATPDEA, in July 2003, USTR promulgated regulations (15 CFR Part 2016) (68 Fed. Reg. 43922) regarding reviews of the eligibility of countries and articles under the ATPA as amended. Under these regulations, USTR conducts reviews and provides an opportunity for the submission of petitions for the withdrawal or suspension of certain benefits of the program. Petitions must indicate the eligibility criterion that the petitioner believes warrants review. USTR, on behalf of the Trade Policy Staff Committee (TPSC), publishes a list of the petitions filed. The Andean Subcommittee of the TPSC conducts a preliminary review of the petitions. The U.S. Trade Representative has not recommended the withdrawal or suspension of ATPA/ATPDEA designation, or the withdrawal, suspension, or limitation of benefits for any of the beneficiary countries based on the results of the reviews of petitions filed under these procedures.

Safeguard Provisions

Section 204(d) of the ATPA authorizes the President to suspend duty-free treatment under the ATPA if temporary import relief is proclaimed for an article pursuant to Chapter 1 of Title II of the Trade Act of 1974 ("global safeguards") or Section 232 of the Trade Expansion Act of 1962. Section 204(e) of the ATPA provides for emergency relief from imports of perishable products from beneficiary countries, and specifies the procedures for using these safeguard provisions.

Since 1991, the U.S. Government has taken two global safeguard measures that affected imports from the region. In February 2000, the President suspended duty-free treatment of steel wire rod and welded line pipe from ATPA beneficiary countries in two separate actions under the U.S. global safeguard law. In 1996, the President instituted a global safeguard action and suspended duty-free treatment of corn brooms for the period November 28, 1996, through November 27, 1999. This affected imports of corn brooms from Colombia.

Reports on the Impact of the ATPA

Section 206 of the ATPA requires the U.S. International Trade Commission (USITC) to submit biennial reports to the Congress on the impact of the ATPA on the U.S. economy generally and on U.S. industries and consumers, and its effectiveness in promoting drug-related crop eradication and crop substitution efforts of beneficiary countries. The USITC submitted its most recent (thirteenth) report covering 2007 to Congress in September 2008.

The USITC reports have consistently found that the overall effect of imports benefiting exclusively under the ATPA program (*i.e.*, those ineligible for other tariff preferences) on U.S. consumers and the economy as a whole, including in the year 2007, has been negligible. The thirteenth report estimated that U.S. imports of ATPA/ATPDEA-preference products could have potentially significant effects on domestic industries producing asparagus; fresh-cut roses; and fresh-cut chrysanthemums. This report also found that the ATPA/ATPDEA continues to have a positive (albeit small and indirect) effect on drug-crop eradication and crop substitution, as well as job growth in export-oriented industries, in the Andean region.

Section 207 of the ATPA/ATPDEA directs the Secretary of Labor, in consultation with other appropriate Federal agencies, to undertake a continuing review and analysis of the impact of the ATPA/ATPDEA on U.S. employment. The Secretary of Labor is required to report to Congress annually on the results of such review and analysis. The Department of Labor's most recent (sixteenth) report covering 2008 was submitted to Congress in 2009. The Department of Labor's reports have consistently found that the ATPA/ATPDEA does not appear to have had an adverse impact on, or to have constituted a significant threat to, overall U.S. employment. The Sixteenth Report found that, at the industry level, trends in U.S. domestic production and U.S. imports from the beneficiary countries since implementation of the ATPA/ATPDEA suggest that increased imports of certain fresh cut flowers and asparagus due to the ATPA/ATPDEA trade preferences may have displaced some growers and workers in the United States; however, given the complexities involved, it is difficult to isolate conclusively the factors responsible for these trends.

U.S. Trade with ATPA/ATPDEA Countries

U.S. trade with the ATPA/ATPDEA countries fell substantially in 2009, following rapid growth in 2008. Two-way trade decreased 21 percent in 2009, following a 37 percent increase in 2008. U.S. imports from ATPA countries fell 26 percent to $21.2 billion in 2009 compared with 2008, and U.S. exports fell 14 percent to $17.1 billion, resulting in a trade deficit of $4.0 billion. Over the past five years, U.S. imports from the region increased 37 percent and U.S. exports grew 123 percent.

Table 2-1. U.S. Trade with ATPA/ATPDEA Countries,1991-2009*

Year	U.S. Exports**	ATPA/ATPDEA Countries' Share of U.S. Exports to the World	U.S. Imports***	ATPA/ATPDEA Countries' Share of U.S. Imports from the World	U.S. Trade Balance
	Million $$	Percent	Million $$	Percent	Million $$
1991	3,798.2	0.9	4,969.5	1.0	-1,171.3
1992	5,319.7	1.3	5,058.7	1.0	261.0
1993	5,359.1	1.2	5,282.3	0.9	76.7
1994	6,445.0	1.3	5,879.5	0.9	565.5
1995	7,820.2	1.4	6,968.7	0.9	851.4
1996	7,718.7	1.3	7,867.6	1.0	-148.9
1997	8,681.8	1.3	8,673.6	1.0	8.2
1998	8,670.1	1.4	8,361.0	0.9	309.1
1999	6,263.2	1.0	9,830.2	1.0	-3,567.0
2000	6,295.1	0.9	11,117.2	0.9	-4,822.1
2001	6,363.3	1.0	9,568.7	0.8	-3,205.3
2002	6,463.8	1.0	9,611.5	0.8	-3,147.7
2003	6,525.7	1.0	11,639.5	0.9	-5,113.8
2004	7,663.6	1.1	15,489.8	1.1	-7,826.2
2005	8,919.1	1.1	20,060.1	1.2	-11,141.0
2006	11,636.5	1.3	22,510.6	1.2	-10,874.1
2007	14,620.5	1.4	20,922.9	1.1	-6,302.4
2008	19,762.7	1.7	28,483.0	1.4	-8,720.3
2009	17,074.9	1.8	21,193.9	1.4	-4,119.0

*Includes trade with Bolivia

**Domestic exports, F.A.S. basis

***Imports for consumption, customs value

Source: Compiled from official statistics of the U.S. Department of Commerce.

U.S. Imports from ATPA/ATPDEA Beneficiaries

U.S. imports from ATPA/ATPDEA countries fell to $21.2 billion in 2009 after reaching a record level of $28.5 billion in 2008. The share of U.S. imports from ATPA/ATPDEA countries among all U.S. imports fell in 2009 to 1.4 percent. (See Table 2-1.)

U.S. imports from ATPA/ATPDEA countries consist primarily of derivatives of raw materials, agricultural products, and apparel. Mineral fuels, mainly petroleum, accounted for 50 percent of imports in 2009, down from 59 percent in 2008, but similar in magnitude to the shares in previous years. In 2009, lower oil prices were primarily responsible for the decreased share, although the quantity of crude oil imports increased. Other leading imports from ATPA/ATPDEA countries in 2009 were precious metals, gemstones and jewelry, primarily nonmonetary gold; coffee; fruits and nuts, primarily bananas; apparel; cut flowers; fish and crustaceans; copper articles, mainly cathodes; unwrought tin; and edible vegetables, primarily asparagus.

About 88 percent of U.S. imports from ATPA/ATPDEA countries enter the U.S. market duty-free under ATPA/ATPDEA, GSP, the United States-Peru FTA, or Normal Trade Relations (NTR) tariff rates (formerly known as Most Favored Nation (MFN) tariff rates). (See Table 2- 2.) All 20 leading imports from the region were eligible for duty-free treatment in 2009. With the implementation of ATPDEA in late 2002, the duty-free portion of U.S. imports jumped from approximately 53 percent in 2002, to 85 percent in 2003, and 88 percent in 2009. Thirty-five percent of U.S. imports from the region entered duty free under NTR tariff rates in 2009. Such traditional U.S. imports from ATPA/ATPDEA countries as coffee, bananas, shrimp, and bituminous coal enter the U.S. market NTR duty-free. Another two percent of U.S. imports entered under the GSP. Forty six percent of U.S. imports from the region entered under ATPA/ATPDEA in 2009, falling from 61 percent in 2008, and compared to an average of 18 percent in the three years prior to the implementation of ATPDEA. In 2009, there was a substantial shift in imports from Peru from ATPA/ATPDEA to the United States-Peru FTA.

U.S. imports under ATPA/ATPDEA fell 44 percent to $9.7 billion in 2009, following a 40 percent increase in 2008 to $17.2 billion from $12.3 billion in 2007. The share of U.S. imports from the region that entered under ATPA/ATPDEA was stable around 60 percent for several years before falling to 47 percent in 2009.

Petroleum-based imports accounted for over three-fourths (76 percent) of U.S. imports under ATPA/ATPDEA in 2009, and were largely responsible for the 44 percent decrease in U.S. imports under ATPA/ATPDEA in 2009 due to the decline in the price of these imports. Apparel was the next largest category of imports under ATPA/ATPDEA, accounting for 6 percent of the total. The third largest category was cut flowers, and copper cathodes ranked fourth. Other important imports were fresh asparagus and vegetable and fruit preparations, including preparations of artichokes, asparagus, certain other fruit juices, bananas, and pimientos. U.S. imports under ATPA/ATPDEA of all of these products declined between 2008 and 2009, although imports of cut flowers declined only a small amount. Imports of gold jewelry, previously a leading import under ATPA/ATPDEA, have plummeted over the past several years, declining by around 90 percent since 2006.

U.S. Imports under the ATPA/ATPDEA by Country

Colombia was the leading source of U.S. imports under the ATPA/ATPDEA in 2009, having surpassed Ecuador in 2008. Colombia supplied 58 percent of U.S. imports under ATPA/ATPDEA in 2009; Ecuador, 28 percent; and Peru, 14 percent. (See Table 2.3.) Both Colombia and Ecuador supplied $6.2 billion of U.S. petroleum imports under ATPA/ATPDEA in 2008, but such imports from Colombia fell 26 percent in 2009 on lower prices and higher volume, while imports from Ecuador fell 61 percent on both lower prices and lower volume. U.S. imports under the ATPA/ATPDEA from each of the countries declined between 2008 and 2009.

Table 2-2. U.S. Imports from ATPA/ATPDEA Countries, Total and Under Import Programs, 2007-2009, (*thousands of dollars*)

Country	Import Program	2007	Percent of total	2008	Percent of total	2009	Percent of total
Bolivia	Total	333,611	100.0	540,435	100.0	504,002	100.0
.	GSP	40,727	12.2	47,632	8.8	123,889	24.6
.	ATPA[1]	91,282	27.4	56,958	10.5	0	0.0
.	ATPDEA	56,865	17.0	83,009	15.4	0	0.0
	MFN free	138,665	41.6	248,325	45.9	282,424	56.0
Colombia	Total	9,251,233	100.0	13,058,845	100.0	11,209,359	100.0
.	GSP	236,416	2.6	235,815	1.8	188,730	1.7
.	ATPA[1]	864,673	9.3	811,454	6.2	796,854	7.1
.	ATPDEA	3,662,986	39.6	6,527,779	50.0	4,792,631	42.8
	MFN free	3,492,051	37.7	4,314,317	33.0	4,175,188	37.2
Ecuador	Total	6,131,024	100.0	9,043,832	100.0	5,245,899	100.0
.	GSP	76,599	1.2	57,137	0.6	52,263	1.0
.	ATPA[1]	289,145	4.7	283,655	3.1	271,525	5.2
.	ATPDEA	4,324,647	70.5	6,311,119	69.8	2,476,921	47.2
	MFN free	1,104,012	18.0	1,261,953	14.0	1,444,768	27.5
Peru	Total	5,207,070	100.0	5,839,906	100.0	4,234,615	100.0
.	PeruU.S.	0	0.0	0	0.0	980,516	23.2
.	GSP	245,529	4.7	271,000	4.6	30,696	0.7
.	ATPA[1]	1,565,012	30.1	1,520,109	26.0	583,305	13.8
.	ATPDEA	1,452,232	27.9	1,648,593	28.2	793,008	18.7
	MFN free	1,727,786	33.2	1,986,905	34.0	1,609,566	38.0
All ATPA countries	Total	20,922,938	100.0	28,483,018	100.0	20,689,873	100.0
	PeruU.S.	0	0.0	0	0.0	980,516	4.7
	GSP	599,271	2.9	611,584	2.1	271,689	1.3
	ATPA[1]	2,810,112	13.4	2,672,176	9.4	1,651,684	8.0
	ATPDEA	9,496,730	45.4	14,570,500	51.2	8,062,560	39.0
	MFN free	6,462,514	30.9	7,811,500	27.4	7,229,522	34.9

1 ATPA in this table refers to the original ATPA (ATPA excluding ATPDEA).

Source: USITC dataweb compiled from official statistics of the U.S. Department of Commerce.

Table 2-3. U.S. Imports for Consumption under the ATPA/ATPDEA, by Country, 2007-2009

Country	2007	2008	2009	2009 share of total
	1,000 dollars	*1,000 dollars*	*1,000 dollars*	Percent
Colombia	4,527,659	7,339,233	5,589,485	57.5
Ecuador	4,613,792	6,594,774	2,748,446	28.3
Peru	3,017,244	3,168,702	1,376,312	14.2
Bolivia	148,148	139,966	0	0.0
Total	12,306,843	17,242,675	9,714,243	100.0

Source: USITC Dataweb compiled from official statistics of the U.S. Department of Commerce.

U.S. imports under ATPA/ATPDEA from Colombia decreased 24 percent to $5.6 billion in 2009, less than from any other ATPA/ATPDEA country. Petroleum-related products were primarily responsible for the decrease, accounting for 82 percent ($4.6 billion) of ATPA/ATPDEA entries from Colombia in 2009, down from an 84 percent share ($6.2 billion) in 2008. Other major U.S. imports under ATPA/ATPDEA from Colombia declined in 2009 compared with 2008, with the exception of cut flowers, the second largest import ($506 million), which increased 1.4 percent. Imports of apparel, the third largest import ($210 million) fell 33 percent. Cut flowers and apparel accounted for 9.1 percent and 3.8 percent of ATPA/ATPDEA entries from Colombia, respectively, in 2009. Other important imports under ATPA/ATPDEA from Colombia were plastics ($53 million), sugar ($34 million), aluminum products ($30 million), ceramics ($24 million), and vegetable and fruit preparations ($20 million), all of which declined in 2009 compared with 2008, except sugar and vegetable and fruit preparations.

ATPA/ATPDEA entries from Ecuador decreased 58 percent to $2.7 billion in 2009, from $6.6 billion in 2008. Petroleum products ($2.4 billion) overwhelmingly dominated such imports from Ecuador, accounting for 88 percent in 2009, lower than the shares of over 90 percent in each of the previous four years. Other important imports under ATPA/ATPDEA from Ecuador in 2009 were cut flowers ($118 million), down 11 percent in 2009 compared with 2008; tuna ($57 million), down 31 percent; vegetables ($41 million), down 5 percent; vegetable and fruit preparations ($36 million), up 28 percent; and fruits, primarily fresh pineapples, fresh mangoes, and frozen fruits ($35 million), up 28 percent.

U.S. imports under ATPA/ATPDEA from Peru decreased 57 percent, from $3.2 billion in 2008 to $1.4 billion in 2009, reflecting sharply lower prices for resource-based products and a shift in entry of some imports from ATPA/APTDEA to the United States-Peru FTA. The leading ATPA/ATPDEA entry from Peru was apparel; although apparel imports declined 47 percent to $408 million in 2009, they accounted for 30 percent of total ATPA/ATPDEA entries from Peru. The second largest U.S. import under ATPA/ATPDEA from Peru was petroleum products, which decreased 56 percent to $384 million in 2009. The third largest import in 2009, and formerly the leading import from Peru under ATPA/ATPADEA, was copper articles, primarily copper cathodes at $241 million, down 73 percent from 2008. Other leading ATPA/ATPDEA imports from Peru in 2009 were vegetable and fruit preparations ($91 million); fruits, primarily grapes and mangoes ($56 million); and fresh asparagus ($45 million). Total U.S. imports of fresh asparagus actually increased 6 percent, but a large share of such imports shifted from ATPA/ATPDEA to the United States-Peru FTA.

U.S. Exports to ATPA/ATPDEA Beneficiaries

U.S. exports to ATPA/ATPDEA countries, including Bolivia, fell 14 percent to $17.1 billion in 2009, less than the 20 percent decrease recorded for all U.S. exports. The ATPA/ATPDEA countries' share of U.S. exports to the world was 1.8 percent in 2009.

The leading category of U.S. exports to ATPA/ATPDEA countries in 2009 was nonelectrical machinery, equipment, appliances, and parts, destined principally for oil and gas extraction, mining, and data processing. U.S. exports of nonelectrical machinery and parts decreased 12 percent to $3.8 billion in 2009, and have consistently accounted for 21-22 percent of total U.S. exports to the region over the past five years. U.S. exports of mineral fuels, primarily refined petroleum products, which ranked second in 2009, decreased one percent to $2.7 billion in 2009. All other categories of U.S. exports among the top ten to the region also decreased in 2009 compared with 2008, including electrical machinery ($1.3 billion), plastics ($1.1 billion), organic chemicals ($823 million), and motor vehicles ($762 million).

Colombia was the largest market for U.S. exports at $8.8 billion, representing 51 percent of U.S. exports to ATPA/ATPDEA countries in 2009. Peru ranked second as a destination for U.S. exports, with $4.4 billion in U.S. goods (26 percent); Ecuador was third, with $3.6 billion (21 percent); and Bolivia was fourth, with $378 million (2 percent). U.S. exports to Colombia and Peru fell 17 percent and 23 percent, respectively, in 2009, but exports to Ecuador and Bolivia rose 14 percent and 5 percent, respectively.

Country Eligibility Reports

This chapter first outlines the detailed country eligibility criteria in the ATPA/ATPDEA and proceeds to discuss each of the four countries' performance under the criteria. Each country report also examines the effects of the ATPA/ATPDEA on trade, investment and economic development in the country and on creating sustainable economic alternatives to coca production. These country reports are based on information provided by U.S. embassies in the region. They are an update to USTR's April 30, 2009, Fourth Report to the Congress on the Operation of the Andean Trade Preference Act as Amended.

As summarized below, the ATPA/ATPDEA contains two types of criteria: mandatory and discretionary. The President may not designate an ATPA/ATPDEA country as a beneficiary if the country fails to meet the mandatory criteria, described in the statute as "limitations on designation," unless the President finds that designation would be in the national economic or security interest of the United States. The President must take the discretionary criteria, described in the statute as "factors affecting designation," into account in determining whether to designate any country as a beneficiary country, but he is not barred from designating a country that fails to meet those criteria as a beneficiary.[3]

Summary of Eligibility Criteria

Mandatory criteria *(for renewed ATPA benefits and ATPDEA benefits)*:
"The President shall not designate any country:

1) if such country is a Communist country;
2) if such country:

- has nationalized, expropriated or otherwise seized ownership or control of property owned by a United States citizen or by a corporation, partnership, or association which is 50 percent or more beneficially owned by United States citizens,
- has taken steps to repudiate or nullify any existing contract or agreement with, or any patent, trademark, or other intellectual property of, a United States citizen or a corporation, partnership, or association, which is 50 percent or more beneficially owned by United States citizens, the effect of which is to nationalize, expropriate, or otherwise seize ownership or control of property so owned, or
- has imposed or enforced taxes or other exactions, restrictive maintenance or operational conditions, or other measures with respect to property so owned, the effect of which is to nationalize, expropriate, or otherwise seize ownership or control of such property, unless the President determines that:

    - prompt, adequate, and effective compensation has been or is being made to such citizen, corporation, partnership, or association,
    - good-faith negotiations to provide prompt, adequate, and effective compensation under the applicable provisions of international law are in progress, or such country is otherwise taking steps to discharge its obligations under international law with respect to such citizen, corporation, partnership, or association, or
    - a dispute involving such citizen, corporation, partnership or association, over compensation for such a seizure has been submitted to arbitration under the provisions of the Convention for the Settlement of Investment Disputes, or in another mutually agreed upon forum, and promptly furnishes a copy of such determination to the Senate and House of Representatives;

3) if such country fails to act in good faith in recognizing as binding or in enforcing arbitral awards in favor of United States citizens or a corporation, partnership, or association which is 50 percent or more beneficially owned by United States citizens, which have been made by arbitrators appointed for each case or by permanent arbitral bodies to which the parties involved have submitted their dispute;
4) if such country affords preferential treatment to the products of a developed country, other than the United States, and if such preferential treatment has, or is likely to have, a significant adverse effect on United States commerce, unless the President:

- has received assurances satisfactory to him that such preferential treatment will be eliminated or that action will be taken to assure that there will be no such significant adverse effect, and
- reports those assurances to the Congress;

5) if a government-owned entity in such country engages in the broadcast of copyrighted material, including films or television material, belonging to United States copyright owners without their express consent or such country fails to work towards the provision of adequate and effective protection of intellectual property rights;
6) unless such country is a signatory to a treaty, convention, protocol, or other agreement regarding the extradition of United States citizens; and
7) if such country has not or is not taking steps to afford internationally recognized worker rights (as defined in section 507(4) of the Trade Act of 1974) to workers in the country (including any designated zone in that country).

The first, second, third, fifth, and seventh criteria shall not prevent the designation of any country as a beneficiary country under this title if the President determines that such designation will be in the national economic or security interest of the United States and reports such determination to the Congress with his reasons therefore."

Discretionary criteria *(for renewed ATPA benefits and ATPDEA benefits)*:

1) "an expression by such country of its desire to be so designated;
2) the economic conditions in such country, the living standards of its inhabitants, and any other economic factors which he deems appropriate;
3) the extent to which such country has assured the United States it will provide equitable and reasonable access to the markets and basic commodity resources of such country;
4) the degree to which such country follows the accepted rules of international trade provided for under the WTO Agreement and the multilateral trade agreements (as such terms are defined in paragraphs (9) and (4), respectively, of section 2 of the Uruguay Round Agreements Act);
5) the degree to which such country uses export subsidies or imposes export performance requirements or local content requirements which distort international trade;
6) the degree to which the trade policies of such country as they relate to other beneficiary countries are contributing to the revitalization of the region;
7) the degree to which such country is undertaking self-help measures to protect its own economic development;
8) whether or not such country has taken or is taking steps to afford to workers in that country (including any designated zone in that country) internationally recognized worker rights;
9) the extent to which such country provides under its law adequate and effective means for foreign nationals to secure, exercise, and enforce exclusive rights in intellectual property, including patent, trademark, and copyright rights;

10) the extent to which such country prohibits its nationals from engaging in the broadcast of copyrighted material, including films or television material, belonging to United States copyright owners without their express consent;
11) whether such country has met the narcotics cooperation certification criteria set forth in section 481(h)(2)(A) *[deemed to be a reference to section 490 of the Foreign Assistance Act of 1991 by section 6(a) of Public Law 102-583]* of the Foreign Assistance Act of 1961 for eligibility for United States assistance; and
12) the extent to which such country is prepared to cooperate with the United States in the administration of the provisions of the Andean Trade Preference Act, as amended."

Discretionary criteria *(for ATPDEA benefits only)*:

1) "Whether the beneficiary country has demonstrated a commitment to undertake its obligations under the WTO, including those agreements listed in section 101(d) of the Uruguay Round Agreements Act, on or ahead of schedule, and participate in negotiations toward the completion of the FTAA or another free trade agreement;
2) the extent to which the country provides protection of intellectual property rights consistent with or greater than the protection afforded under the Agreement on Trade-Related Aspects of Intellectual Property Rights described in section 101(d)(15) of the Uruguay Round Agreements Act;
3) the extent to which the country provides internationally recognized worker rights, including:

- the right of association;
- the right to organize and bargain collectively;
- a prohibition on the use of any form of forced or compulsory labor;
- a minimum age for the employment of children; and
- acceptable conditions of work with respect to minimum wages, hours of work, and occupational safety and health;

4) whether the country has implemented its commitments to eliminate the worst forms of child labor, as defined in section 507(6) of the Trade Act of 1974;
5) the extent to which the country has met the counternarcotics certification criteria set forth in section 490 of the Foreign Assistance Act of 1961 (22 U.S.C. 2291(j)) for eligibility for United States assistance;
6) the extent to which the country has taken steps to become a party to and implements the Inter-American Convention Against Corruption;
7) the extent to which the country applies transparent, nondiscriminatory, and competitive procedures in government procurement equivalent to those contained in the Agreement on Government Procurement described in section 101(d)(17) of the Uruguay Round Agreements Act, and contributes to efforts in international fora to develop and implement rules on transparency in government procurement; and
8) the extent to which the country has taken steps to support the efforts of the United States to combat terrorism."

Bolivia

U.S.-Bolivia Trade (Millions of Dollars)

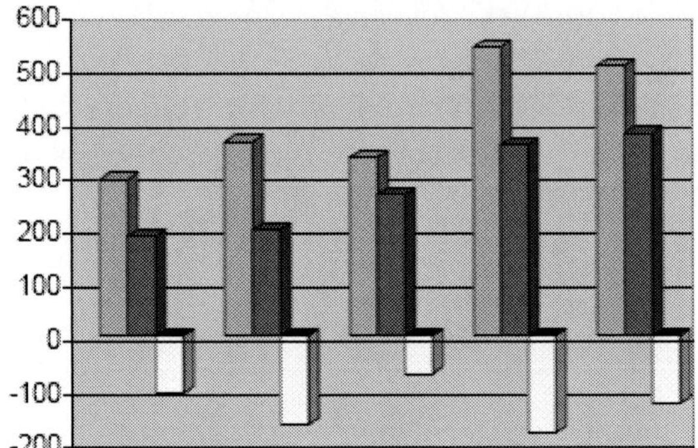

	2005	2006	2007	2008	2009
U.S. Imports	293	362	334	540	504
U.S. Exports	186	197	263	358	378
Trade Balance	-108	-165	-71	-182	-127

Population: 9,775,246; (July 2009 est.) GDP per capita (PPP): $4,600 (2009 est.).
Source: 2010 World Fact Book.

Preferential Tariff Treatment

In 2009, U.S. goods imports from Bolivia totaled $504 million, a 7 percent decrease from 2008.[4] Bolivia accounted for 2.4 percent of total U.S. imports from the four Andean countries in 2009. U.S. imports under preference programs (ATPA/ATPDEA and GSP) from Bolivia decreased 34 percent, from $188 million in 2008 to $124 million in 2009, a decrease of $64 million, reflecting changes resulting from the denial of benefits under ATPA/ATPDEA to Bolivia. Imports of petroleum and petroleum products, which amounted to $72 million under ATPDEA and 51 percent of imports under ATPA/ATPDEA in 2008, do not qualify for duty-free entry under GSP. (NTR duty rates on petroleum and petroleum products are extremely low—5.25¢ or 10.5¢ per barrel on products commonly imported from Bolivia—so preferences have only a very small impact on such imports.) Since most of Bolivia's major exports that had qualified for ATPA (excluding ATPDEA) preferences are also eligible for GSP preferences, these products were able to be entered duty-free under GSP in 2009. Most notable of these products were various types of precious metal jewelry and articles of precious metals. Imports of these products under preference programs increased $23 million from 2008 to 2009 to a total of $83 million, an increase of 38 percent.

Expropriations

The new Bolivian Constitution provides that property may be expropriated for the public good or when the property does not fulfill a "social purpose." It also stipulates that just compensation must be provided. Regulatory laws that grant concessions to exploit natural resources such as hydrocarbons and minerals also provide a means of expropriating land and guaranteeing rights of way needed to develop concessions. A United States-Bolivia bilateral investment treaty (BIT) entered into force in June 2001. The BIT provides that expropriation of U.S. investments can only be carried out for a public purpose, in a nondiscriminatory manner, in accordance with due process of law, and upon payment of prompt, adequate, and effective compensation.

In 2005, the Bolivian government enacted a law requiring that hydrocarbons companies negotiate new service contracts that grant control over the production chain to the state, and that provide *Yacimientos Petrolíferos Fiscales Bolivianos* (YPFB), the state-owned oil company, a share of the companies' equity. All production companies signed new contracts in October 2006, and agreed to pay 50 percent in taxes and royalties, as well as provide YPFB with an equity stake ranging from zero to 32 percent. In May 2008, Bolivia moved to further consolidate state control over the hydrocarbon companies privatized in the 1990s, e.g. *Transredes*, the principal pipeline operator partially owned by Ashmore Energy International (AEI) of Houston, Texas, by mandating that the state have controlling ownership of 50 plus one percent. In 2009, the Bolivian government and *Transredes* reached an agreement whereby the government paid approximately $230 million to acquire 97 percent of the company.

Arbitral Awards

The United States-Bolivia BIT provides for recourse to international arbitration in the event of disputes between U.S. investors and the Bolivian government. Bolivia's Investment Law (Law 1182 of 1990) provides for arbitration in accordance with the Bolivian Constitution and international norms, and the Arbitration and Conciliation Law (Law 1770 of 1997) outlines arbitration procedures and enforcement mechanisms. These laws state that international agreements, such as the International Convention on the Settlement of Investment Disputes between States and Nationals of Other States (ICSID) and the 1958 Convention on the Recognition and Enforcement of Foreign Arbitral Awards (the "New York Convention"), must be honored. However, the Constitution stipulates that hydrocarbon companies may not invoke international arbitration for any reason nor appeal to diplomatic claims, nor will the government recognize international or foreign rulings. The Constitution assigns to the Constitutional Court responsibility for addressing conflicts between the Constitution and Bolivia's international agreements. In November 2007, Bolivia became the first country to withdraw from ICSID.

Reverse Preferences

The U.S. Government has no indication that Bolivia has granted such preferences to the products of a developed nation.

Intellectual Property

Patents, trademarks, and industrial designs are protected by Andean Community Decisions 486 (Common Industrial Property Regime) and 345 (Common Provisions on the Protection of the Rights of Breeders of New Plant Varieties). Copyrights are protected by Andean Community Decision 351 (Common Regime on Copyright and Neighboring Rights). However, enforcement of existing laws to protect intellectual property rights is weak, and piracy in Bolivia continues largely unabated.

The copyright law (Law 1322, 1992) protects literary, artistic, and scientific works for the lifetime of the author plus 50 years. The law also provides protection for software and databases.

Bolivian copyright protection includes the exclusive right to copy or reproduce works; to revise, adapt, or prepare derivative works; to distribute copies of works; and to publicly communicate works. Although the exclusive right to translate works is not explicitly granted, the law does prevent unauthorized adaptation, transformation, modification, and editing.

The copyright law protects the rights of Bolivian authors, foreign authors domiciled in Bolivia, and foreign authors published for the first time in Bolivia. Foreigners not domiciled in Bolivia are protected to the extent provided in international conventions and treaties to which Bolivia is a party. Additional protection is provided by the film and video law (Law 1302, 1991) which established a National Movie Council (CONACINE) to oversee the domestic film industry and requires that all films and videos shown or distributed in Bolivia be registered with the organization.

The existing copyright law recognizes copyright infringement as a public offense and the 2001 Bolivian Criminal Procedures Code provides for the criminal prosecution of intellectual property rights (IPR) violations. However, the International Intellectual Property Alliance estimates that piracy levels have reached 100 percent for motion pictures and over 90 percent for recorded music. The U.S. Government is not aware of any allegations of unauthorized broadcast of U.S. copyrighted works by a government-owned entity.

The Bolivian government is a member of several international conventions that concern intellectual property, including:

- World Intellectual Property Organization (WIPO) Convention;
- Paris Convention for the Protection of Industrial Property; and
- Berne Convention for the Protection of Literary and Artistic Works.

Bolivia is also a signatory to the WIPO Copyright Treaty and the WIPO Performances and Phonograms Treaty. The Bolivian congress has not yet ratified these treaties.

Extradition

An extradition treaty with the United States permits the extradition of U.S. citizens.

Workers' Rights

Bolivia has ratified all eight International Labor Organization core labor conventions. Bolivian labor laws provide for a range of benefits for full-time salaried employees. Bolivia's labor code assures workers the right to establish and join organizations of their choosing. Bolivian labor law does not restrict unions from affiliating with international labor confederations.

To call a legal strike, private sector workers must first engage in government mediation and obtain authorization to strike by a vote of 75 percent of workers. Laborers rarely meet these requirements, but strikes and protests are common, and the government does not normally prosecute strikers. While solidarity strikes are illegal under the current labor code, the government does not routinely enforce this law and in practice allows such strikes. The government has the power to declare a strike illegal and has done so on occasion.

With the exception of health and gas industry workers and teachers, the labor code formally denies civil servants the right to organize and prohibits strikes in public services, including banks and public markets. Still, the rate of unionization in the public sector (just over 50 percent of salaried workers) is twice that of the private sector, and strikes are common.

Bolivian law prohibits forced or compulsory labor, including by children; however, in 2005 the ILO reported that between 26,000 and 30,000 persons, including children and mostly of indigenous origin, were victims of forced labor, harvesting Brazil nuts in the *Beni* Department. Similar conditions were reported to exist in the sugar industry in the *Santa Cruz* Department.

According to the International Labor Organization, 313,529 children between the ages of seven and seventeen work in Bolivia, and approximately 142,000 are girls. Although the law prohibits persons under 18 years of age from work in the sugarcane fields, approximately 10,000 rural migrant children (7,000 of whom are under the age of 14) reportedly engage in such work. Children also worked in mining gold, silver, and tin and in other dangerous occupations in the informal sector.

On November 28, 2002, the Bolivian government ratified ILO Convention 182 on the Worst Forms of Child Labor. Bolivia has taken steps to implement its commitments under this Convention by creating an inter-institutional commission and initiating the development of a national plan to eradicate the worst forms of child labor. The government continued to work with non-governmental organizations to discourage the use of child labor in the mining and sugar sectors by participating in internationally funded programs to provide educational alternatives to children who otherwise would work in mines or sugarcane fields. Nonetheless, according to the human rights ombudsman, as of 2008, 3,800 children still worked in mining.

Economic Conditions

Bolivian has remained relatively immune from the worldwide economic crisis. In 2009, GDP continued strong growth at an estimated 3.7 percent, one of the highest rates in the region. Inflation fell significantly from 11.8 percent in 2008 to 0.3 percent. The financial sector is strong with more than $3 billion in excess liquidity. International reserves rose from $3.2 billion in 2006 to $8.6 billion in 2009, covering 21 months of imports or all deposits in the financial system, in local and foreign currencies. According to the United Nations Conference on Trade and Development (UNCTAD), the stock of Foreign Domestic Investment (FDI) in Bolivia increased from $1 billion in 1990 to $6 billion in 2008. Also, the Central Bank of Bolivia reported that the International Investment Position registered a net credit of $2.7 billion, or 16 percent of annual GDP in 2009. Total FDI from all countries in 2009 was $748.5 million. Of this, $172 million was from the United States, which was the country's top investor in 2009, contributing 23 percent of all FDI. Fiscal and external accounts registered surpluses the last two years.

With the election of President Morales in 2005, the government moved away from market-based policies and toward greater state involvement in the economy. In December 2009, President Morales was reelected and his party obtained a majority in both houses of the Bolivian legislature. The government has continued to stress the need for greater state control of the economy and has committed to nationalize additional enterprises.

Market Access

Bolivia generally provides equitable and reasonable market access for U.S. exports. Bolivia's current tariff structure was approved in November 2007. Under this scheme, capital goods designated for industrial development may enter duty-free, non-essential capital goods are subject to a five percent tariff, and most other goods are subject to tariffs of 10-20 percent. In May 2009, Bolivia established by Supreme Decree 125 a separate 35 percent tax for textile products and wooden furniture.

Bolivia also enacted a Ministerial Resolution in December 2008 that established the 2009 Bolivian Customs Import Tariff This resolution brings Bolivia into accordance with Decision 653 of the Andean Community taken in November 2006, which approved the common description and coding nomenclature for the goods of the Andean Community member countries.

Bolivia's trade policy generally does not apply specific restrictions to trade in goods and services, such as permits or prior licenses, with the exception that all importers must register with the Bolivian National Customs Office. The Bolivian government imposes restrictions where there is a potential for danger to human, animal, or plant health; to protect the country's artistic or cultural heritage; and to ensure the security of the state.

Participation in Free Trade Negotiations

In May 2004, the United States initiated negotiations on an FTA with Colombia, Ecuador, and Peru. To date, the United States has concluded FTAs with Peru and Colombia. Bolivia initially participated as an observer with a view to becoming party to a free trade agreement at a later stage, but the United States did not initiate negotiations with Bolivia.

Subsidies or Other Requirements that Distort International Trade

While Bolivia has eliminated many of its export subsidy programs, the government has notified the World Trade Organization (WTO) that it provides export subsidies through its "Free Trade Zones" and "Temporary Import Regime for Export Promotion."

Bolivia also limits some agricultural exports unless producers can show that internal demand has been met at "fair prices." Exporters must request a certificate of internal sufficiency of supply and "fair" price from the Ministry of Production and Microenterprises before selling products abroad. Products that have recently been subject to this provision include sugar, beef, poultry, and vegetable oils.

Regional Trade Policies

Bolivia, along with Chile, Colombia, Ecuador, Peru, and Venezuela, is an associate member of the Common Market of the South (Mercado Común del Sur – MERCOSUR) group which includes Argentina, Brazil, Paraguay, and Uruguay. MERCOSUR has virtually eliminated tariff and non-tariff barriers on most intra-regional trade between members with the implementation of a Common External Tariff (CET) system. Associate members enjoy tariff reductions, but are not subject to the CET system.

Bolivia is also a member of the Andean Community of Nations (Comunidad Andina de Naciones or CAN) with Colombia, Ecuador, and Peru. This agreement has significantly reduced most internal trade barriers.

Narcotics and Counter-terrorism Cooperation

As described in the Executive Summary, Bolivia is not currently an ATPA/ADPDEA beneficiary country due to its failure to meet the program's eligibility criteria related to counternarcotics cooperation.

According to U.S. Government estimates, Bolivia's 2009 coca cultivation was approximately 35,000 hectares, a nine percent increase over the previous year. UN studies estimate that coca cultivation increased by six percent to 30,500 hectares in 2008. UN data for 2009 is not yet available. The United States believes that potential cocaine production increased from 130 metric tons in 2007 to 195 metric tons in 2008 due to the use of more efficient Colombian-style cocaine processing methods, and that potential production remained the same in 2009.

The Bolivian government continued to conduct interdiction and eradication operations. In the first quarter of 2010, the Bolivian government seized 9.45 metric tons of cocaine base, 0.95 metric tons of cocaine hydrochloride (HCI), and 240 metric tons of illegally grown coca leaf. In 2009, the Bolivian government eradicated 6,341 hectares of coca. The Bolivian government increased its stated eradication goal to 7,000 hectares for 2010, and in the first quarter has eradicated 675 hectares. Still, eradication efforts have not been sufficient to achieve a net reduction in hectares of coca cultivation, as eradication of coca seedbeds has dropped significantly (destruction of 10 square meters of coca seedbed prevents one hectare of coca cultivation). Bolivia also is working to improve counternarcotics cooperation with Brazil, Argentina, and other neighbors. The United States remains committed to working with Bolivia to achieve concrete counternarcotics results.

The Bolivian government continues to work closely with USAID and other donors on alternative development. USAID estimates that the cultivation of alternative crops and pastures in the *Cochabamba Tropics* and the *Yungas* of *La Paz* area increased steadily, from 40,613 hectares in 1986 to an estimated 150,000 hectares in 2006. Community development activities in the *Yungas* and agricultural extension services and improved road access in *Cochabamba* have proven effective ways of reaching increasing numbers of families in those regions. The cumulative number of farm families assisted through integrated alternative development projects in the *Chapare* and *Yungas* regions totaled 52,190 through 2006, or more than half of all farm families in those regions. In the last two years, 26,000 families were benefited, 8,716 new jobs were created, $44.2 million of alternative development products' sales were generated, and 24,276 hectares of new or improved crops and areas under forest management plans were directly supported with U.S. assistance. High-value licit crop exports such as bananas, pineapple, canned palm hearts, coffee, and cacao increased from $7.5 million in 2001 to $37.8 million in 2008.

Government Procurement

Government expenditures account for a significant portion of Bolivia's Gross Domestic Product (approximately 33 percent according to the IMF). The central government, state, and local governments, and other public entities are important buyers of machinery, equipment, materials, and other goods and services.

Suppliers must comply with prerequisites established in bidding documents exclusive to each purchase. Bid specifications containing technical and commercial requirements are available through the relevant government entity and local newspapers. The entity's chief official determines qualifying procedures and makes award decisions. Officials consider both price and quality when awarding contracts.

Domestic bidders receive a 10 to 15 percent preference, depending on the bid, to encourage local industrial development. Government procurement under $100,000 must also give priority to the small Bolivian business or small enterprise sector, micro producers associations, and peasant associations. Vendors that fall under these categories are required to provide fewer guarantees and prerequisites than the regular business sector. Bolivian companies are given priority for government procurement bids from $142,000 to $5.7 million. Importers of foreign goods can participate in these procurements only when locally manufactured products and service providers are unavailable or when the Bolivian government does not select a domestic supplier; in such cases, the government can call for international bids. International public bids are called for when purchases exceed $5.7 million.

The Ministry of Defense and the Ministry of Government are allowed to make exceptional purchases of unlimited amounts. The government may issue tenders for national security purchases for the armed forces or for goods and services of national interest with no limit in value.

Bolivia is not a signatory to the WTO Agreement on Government Procurement.

Colombia

U.S.-Colombia Trade (Millions of Dollars)

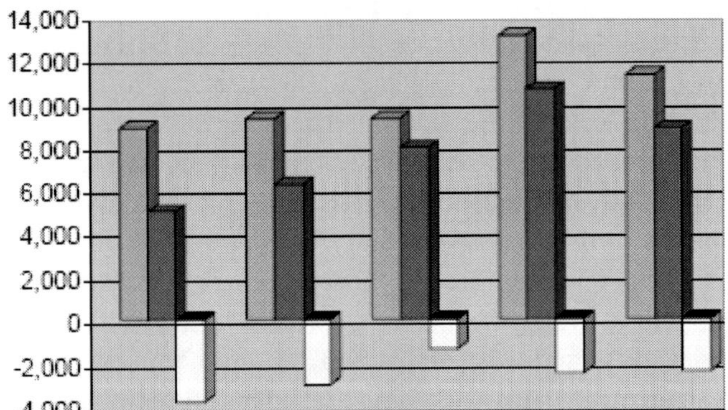

	2005	2006	2007	2008	2009
U.S. Imports	8,770	9,240	9,251	13,059	11,209
U.S. Exports	4,962	6,236	7,884	10,568	8,752
Trade Balance	-3,808	-3,004	-1,367	-2,491	-2,457

Population: 43,677,372; (July 2009 est.) GDP per capita (PPP): $9,200 (2009 est.)
Source: 2010 World Fact Book.

Effect of ATPA/ATPDEA

In 2009, U.S. goods imports from Colombia totaled $11.2 billion, a 14 percent decrease from 2008. U.S. imports under the ATPA/ATPDEA from Colombia were $5.6 billion in 2009, down 24 percent from $7.3 billion in 2008. Petroleum-related products were primarily responsible for the decrease, accounting for 82 percent ($4.6 billion) of ATPA/ATPDEA entries from Colombia in 2009, down from an 84 percent share ($6.2 billion) in 2008. Other major U.S. imports under ATPA/ATPDEA from Colombia declined in 2009 compared with 2008, with the exception of cut flowers, the second largest import ($506 million), which increased 1.4 percent. Imports of apparel, the third largest import ($210 million) fell 33 percent. Cut flowers and apparel accounted for 9.1 percent and 3.8 percent of ATPA/ATPDEA entries from Colombia, respectively, in 2009. Other important imports under ATPA/ATPDEA from Colombia were plastics ($53 million), sugar ($34 million), aluminum products ($30 million), ceramics ($24 million), and vegetable and fruit preparations ($20 million), all of which, except sugar and vegetable and fruit preparations, declined in 2009 compared with 2008.

Expropriations

The 1991 Constitution protects individual rights against the actions of the state and upholds the right to private property. The Constitution permits acquisition of private property in cases of public necessity (e.g., a public transit system) and social interest (e.g., agrarian reform). Colombian law guarantees indemnification in such cases. Confiscation of property used in, or that is the fruit of, criminal activities is allowed.

Arbitral Awards

Law 315 permits the inclusion of a binding arbitration clause in contracts between foreign investors and Colombian entities, private and public. The law allows parties to set their own arbitration terms, including location, procedures, rules, and the nationality of arbitrators. In the absence of an arbitration clause, Colombian law mandates that disputes go before a Colombian judge for settlement. Colombia is a signatory to the New York Convention and the ICSID Convention, and a member of the Multilateral Investment Guarantee Agency (MIGA).

Reverse Preferences

Colombia has signed free trade agreements with both Canada and the European Free Trade Association, though neither agreement has entered into force. However, Colombia has also signed a free trade agreement with the United States which is pending Congressional action.

Intellectual Property

Patents, trademarks and industrial designs are protected by Andean Community Decisions 344 (the Common Industrial Property Regime) and 345 (the Common Regime to Protect Plant Varieties). Copyrights are protected by Andean Community Decision 351 (the Common Regime on Copyright and Neighboring Rights). These decisions, which were adopted in 1993 and 1994, are comprehensive and represent a significant improvement over earlier standards of protection for intellectual property in the Andean Community countries.

The Colombian government is a member of several international conventions that concern intellectual property, including the following:

- Convention Establishing the World Intellectual Property Organization (WIPO);
- Berne Convention for the Protection of Literary and Artistic Works;
- Paris Convention for the Protection of Industrial Property;
- Patent Cooperation Treaty;
- WIPO Performances and Phonograms Treaty; and
- WIPO Copyright Treaty.

In Colombia, the grant, registration and administration of intellectual property rights (industrial property and copyright) are carried out by four different government entities. The Office of the Superintendent of Industry and Commerce acts as the Colombian patent and trademark office. The Colombian Agricultural Institute is in charge of the issuance of plant variety protection and agro-chemical patents. The Ministry of Social Protection is in charge of the issuance of pharmaceutical patents, while the Ministry of Interior and Justice is in charge of the issuance of literary copyrights. Each of these entities experiences significant financial and technical resource constraints. Moreover, the lack of uniformity and consistency in IPR registration and oversight procedures limits the transparency and predictability of the IPR enforcement regime.

In 2002, the Colombian government issued Decree 2085, which improved the protection of undisclosed data for pharmaceutical products. The decree grants a five year period for undisclosed data used to obtain a health registration.

Colombia's Special Investigative IPR Unit, within the Prosecutor General's Office, has focused its efforts against violations of copyrights and theft of patent and trademark rights. In spite of increased actions to combat IPR violations, deterrent penalties and serious criminal sentences are still rare.

In an effort to improve Colombia's enforcement efforts, President Uribe signed a criminal reform law in 2006, establishing new offenses and increasing the penalties for violation of intellectual property rights, including the illegal broadcasting of copyrighted material.

The United States-Colombia Trade Promotion Agreement (CTPA) was signed in 2006 and, upon entry into force, would provide for improved standards for the protection and enforcement of a broad range of intellectual property rights.

Extradition

An extradition treaty with the United States permits the extradition of U.S. citizens.

Workers' Rights

Although the Colombian government has taken significant steps to improve enforcement of worker rights, concerns remain, in particular regarding violence against union members. In 2009, a government protection program provided protection measures to 1,550 trade unionists, accounting for 14 percent of persons under government protection. The Colombian government is also taking steps to combat actions taken with impunity and address a backlog of cases of crimes against trade unionists and other vulnerable groups. With U.S. Government assistance, in 2008 Colombia completed the transition to an accusatorial-style criminal justice system, replacing the inquisitorial system that had proven cumbersome and inefficient.

In addition, the Colombian Prosecutor General's Office expanded its Human Rights Office in 2006 to include a sub-unit focusing on the investigation and prosecution of murder cases in which the victims were labor union members. The sub-unit began with eight prosecutors and in 2008 expanded to 19 prosecutors, 19 assistant lawyers, and 78 investigators. It works closely with local prosecutors from around the country who are also handling murder cases in which the victims were labor union members. Since 2000, the Prosecutor General's Office has obtained 248 convictions involving 350 individuals in crimes with union member victims, with 199 of these convictions (80 percent of total convictions) coming since the initiation of the labor subunit. The sub-unit has three convictions thus far in

2010. In addition, since 2008 the Colombian judiciary has assigned three specialized judges to hear exclusively cases involving violence against unionists and in 2009, the Colombian Congress passed a law to increase prison sentences and extend the statute of limitations for homicides against union members.

The ILO sent a high-level mission to Colombia in October 2009 to review labor issues. The mission met with government officials, trade union leaders, and business representatives, and reported some progress on the violence issues as well as certain labor code reforms. In a 2010 report, the ILO Committee of Experts recognized Colombia's efforts to combat violence in general and noted a decrease in violent acts against trade unionists. The ILO also commended Colombia for strengthening criminal penalties and prison sentences for perpetrators of violence against union members. The ILO expressed hope in this report that Colombia's actions will lead to an effective way to address violence against union members and prosecute those responsible for these crimes.

Colombia has ratified all eight of the core International Labor Organization conventions. Colombian law recognizes the rights of workers to organize, bargain collectively, and strike.

Unions are free to affiliate with international labor confederations. The labor code provides for automatic recognition of unions that obtain 25 signatures from potential members and comply with a registration process. There are penalties for interfering with workers' freedom of association, and the labor code prohibits the dissolution or suspension of trade unions by administrative fiat. In 2008, Colombia's Constitutional Court issued a ruling concerning the process for registering new unions with the Ministry of Social Protection (MSP), and this action seems to have resolved longstanding concerns that the process was slow and used to block union formation.

The Constitution provides for the right to strike, and workers exercise this right in practice. However, members of the armed forces, police, and persons executing "essential public services," are not permitted to strike. Before staging a strike, public sector unions must negotiate directly with management. Confederations and federations are also prohibited from striking. The law prohibits the use of strikebreakers. Based on new labor legislation that went into effect in 2008, the MSP can no longer send strikes that are not resolved within 60 days to a tripartite arbitration tribunal, where a binding resolution was issued. As confirmed by the Government of Colombia to the ILO, both parties must now agree to arbitration. The new law, as amended by a subsequent Constitutional Court decision, also moved the power to declare strikes illegal from the executive branch to the judicial branch. Colombia's Free Trade Zones are covered under national labor laws.

Specific concerns remain about the consistency of Colombia's labor laws with core labor standards, especially allegations of widespread misuse of cooperatives to prevent workers from forming unions and bargaining collectively. In response to concerns identified by the ILO, Colombia has enacted new laws that require workers' cooperatives to pay into the social security system and benefits programs, and levy heftier fines on cooperatives that do not comply with current laws. Despite these efforts, labor groups claim that cooperatives remain largely unregulated and continue to be used by employers to deny basic worker rights. The ILO has also noted concerns with the Colombian law that allows employers and non-union workers to conclude a "collective pact" when a union represents less than one-third of the employees in a workplace. The ILO committee of experts has noted that bargaining with non-union workers should only be permitted in the absence of unions.

Forced or compulsory labor is prohibited by law. The minimum age of employment is fifteen, compatible with ILO Convention 138. Although the labor code mandates special authorization for minors between fifteen and seventeen years of age to work, child labor remains an issue. The Colombian government is making efforts to address the problem through several initiatives, including ILO child labor programs funded by the U.S. Department of Labor. Colombia has ratified ILO Convention 182 on the worst forms of child labor. The Colombian government has designated authority to implement and enforce child labor laws to the Family Ombudsman's offices, Human Rights Ombudsman's offices, Family Welfare Institute and community police officers.

The government establishes a uniform minimum wage every year through tripartite negotiations among representatives of business, organized labor, and the government. Colombia has extensive regulations providing for the occupational safety and health of workers, but regulations are difficult to enforce due to an under-resourced labor inspectorate and the large percentage of workers in the informal sector who are not covered by the social insurance systems.

Economic Conditions

The revival of Colombia's economy in recent years can be attributed to increased security, strong internal demand, a resilient global market for commodities, ATPA/ATPDEA-driven exports, and, increasingly, the numerous free trade agreements and bilateral investment treaties Colombia has negotiated. Real GDP growth in 2009 was 0.4 percent, relatively strong given the global downturn and negative growth in most of the region. Growth between 2003 and 2007 averaged 5.6 percent. According to UNCTAD and Central Bank figures, the stock of global FDI in Colombia increased from $3.9 billion in 1992 to an estimated $72 billion in 2009, with annual flows increasing from $1.4 billion in 1994 to approximately $9.5 billion in 2009. The stock of U.S. FDI in Colombia was $9.9 billion in 2008, a 22 percent increase from 2007. Unemployment rose to 14 percent in January 2010. Poverty rates dropped from 54 percent in 2002 to 46 percent in 2008.

The Uribe Administration has pushed an aggressive trade agenda, which includes FTAs, BITs and Double Taxation Agreements (DTA). Besides the CTPA, Colombia signed FTAs with Chile in 2006; Central America's North Triangle (Guatemala, Honduras and El Salvador) in 2007; Canada and the European Free Trade Association, or EFTA (Switzerland, Norway, Iceland and Liechtenstein) in 2008; and concluded negotiations in 2010 with the European Union. Colombia is now negotiating FTAs with Panama and South Korea.

Market Access

Colombia has opened its economy considerably since the early 1990s. Customs duties have been cut and many non-tariff barriers eliminated. Most duties have been consolidated into three tariff levels: zero percent to five percent on capital goods, industrial goods and raw materials not produced in Colombia; 10 percent on manufactured goods with some exceptions; and 15 percent to 20 percent on consumer and "sensitive" goods.

Some important exceptions include automobiles, which are subject to a 35 percent tariff, and many agricultural products, which fall under a variable "price band" import duty system. The price band system includes 14 product groups and covers more than 150 tariff lines. When international prices surpass the price band ceiling, tariffs are reduced; when prices drop below the price band floor, tariffs are raised. At times this results in duties approaching or exceeding 100 percent for important U.S. exports to Colombia, including corn, wheat, rice, soybeans, pork, poultry, cheeses, and powdered milk. These duties have negatively affected U.S. access. Moreover, as Colombia's free trade agreements with other countries enter into force and tariffs gradually phase out, the United States will continue to lose market share, particularly in agricultural commodities.

The United States and Colombia have resolved a number of sanitary and phytosanitary (SPS) barriers to agricultural trade. In 2006, Colombia formalized its recognition of the equivalence of the U.S. meat and poultry inspection systems. The two sides reached agreement on the specific contents of U.S. sanitary certificates accompanying U.S. poultry and poultry products to Colombia. However, the Ministry of Agriculture through its sanitary and phytosanitary regulatory agency, the Colombian Agricultural Institute (ICA), has imposed separate import requirements, which have negatively impacted U.S. exports of cooked poultry meat and egg products. Since 2007, the National Institute for Surveillance of Food and Medicines (INVIMA) has been applying food safety measures which appear to be inconsistent with international standards, and U.S. officials are working with INVIMA to resolve these issues.

Participation in Free Trade Negotiations

On February 27, 2006, the United States and Colombia announced the conclusion of negotiations on a comprehensive, state-of-the-art trade agreement. On November 22, 2006, the United States-Colombia Trade Promotion Agreement (CTPA) was signed in Washington, D.C. by Deputy U.S. Trade Representative John K. Veroneau and Colombian Trade Minister Jorge Humberto Botero. The United States and Colombia amended the CTPA in June 2007, to include provisions reflecting the May 10 bipartisan agreement with the U.S. Congress. The Colombian legislature ratified the CTPA in 2007. The U.S. Congress has not yet voted on legislation approving and implementing the agreement.

Subsidies or Other Requirements that Distort International Trade

Colombia has notified the WTO that its free trade zone (FTZ) regime, the special import-export (Plan Vallejo) system, and the tax reimbursement certificate (CERT) program, contain export subsidies. The Colombian government issued Law 1004 in December 2005, which provides for a 15 percent profit tax on industrial and services companies operating within FTZs. The profit tax rate for companies outside of FTZs is 33 percent. The Plan Vallejo program allows for tariff exemptions on the import of capital goods and raw materials used to manufacture goods that are subsequently exported. The CERT program had been reactivated in 2008 to fight the effects of a strong peso, but no certificates have been issued since August of that year.

Regional Trade Policies

Colombia is a member of the Andean Community of Nations (CAN). Colombian exports to CAN countries (including Venezuela, which is nominally bound by its CAN commitments for five years from its 2006 withdrawal) totaled $6.1 billion in 2009, about 18 percent of Colombia’s entire exports. Imports from these countries totaled $2 billion in 2009, about 6.5 percent of total imports. Trade with Venezuela dropped by almost 70 percent after Venezuela imposed unilateral restrictions on Colombian exports in 2009. Colombian exports to

MERCOSUR were $694 million in 2009, while imports, primarily from Brazil, reached $2 billion. Imports from Mexico were $2.1 billion in 2009.

The Colombian government already has negotiated or is pursuing trade accords with many countries in the region. It has free trade on most goods with Bolivia, Ecuador, and Peru within the Andean Community arrangement. Colombia is a member of ALADI, which promotes economic integration and cooperation in the region. Colombia signed a trade agreement with the members of MERCOSUR in 2004. Colombia is in the process of implementing its FTA with Guatemala, Honduras, and El Salvador. In 2009, Colombia's FTA with Chile entered into force. Also in 2009, Colombia and Mexico concluded negotiations of an updated free trade agreement, which will replace the more limited G-2 agreement of 1995. The Colombian government is working actively to join APEC.

Narcotics and Counter-terrorism Cooperation

The Colombian government continues to make significant progress in its vigorous fight against the production and trafficking of illicit drugs. In recent years Colombia has met or exceeded all of its identified narcotics cooperation certification criteria under the U.S. Foreign Assistance Act of 1961. Colombia is actively investigating and prosecuting cases against drug traffickers and cooperating with U.S. judicial authorities to provide evidence and witnesses for prosecutions of extradited Colombian nationals facing trial in the United States. The Colombian government has also begun to address increasing domestic drug consumption and has raised the profile of drug prevention and treatment efforts. Colombia is a party to the 1988 UN Drug Convention.

Total eradication of coca in Colombia in 2009 was 165,272 hectares. The Colombian security forces' seizure of 288 MT of cocaine and cocaine base last year was a record, and significant quantities of heroin and precursor chemicals were also taken from the market. They also destroyed 3,080 hydrochloride (HCl) and coca base processing labs. According to the Drug Enforcement Agency, the price of cocaine increased by 72 percent and purity decreased by 45 percent from January 2007 to December 2009. Record seizures and sustained coca eradication played a role in producing an increase in the price and a reduction in purity of cocaine in the United States.

Citing record coca eradication in 2008, the U.S. Government and the United Nations reported separately significant declines in Colombian cocaine production potential and coca cultivation in Colombia in 2009. The U.S. Government reported that cultivation in 2008 was down 29 percent compared to 2007 – the largest ever decline in cultivation cited by the U.S. Government and the first reported drop since 2002. The U.S. Government, crediting sustained aerial eradication operations in 2008, also reported a decline in pure cocaine production potential to 295 MT, 39 percent less compared to 2007 and 58 percent less than the reported 2001 high of 700 MT.

The Colombian government remains a key ally of the United States in the fight against drug trafficking, and Colombian officials have repeatedly emphasized in public that the narcotics threat is a major challenge to solidifying stability and the rule of law in Colombia. The United States works closely with Colombian law enforcement and military authorities to eradicate coca and opium poppy, detect and seize illegal drug shipments, prosecute drug traffickers and terrorists, and extradite those who have violated U.S. law, while providing alternative development options to deter replanting of coca and encourage legal livelihoods. Colombia's commitment to addressing the drug trade is also exemplified by its willingness to work closely with the United States on the transfer of operational and financial responsibility for several counternarcotics programs.

Colombia's increased law enforcement efforts and expansion of government control into previously hard-to-govern areas is ongoing under President Uribe's National Consolidation Plan. Under this approach, security, counternarcotics, rule of law, and economic and alternative development opportunities are being closely coordinated in critical regions of the country to facilitate stability and democratic growth. Homicides, kidnappings, and acts of terrorism have dropped dramatically over the last decade, and the United States is supporting Colombian government efforts to expand government institutions and services into rural and former conflict regions.

Colombian security forces captured or killed a number of mid-level FARC leaders, promoted the reintegration into society of former combatants, and reduced the amount of territory in which guerillas could freely operate. The Colombian military disrupted the FARC's communications network, destroyed major caches of weapon and supplies, and reduced the group's financial resources through counternarcotics and other security operations.

Government Procurement

Colombia is an observer, but not a signatory, to the WTO Agreement on Government Procurement.

Law 816 of 2003 mandates that all public entities accord preferential treatment to bids that incorporate Colombian goods or services. Under Law 816, national companies are given a 10 percent to 20 percent "bonus" in their evaluation score, and companies using Colombian goods or services are given a five percent to 15 percent "bonus." Bids without any local content are scored between five percent and 20 percent lower than bids with such a component. Additionally, Law 816 requires that foreign suppliers without local headquarters in Colombia obtain certification from a Colombian mission in the supplier's home country that government procurement laws in the supplier's home country meet reciprocity requirements. This law has created a barrier to participation by U.S. suppliers in Colombian government procurement. Colombia will have to remove these barriers when the CTPA enters into force.

Ecuador

Effect of ATPA/ATPDEA

In 2009, U.S. goods imports from Ecuador totaled $5.2 billion, a 42 percent decrease from 2008. ATPA/ATPDEA entries from Ecuador decreased 58 percent to $2.7 billion in 2009, from $6.6 billion in 2008. Petroleum products ($2.4 billion) overwhelmingly dominated such imports from Ecuador, accounting for 88 percent in 2009, lower than the shares of over 90 percent in each of the previous four years. Other important imports under ATPA/ATPDEA from Ecuador in 2009 were cut flowers ($118 million), down 11 percent in 2009 compared with 2008; tuna ($57 million), down 31 percent; vegetables ($41 million), down 5 percent; vegetable and fruit preparations ($36 million), up 28 percent; and fruits, primarily fresh pineapples, fresh mangoes, and frozen fruits ($35 million), up 28 percent.

U.S.-Ecuador Trade (Millions of Dollars)

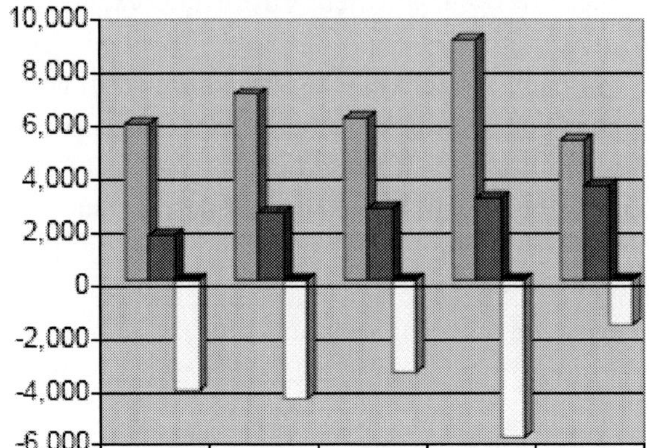

	2005	2006	2007	2008	2009
U.S. Imports	5,874	7,011	6,131	9,044	5,246
U.S. Exports	1,733	2,548	2,709	3,150	3,589
Trade Balance	-4,141	-4,463	-3,422	-5,894	-1,656

Population: 14,573,101; (July 2009 est.) GDP per capita (PPP): $7,300 (2009 est.)
Source: 2010 World Fact Book.

Expropriations

Under Ecuadorian law, individuals have the right to petition a judge to establish the appropriate price for expropriated property. The Agrarian Development Law restricts the grounds for expropriation of agricultural land and provides for adjudication of disputes in the courts. While cases of land expropriation have been infrequent, the Ecuadorian government has announced that it intends to start expropriating "unused" agricultural land and provide it to small landless producers (under Ecuadorian law, land that has been "unused" for two years may be expropriated). Under the United States-Ecuador BIT, expropriation of U.S. investments can only be carried out only for a public purpose, in a nondiscriminatory manner, in accordance with due process of law, and upon payment of prompt, adequate, and effective compensation.

Arbitral Awards

The United States-Ecuador BIT provides for international arbitration of disputes at the investor's initiative. However, developments in the past year give rise to concerns as to the government's commitment to international arbitration for the settlement of investor disputes. In September 2009, the government requested the Ecuadorian National Assembly approve termination of 13 BITs, including the BIT with the United States, stating that the BIT's provisions on international arbitration and national treatment conflict with the country's 2008 Constitution. As of publication, the National Assembly had returned the request to the Executive, pending a Constitutional Court opinion; for the moment, the United States-Ecuador BIT remains in force. Separately, in July 2009, the government submitted written notice of its withdrawal from ICSID, again citing conflicts with the 2008 Constitution.

Ecuador's withdrawal from the ICSID became effective on January 7, 2010; however, the government continues to participate in pending international arbitration cases.

In March 2010, a U.S. company won an arbitral award against Ecuador for violating the United States-Ecuador BIT by failing to provide effective means of resolving commercial disputes in Ecuadorian courts. The case relates to claims filed in Ecuador by the company in the early 1990s, the resolution of which the arbitral tribunal held to have been unduly delayed. The government has indicated that it intends to contest the arbitral award. In September 2009, the same U.S. company filed another arbitration under the BIT, claiming, among other things, government mistreatment in connection with a longstanding lawsuit pending against the company in an Ecuadorian court. The Ecuadorian government sought a stay of the arbitration in U.S. federal court, but that request was denied. The Ecuadorian government is appealing this decision.

Reverse Preferences

The U.S. Government has no indication that Ecuador has granted such preferences to the products of a developed nation.

Intellectual Property

Ecuador's intellectual property regime is governed by the "Law on Intellectual Property" adopted in 1998 and by various Andean Community decisions. The law provides criminal and administrative relief to right holders. Patents, trademarks, and industrial designs are protected by Andean Community Decisions 344 (the Common Industrial Property Regime) and 345 (the Common Regime to Protect Plant Varieties). Copyrights are protected by Andean Community Decision 351 (the Common Regime on Copyright and Neighboring Rights) and Decision 486 (the Common Regime on Industrial Property). The Ecuadorian Intellectual Property Institute (IEPI) was established in January 1999 to handle patent, trademark, and copyright registrations on the Ecuadorian government's behalf.

The Ecuadorian government is a member of several international conventions that concern intellectual property, including the following:

- Convention Establishing the World Intellectual Property Organization (WIPO);
- Berne Convention for the Protection of Literary and Artistic Works;
- Patent Cooperation Treaty;
- WIPO Copyright Treaty;
- WIPO Performances and Phonograms Treaty; and
- Paris Convention for the Protection of Industrial Property.

Works are protected under copyright law for the life of the author plus 70 years. A 2006 decision by Ecuador's Supreme Court upheld the right of music composers to be compensated by television and radio stations who broadcast their compositions. The Ecuadorian government has not taken action, however, to clarify that Article 78 of the 1999 Law on Higher Education does not permit software copyright infringement by educational institutions.

Trademark registration is permitted for renewable 10 year periods. Ecuador's IPR law provides protections for well-known trademarks. The time for processing trademark applications has been reduced from 24 months in 2007 to four months in 2009. Local registration of unauthorized copies of well-known trademarks has also been reduced.

The IPR law also provides protection for industrial designs and extends protection to industrial secrets and geographical indications. Semiconductor chip layouts are protected. Plant varieties and other biotechnology products are also protected.

In 2009, IEPI continued an anti-piracy campaign entitled "Ecuador is Original," which features popular Ecuadorian recording artists promoting an anti-piracy message. The campaign was disseminated via national radio, IEPI's website, and You Tube. In 2009, IEPI also organized several seminars to increase public awareness of the importance of copyrights, trademarks, and patents.

Despite the laws on the books, intellectual property rights protection and enforcement remain major problems in Ecuador. The national police and the Customs Corporation of Ecuador (CAE) are responsible for carrying out IPR enforcement orders, but it is sometimes difficult to have court orders enforced.

IEPI and Ecuadorian Customs have enforcement actions in their areas of competence where they can act with or without a formal complaint by the right holder, through administrative sanctions imposed by IEPI or the interception of counterfeit goods by Customs. Both the number of administrative actions initiated by right holders that IEPI has resolved and seizures by Ecuadorian Customs fell in 2009. In 2008, the Prosecutor General's office and Ecuadorian Customs created special IPR units focused on investigations, fines, and seizures. However, the effectiveness of these units appears to be limited. The Ecuadorian government has not yet established specialized IPR courts as required under its current IPR law.

Piracy in products with copyright and trademark protection is pervasive. Pirated CDs and DVDs are found on many street corners and in shops, and the import and sale of products that infringe registered trademarks are common. Sellers of pirated goods sell their illegal wares with little fear of prosecution. In April 2001, USTR removed Ecuador from its Special 301 Watch List to reflect improvements in Ecuador's IPR regime. However, weakened enforcement efforts led to Ecuador's re-listing in 2003, and it has remained on the Watch List since that time.

The IPR law extends patent protection for 20 years from the date of filing. A 2006 Superior Court decision upheld the right of patent holders to have infringing copies of their patented products removed from the market. However, the Ministry of Industry has accepted for review a petition filed in September 2009 alleging that a 2007 case of a U.S. pharmaceutical company successfully defending its patent constituted an abuse of market position. The petition is still under review by the Ministry of Industry.

The amount of time required to process a patent application has been reduced from nine years in 2007 to six years in 2009. IEPI aims to further reduce the processing time to five years.

The Ecuadorian government has implemented a policy concerning compulsory licensing of certain patented inventions. Presidential decrees establishing policy frameworks for issuing compulsory licenses for patented pharmaceutical products and agrochemicals were issued in October 2009 and December 2009, respectively. On January 15, 2010, IEPI issued detailed requirements and procedures for applying for compulsory licenses for pharmaceutical products; procedures for agricultural chemicals are not yet in place.

IEPI has established two types of compulsory licenses for pharmaceuticals, those for public noncommercial use and those for commercial use. The resolution defines public non-commercial use as "the acquisition of pharmaceuticals by any Ecuadorian public sector entity in order to meet the needs of its health programs." A license for non-commercial use allows for the production or importation of a product, primarily for domestic use.

Licenses for commercial use are limited to production (there is no importation provision), primarily to supply the domestic market. In addition, a potential licensee must also provide evidence that they have attempted to obtain the authorization of the right holder on "reasonable commercial terms and conditions" and that they did not receive a favorable response within 45 days. For both types of licenses, the resolution states that IEPI will establish the level of remuneration to the patent holder.

On April 14, 2010, the Ecuadorian government issued its first compulsory license. The license stated that it was for public non-commercial use of an HIV/AIDS treatment drug patented by a U.S. company.

Extradition

An extradition treaty with the United States permits the extradition of U.S. citizens.

Workers' Rights

Ecuador has ratified all eight of the ILO core labor conventions.

Most workers in the private and parastatal sectors have the constitutional right to form trade unions and local law allows for unionization of any company with at least 30 employees. Private employers are required to engage in collective bargaining with recognized unions. The labor code prohibits discrimination against unions and requires that employers provide space for union activities. It also provides for resolution of conflicts through a tripartite arbitration and conciliation board process, although the tripartite boards were no longer meeting as of February 2009.

Except for public servants and workers in some parastatals, workers by law have the right to strike in most sectors. Under the law, employees that do not fall into the technical, administrative, or professional categories may join a union and bargain collectively. Public sector employees in strategic sectors, as designated in the new Constitution, may not take any action that paralyzes those sectors, including striking. The Constitution lists health, environmental sanitation, education, justice, the fire brigade, social security, electrical energy, drinking water and sewerage, hydrocarbon production, the processing, transport and distribution of fuel, public transport, and post and telecommunications as strategic sectors. Most public employees maintained membership in a labor sector association. Such associations are not allowed to strike or bargain collectively.

Legally striking employees are entitled to full pay and benefits and may occupy the premises under police protection, although there are restrictions on solidarity strikes. The law does not require reinstatement of workers fired for union activity, but does require compensation and fines. Although trade union political influence has declined in recent years, labor groups occasionally attempt to stage national strikes to protest economic reform measures.

Ecuador's 2008 Constitution provides additional language regarding worker rights. Revisions to the Labor Code to reflect this are expected eventually. The Constitution includes new language promoting the democratic, participatory, and transparent functioning of labor unions. It prohibits any type of outsourcing or partial contracting for activities that are part of a company's core business. Outsourcing had been used in the past by some companies to have a more flexible workforce, prevent formation of unions and to avoid some labor obligations. Most companies have re-hired workers on a permanent basis. In the past, most workers in export processing zones were hired on temporary contracts, and did not appear to be protected by some elements of the labor code. The status of these types of contracts under the 2008 Constitution is unclear.

The Constitution and the labor code prohibit forced labor. The law also prohibits the employment of persons under the age of fifteen, except in special circumstances, such as an apprenticeship. Enforcement of this provision is uneven, especially in rural communities. Ecuador's National Institute of Statistics and Census' National Child Labor Survey found that the number of children between the ages of five and fourteen working illegally fell from 550,000 in 2001 to 367,000 in 2006. The children were working primarily in rural areas in the informal sector. The Ecuadorian government utilizes 29 child labor inspectors. These inspectors have the authority to cite violations and sanction companies and employers found to have illegally hired child labor. During the year the inspectors conducted 3,992 workplace inspections and removed 2,056 minors working in dangerous conditions in violation of labor laws.

Ecuador's labor code provides for a 40 hour work week, 15 calendar days of annual paid vacation, restrictions on child labor, general protection of worker health and safety, minimum wages and bonuses, 90 days of maternity leave, and employer-provided benefits. Ecuador's legislative commission passed a 15 day paternity leave law on February 9, 2009. By law, companies must distribute at least 15 percent of pre-tax profits to their employees.

Workers have the constitutional right to a healthy and safe work environment. A worker may request that an inspector from the Ministry of Labor and Employment investigate a workplace hazard; if confirmed, the inspector may close down the workplace. Response time for inspectors ranges from three days in major cities to much longer in the countryside.

The minimum wage was increased 18 percent in 2008, another 9 percent in 2009 and 10 percent in 2010, but there are concerns that a family earning only 1.6 minimum wages would not have sufficient income to afford the basic consumption basket ($528.90 in December 2009). Most organized workers in state industries and in the formal sector (private enterprises) earn more than the minimum wage and are provided other significant benefits through collective bargaining. However, the majority of workers are employed in the large informal sector, and these workers do not have recourse to the minimum wage, social security, or legally mandated benefits.

Economic Conditions

In March 2000, Ecuador adopted the U.S. dollar as its national currency in response to a serious economic crisis. Dollarization, combined with responsible fiscal policies, helped tame inflation and bring the country back to positive growth and economic stability. The economy grew 3.9 percent in 2006 but slowed to 2.5 percent in 2007, constrained by declining petroleum production and reduced private sector investment. The economy grew by 7.2 percent in 2008 due to high oil prices and increased government spending. However, by the end of 2008 the Ecuadorian economy began to experience the consequences of the global economic crisis, as oil prices dropped sharply, remittances from Ecuadorians abroad fell, and Ecuador realized a trade deficit for the last four months of the year, causing its balance of payments to deteriorate. These trends continued through the first quarter of 2009. Starting with the last quarter of 2008, Ecuador experienced three consecutive quarters of economic contraction.

Ecuador's balance of payments improved in the second and third quarters of 2009 with an improvement in the trade balance, mainly the result of rebounding oil prices, a recovery in remittance inflows from abroad, and import restrictions. By the third quarter of 2009, as the world economic crisis eased and international oils prices rebounded, Ecuador's economy began to recover. Ecuador's Central Bank estimated 0.36 percent economic growth for 2009. Ecuador registered a trade deficit of $332 million in 2009. Annual inflation was 8.8 percent in 2008, but fell to 4.3 percent in 2009.

In April 2006, Ecuador revised its hydrocarbons law requiring companies to share at least 50 percent of extraordinary revenues with the government. In 2007, this share was increased to 99 percent, prompting some companies to sell their assets to the government and leave the country, and others to initiate international arbitration cases claiming the government breached its contract by unilaterally changing the rules. The windfall tax rate was subsequently lowered to 70 percent for new contracts. In 2006 and 2007 the Ecuadorian government sought to renegotiate petroleum production contracts with foreign oil companies, but did not reach agreement. In 2008, the government signed new short-term agreements with a number of foreign oil companies but stated that it intended to negotiate long-term agreements based on a new service contract model, transitioning away from production sharing contracts. A few companies have converted to service contracts, but most others negotiated interim production sharing agreements.

In September 2009, the government circulated a draft Hydrocarbons Law, but it has yet to submit the legislation to the National Assembly. While last year the government discussed in general terms a new model for service contracts, it did not provide the text of the new model to foreign oil companies until March 1, 2010. The government has stated that the foreign oil companies must sign new service contracts immediately, even though the new Hydrocarbons Law is not in place yet.

In December 2008, the Ecuadorian government defaulted on a commercial bond issuance, and in March 2009 defaulted on another commercial bond issuance. The government has continued to pay a third commercial bond issuance and has remained current on its obligations to multilateral lenders. The government presented a repurchasing proposal in April 2009, which allowed the repurchase of 73 percent ($ 2.9 billion) of the commercial debt in June 2009. This repurchase severely drained the government's liquidity and therefore reduced the level of the country's international reserves. However, the increase in international oil prices has contributed to increase reserve levels to $4.0 billion by April 1, 2010.

During the first nine months of 2008, the Ecuadorian government lowered the maximum interest rates for the banking sector on a monthly basis. However, since October 2008, downward adjustments of rates for corporate, small business, and housing lending have been frozen. Between June 2009 and January 2010, the interest rate ceiling for consumer credit was temporarily increased in an effort to reduce pressure on the financial sector. In May 2010, interest rates for microfinancing were reduced.

Outside of regulated sectors such as petroleum, mining, and banking, a number of companies reported that they enjoyed growing business for much of 2008 and 2009. A number of companies report that they have good access and a constructive relationship with the Correa Administration, although the private sector has noted concern with a number of the government's economic policies.

Ecuador's Central Bank has changed the methodology it uses to calculate foreign direct investment (FDI), and now only publishes net flows. According to the Central Bank, the net flow of FDI into Ecuador was $195 million in 2007, $993 million in 2008 and $467 million through the third quarter of 2009. In 2008, most of the FDI inflow was associated with renewal of telecommunication concessions. In 2009, FDI appears concentrated in the mining, transportation, and communication sectors.

According to Central Bank statistics, the net flow of U.S. FDI into Ecuador was $50 million in 2007, in contrast to net outflows of $18 million in 2008 and $34 million through the third quarter of 2009. According to the U.S. Bureau of Economic Analysis, the stock of U.S. FDI in Ecuador in 2008 was $1.3 billion, up from $977 million in 2007. For Ecuador to take full advantage of the potential investment benefits associated with the ATPA/ATPDEA, it would need to improve its investment climate by providing greater transparency and certainty for foreign investors.

Market Access

Ecuador's accession to the WTO in 1996 was an important step in improving access to Ecuador's market. However, a number of trade barriers remain, including a lack of transparency and inefficiency in the sanitary registration process, that have delayed and even blocked the entry of some agricultural imports from the United States.

Since 2007, Ecuador has taken a number of steps to reduce import tariffs on raw materials, inputs, and capital goods, while increasing tariffs on consumer goods. In August 2008, Ecuador also eliminated tariffs on airplanes and airplane parts. However, in January 2009, Ecuador imposed higher tariffs and quotas on a large number of imports from all countries, including those from the United States, at levels which exceeded their WTO bound rates. On February 18, 2009, Ecuador notified the WTO that it was invoking the WTO's balance of payments safeguard provisions as a justification for these measures. In response to concerns raised during meetings of the WTO Committee on Balance of Payment Restrictions, Ecuador committed to converting most quotas to tariffs, and to remove all trade measures imposed for balance of payments purposes no later than January 22, 2010. Ecuador did not remove the safeguard measures by January 22, 2010, but instead began implementing a phase-out of the measures that is to be completed by July 23, 2010. The U.S. Government has raised concerns within the WTO Committee on Balance of Payment Restrictions over Ecuador's failure to keep to the January 22, 2010 deadline for eliminating the safeguards, and continues to consult with Ecuador on this issue.

Although Ecuador phased out prior authorization requirements for most imports, Ecuador still requires prior authorization for importing approximately 80 agricultural products. For certain sensitive products such as corn, soybean meal, dairy, and poultry, the Minister of Agriculture or a designee must sign the import authorization. The Ministry of Health is required to provide prior authorization for imports of processed, canned, and packaged products in the form of a sanitary registration. The ability to import some products, such as rice, corn, soybeans, and soybean meal, depends on the Ministry of Agriculture's use of "consultative committees," which authorize imports of bulk commodities based on a complex supply and demand assessment.

Ecuador's import ban on all U.S. live cattle, beef, and beef products due to BSE-related concerns following the detection of a BSE positive animal in the United States in 2003 has remained in effect. However, Andean Community Resolution 1314, promulgated on April 20, 2010, allows each member (Ecuador, Bolivia, Colombia, and Peru) to develop its own regulations regarding the importation of live cattle from the United States. Development of those regulations in Ecuador is ongoing.

AGROCALIDAD, the new agency established in December 2008 with responsibility for animal and plant health and food safety, began by recruiting 90 new professional staff. The Ministry of Agriculture has recently announced plans to reorganize the agency with responsibilities for implementation of animal and plant health programs, such as the foot-and-mouth eradication efforts, being shifted to the Ministry, with AGROCALIDAD being solely responsible for the development and enforcement of sanitary and phyto-sanitary regulations.

As a member of the CAN, Ecuador grants and receives exemptions on tariffs for trade with its CAN partners. A common external tariff (CET) on some products for third party imports into the Andean Community was implemented on January 31, 2006.

In December 2008, the Ecuadorian Quality Council (CONCAL) issued new conformity assessment procedures for several products including lubricants, some automotive parts, tires, apparel, footwear, and appliances, among others. These measures did not provide a transition period for exporters and importers to adjust to the new measures; the immediate implementation disrupted some exports. In January 2009, CONCAL issued a new conformity assessment regulation that relaxed conformity assessment procedures.

Ecuador previously had a pre-shipment inspection (PSI) regime, which added six to eight weeks to shipping times. In October 2007, the PSI regime was replaced with a risk analysis system run by the Ecuadorian Customs Agency. Under the system, low-risk importers benefit from fewer physical inspections and expedited release of their cargo. The law also included changes to customs processes and requirements in an effort to reduce costs and minimize delays for importers.

Ecuador's foreign investment policy is governed largely by the national implementing legislation for Andean Community Decisions 291 and 292 of 1991 and 1993, respectively Foreign investors are accorded the same rights of entry as Ecuadorian private investors, may own up to 100 percent of enterprises in most sectors without prior government approval, and face the same tax regime. Constitutional provisions directing the State to prioritize domestic private investment could impact the right of entry in the future. In December, 2007, the Ecuadorian government passed a broad tax reform package, which included establishing a 0.5 percent tax on capital outflows. This tax was increased to one percent in December 2008 and to two percent effective January 1, 2010. There are no performance requirements associated with foreign investment in Ecuador other than local content requirements in the automotive sector.

Certain sectors of the economy are reserved to the state. All foreign investment in petroleum and mining exploration and development in Ecuador must be carried out under a contract with the government. Foreign investment in domestic fishing operations is subject to approval by the National Fishery Development Council based on a favorable report from the National Fishing Institute. Commercial fishing by foreign companies is permitted provided that the catch is processed in Ecuador.

Participation in Free Trade Negotiations

In May 2004, the United States initiated negotiations on an FTA with Colombia, Ecuador, and Peru. Bolivia participated as an observer. To date, the United States has concluded FTAs with Peru and Colombia. Negotiations with Ecuador were suspended and were not concluded. In July 2009, Ecuador suspended negotiations with the European Community on an association agreement, but is exploring resumption of these negotiations.

Subsidies or Other Requirements that Distort International Trade

Ecuador does not use export subsidies.

Ecuador maintains a local crop absorption program based on Ministerial Agreement 067 of February 20, 1978. This measure prohibits imports of soybean meal and corn during the local harvest season. Ecuador committed to eliminate this ruling during its WTO accession. Nevertheless, it is still being implemented and enforced through Ministerial Agreement 347 of December 14, 2004. Through this program, the industry is obliged to purchase 100 percent of the local production of the aforementioned commodities, usually at high prices set by consultative committees that are often dominated by local producers, before imports of these commodities are allowed.

Ecuador's 2008 Constitution declares Ecuador free of biotechnology crops and seeds. However, the Constitution grants the President the authority to allow for imports of agricultural crops and seeds that may have been produced using biotechnology under exceptional circumstance in the national interest. These provisions require further implementing legislation and regulations. A new Food Sovereignty Law, which was expected to further define the framework for biotechnology products in Ecuador, is in the final stages of the approval process. The law is very general and requires implementing regulations for clarification. The law would provide a broad legislative framework for the use of biotechnology. In the interim, biotechnology cultivation and imports have continued normally. Interested private sector industries are working with Ecuadorian authorities to develop implementing regulations that will not impede trade in products derived from biotechnology.

Regional Trade Policies

As noted above, Ecuador is a member of the Andean Community. According to the Ecuadorian government, the Andean Community absorbed 16 percent of Ecuador's exports and provided 22 percent of its imports in 2009. Ecuador has signed a number of cooperation agreements with countries in the region, including Venezuela and Peru, on topics including energy and social development. Ecuador is also a member of the Latin American Integration Association (ALADI). ALADI countries purchased 24 percent of Ecuador's exports and supplied 37 percent of its imports in 2009. Ecuador has broad agreements for the liberalization of trade in goods with Chile and MERCOSUR. In 2008, Ecuador signed an association agreement with Chile, which included extending and broadening the existing economic complementation agreement. Ecuador also has agreements with Cuba and Mexico that establish tariff preferences for a limited number of products.

Narcotics and Counter-Terrorism Cooperation

For fiscal year 2010, Ecuador was found to have not failed demonstrably in its counternarcotics cooperation with the United States in a Presidential Determination announced in September 2009. Ecuador is not a significant coca-producing country, but is exploited significantly as a transit zone and, to a lesser but growing extent, for processing. With the support of the U.S. Government, Ecuador maintains an active drug detection and interdiction program. Its programs focus on interdiction, police training, drug detection, information sharing, demand reduction, and control of money laundering. The U.S. Government has also supported the implementation of a new criminal procedures code, adopted in 2001, with police and judicial training. In October 2005, Ecuador adopted a new money laundering law, and the U.S. Government has been supporting its implementation. The Ecuadorian government is now working to strengthen its Financial Intelligence Unit to better monitor financial transactions and identify illegal activities.

Ecuador's National Drug Council (CONSEP) activity against trafficking in controlled precursor chemicals continued at a high level. However, CONSEP is still not funded at a level consistent with its broad responsibilities. The Ecuadorian government has continued to reinforce its security presence in the northern border area with an increased number of military operations each year since 2007.

The Counternarcotics Directorate (DNA) of the National Police was increased from 1,385 to 1,700 members in 2009, and remains at that level. New DNA bases and stations were opened with U.S. Government assistance in 2007 in Carchi Province at Tulcan and the Port of Esmeraldas in Esmeraldas Province, both near the Colombian border. New DNA facilities are under construction now at the Port of Guayaquil and near Ecuador's Southern Border in Catamayo, also with U.S. assistance.

The Ecuadorian government continues to work with the U.S. Government to reduce trafficking through Ecuador. Ecuador has criminalized the production, transport, and sale of controlled narcotic substances. Although smuggling of precursor chemicals through Ecuador remains a problem, the Ecuadorian government is making efforts to monitor and control these chemicals and to interdict processing laboratories. Nonetheless, it appears that despite Ecuadorian efforts, transshipment of narcotics through Ecuadorian maritime and land routes to the United States has increased in recent years, although the flow is likely flat at the moment.

In general, Ecuadorian law enforcement agencies cooperated well with U.S. and certain other foreign law enforcement agencies in 2009. However, Ecuadorian government actions in early 2009 that prompted the U.S. Government to end its cooperation with specialized police units, and the subsequent expulsion of members of the U.S. Mission, have continued to have negative effects on the traditionally close cooperation between the two governments. For example, there continues to be disagreement over U.S. government requirements for vetting of specialized police units. Nonetheless, cooperation continues with some police units and on a case-by-case basis, such as the action in April 2010 that was taken based on U.S. and Colombian Interpol warrants to arrest and deport Ramon Quintero, founding member of the Colombian North Valley Cartel. However, in a separate case, in April 2010, the President of Ecuador denied the U.S. request for extradition of narcotics trafficker and Colombian citizen Danilo Nieves to the Southern District of California. Despite an attempt by Nieves to avoid extradition and gain freedom by submitting requests to the Ecuadorian government for refugee status and asylum, which were denied, he remains incarcerated, as Ecuadorian prosecutors pursue new charges against him for the use of false identification documents. A judge has approved preventative detention based on these new charges. If found guilty, Nieves could serve another six to nine years in prison.

There are serious concerns that flaws in Ecuador's Law of Migration, or its application, may allow criminals to avoid justice by filing refugee/asylum petitions in Ecuador, turning the country into a haven for drug traffickers. The recent request by Colombian drug trafficker Danilo Nieves for refugee/asylum status prompted similar requests in May 2010 from two Mexicans and a Colombian who were facing deportation after completing sentences in Ecuador for drug trafficking. Their refugee/asylum petitions have provided them with temporary protection from deportation following their release from prison and their current whereabouts are unknown. Ecuador's current legislation affords any applicant for refugee status a lengthy review process during which time he or she cannot be deported.

Maritime cooperation has increased in recent years in response to a surge in maritime smuggling out of Ecuador. Ecuadorian forces, in cooperation with the United States, through training and access to new equipment, have adapted to a shift in trafficking patterns on the high seas from large multi-ton loads in fishing vessels to smaller loads on go-fast vessels that stay closer to shore. In the past several years, there has been a greater tendency toward the use of self-propelled semi-submersible vessels, which are capable of carrying multi-ton loads for long distances. Overall, traffickers appear to be bringing larger quantities of their product into Ecuador and storing them there for longer periods of time.

In September 2009, operations ceased at the Forward Operating Location at the Ecuadorian Air Force base in Manta as Ecuador's government did not renew the program's lease. It is still unclear whether the Ecuadorian government will permit follow-on activities to replace surveillance coverage of the Eastern Pacific.

Ecuador is a party to the UN Convention for the Suppression of the Financing of Terrorism, and in 2006, the Ecuadorian government ratified the Inter-American Convention against Terrorism. Ecuador is making efforts to improve control of its borders, but in 2008, it established an "open visa policy" allowing tourists from all countries to enter for up to 90 days without first obtaining a visa. Since then, Ecuador has seen a marked increase of entries by travelers from countries with high emigration rates and by "Special Interest Aliens" traveling from countries of concern, exacerbating its problems with alien smuggling. Other issues of concern include Ecuador's weak financial controls, widespread document fraud, and its reputation as a strategic corridor for arms, ammunition, and explosives destined for Colombian terrorist groups.

Ecuador has not criminalized terrorist financing, and the Financial Action Task Force (FATF) and Financial Action Task Force of South America have encouraged the Ecuadorian government to adopt appropriate counterterrorism financing legislation and regulations. On February 18, 2010, FATF identified Ecuador as a jurisdiction with strategic deficiencies in Anti-Money Laundering/Combating the Financing of Terrorism (AML/CFT). FATF's public statement noted that Ecuador had not committed to an action plan developed with the FATF to address key deficiencies related to AML/CTF as of February 2010, and called on its member countries to consider the risks arising from these deficiencies.

In international rankings, Ecuador has been reported to suffer from high levels of corruption. Weak judicial institutions, susceptibility to political influence, and lack of transparency in regulatory bodies are frequently cited as root causes of corruption in Ecuador. There are few non-governmental institutions that fight corruption. President Correa has cited fighting corruption as an important administration goal. Ecuador's 2008 Constitution creates a Transparency and Social Control branch of government tasked with preventing and combating corruption, among other issues.

Government Procurement

Ecuador's public contracting law grants priority to locally produced products and services in public purchases, although foreign suppliers can compete for the contracts. The law created the National Institute of Public Contracting (INCOP) to oversee transparency and timeliness of the contracting process. Foreign bidders must be registered in Ecuador and have a local legal representative in order to participate in government procurement. Ecuador is not a signatory or an observer to the WTO Agreement on Government Procurement.

Peru

U.S.-Peru Trade (Millions of Dollars)

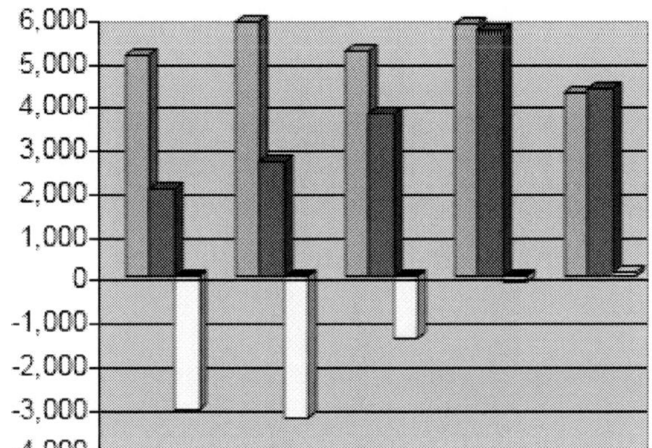

	2005	2006	2007	2008	2009
U.S. Imports	5,123	5,897	5,207	5,840	4,235
U.S. Exports	2,038	2,655	3,764	5,687	4,356
Trade Balance	-3,085	-3,242	-1,443	-153	121

Population: 29,546,963; (July 2009 est.) GDP per capita (PPP): $8,600 (2009 est.)
Source: 2010 World Fact Book.

Effect of ATPA/ATPDEA

In 2009, U.S. goods imports from Peru totaled $4.2 billion, a 28 percent decrease from 2008. U.S. imports under ATPA/ATPDEA from Peru decreased 57 percent, from $3.2 billion in 2008 to $1.4 billion in 2009, reflecting sharply lower prices for resource-based products and a shift in entry of some imports from ATPA/APTDEA to the United States-Peru Trade Promotion Agreement (PTPA). The leading ATPA/ATPDEA entry from Peru was apparel, which declined 47 percent to $408 million in 2009, accounting for 30 percent of total ATPA/ATPDEA entries from Peru. The second largest U.S. import under ATPA/ATPDEA from Peru was petroleum products, which decreased 56 percent to $384 million in 2009. The third largest import in 2009 was copper articles, primarily copper cathodes, and which was formerly the leading import under ATPA/ATPDEA from Peru, at $241 million, down 73 percent from 2008. Other leading ATPA/ATPDEA imports from Peru in 2009 were vegetable and fruit preparations ($91 million); fruits, primarily grapes and mangoes ($56 million); and fresh asparagus ($45 million). Total U.S. imports of fresh asparagus actually increased 6 percent, but a large share of such imports shifted from ATPA/ATPDEA to the PTPA.

Expropriations

Pursuant to Peru's Constitution, the government can only expropriate private property on public interest (e.g., for public works projects) or national security grounds. Any expropriation requires the passage of a specific act of the Congress. The Peruvian government has expressed its intention to comply with international law standards concerning expropriations, and it has agreed to adhere to such standards in the PTPA (including payment of prompt, adequate, and effective compensation). Adequate payment to owners of agricultural lands expropriated by the Peruvian government in the late 1960s and early 1970s is still under discussion with some foreign investors. In 2006, the Peruvian government resolved one such claim involving an American company.

Arbitral Awards

Peru has consented to binding international arbitration of investment disputes between foreign investors and the Peruvian government, in accordance with national legislation or international treaties in force. A December 1992 decree and the 1993 Constitution provide for international arbitration of disputes between foreign investors and the government or state-controlled firms. Peru is a party to the New York Convention. Peru became a contracting party to the ICSID Convention in 1993. Disputes between foreign investors and the state regarding contracts predating Peru's accession to the ICSID Convention, and otherwise not covered by an international agreement, must be submitted to national courts.

Reverse Preferences

A free trade agreement between Peru and Canada entered into force on August 1, 2009. Peru has also a free trade agreement in effect with the United States.

Intellectual Property

The Peruvian government is a member of several international conventions that concern intellectual property, including the following:

- Convention Establishing the World Intellectual Property Organization (WIPO);
- WIPO Copyright Treaty;
- WIPO Performances and Phonograms Treaty;
- Berne Convention for the Protection of Literary and Artistic Works;
- Patent Cooperation Treaty;
- Paris Convention for the Protection of Industrial Property;
- The Convention Relating to the Distribution of Programme-Carrying Signals Transmitted by Satellite (1974);
- The Budapest Treaty on the international Recognition of the Deposit of Microorganisms for the Purpose of Patent Procedure (1977), as amended in 1980;
- The WIPO Copyright Treaty (1996);
- The WIPO Performances and Phonograms Treaty (1996);
- The Patent Cooperation Treaty (1970), as amended in 1979; and
- The Trademark Law Treaty (1994).

As a result of the PTPA, Peru made changes to its legal regime to raise its standards for intellectual property protection and enforcement. Some of these improvements include: protecting trademarks used in Internet domain names; strengthening measures to prevent the circumvention of technological devices for preventing Internet-based copyright piracy; removing burdens for patent registration; protecting against unfair commercial use of test data and other undisclosed information submitted in connection with regulatory approval for pharmaceutical and agricultural chemical products; and providing deterrent-level penalties for piracy and counterfeiting. The U.S. Government will monitor Peru's implementation of these obligations. Peru is listed on the 2009 Special 301 Watch List.

Despite some Peruvian government efforts to improve enforcement, including increased raids on large-scale distributors and users of pirated material, piracy remains widespread, due notably to a failure to apply deterrent penalties. The government, in coordination with the private sector, has conducted numerous raids over the last few years on large-scale distributors and users of pirated goods and has increased other types of enforcement. However, lack of adequate prosecution and sentencing has allowed many IPR infringers to resume their operations after these raids.

Extradition

An extradition treaty with the United States permits the extradition of U.S. citizens.

Workers' Rights

Peru has ratified all eight core conventions of the International Labor Organization (ILO).

Since the election of then-President Toledo in 2001, Peru has made significant labor reforms, and President Garcia's second administration continued on this path by taking several steps to modernize Peru's labor code and ensure that Peru's labor laws are consistent with internationally recognized labor rights. In 2003, Peru passed a major law reform strengthening labor rights and addressing many of the observations raised by the ILO. The law included reforms such as reducing the number of workers needed to form a union, limiting the power of the labor authority to cancel a union's registration, and lessening the requirement to show "dual majority" support in order to conclude a collective bargaining agreement covering workers in a "branch of activity" or occupation. In 2007, Peru passed a series of reforms to regulate the use of subcontracting and temporary work contracts, in order to provide strict government oversight of these mechanisms and protect workers' rights to organize and bargain collectively. The 2007 reforms also addressed issues regarding strikes and anti-union discrimination. Nonetheless, labor advocates expressed concerns as to whether the reforms are sufficient to fully protect temporary or subcontracted workers.

On January 15, 2010, President Garcia signed the new Labor Procedural Law which mandates the reduction of time taken for judicial decisions on labor conflicts to six-months -- a process that used to take four to eight years. The new system of labor courts requires that both sides present oral arguments (not previously allowed) and decisions are to be rendered without undue delay. Workers or worker organizations filing claims of labor violations are to be provided free representation.

Peru's Constitution and the Law of Collective Labor Relations provide for freedom of association for all citizens. Labor regulations provide that workers may form unions based on their occupation, employer affiliation, or geographic territory. Workers are not required to seek authorization prior to forming a trade union, nor may employers legally condition employment on union membership or non-membership.

There are no restrictions on the affiliation of labor unions with international bodies. Several major unions and labor confederations belong to international labor organizations such as the International Trade Union Confederation (ITUC), the international trade secretariats, and regional bodies.

Peru's Constitution recognizes the right to strike, but there are limitations and exceptions based on public interest considerations. It also requires strikers to notify the Ministry of Labor before carrying out a job action, which is contrary to ILO policy that this responsibility should rest with an independent body. Peru's Law on Collective Labor Relations defines a strike as a collective suspension of work conducted in a peaceful and voluntary manner by workers who leave the work site. Supreme Decree 024-2007 established new procedures for calling strikes, including a revised requirement that allows labor unions to declare a strike with a simple majority of voting members, as opposed to the previous rule which required a two-thirds majority vote.

Peru's Constitution provides for collective bargaining, but specifies that this right must be exercised in harmony with broader social objectives and ensures that the collective bargaining agreements are binding. Supreme Decree 013-2006-TR clarified that employers cannot unilaterally change previously agreed-upon collective bargaining agreements, and reduced arbitration costs for collective bargaining agreements. Peru's four Export Processing Zones (EPZs) are not exempt from national labor laws.

The Peruvian Congress unanimously passed the General Labor Inspection Act which went into effect in 2006. The law helps strengthen and professionalize labor inspections by establishing guidelines for labor inspections, setting up separate offices for investigations and for fines, and establishing a National Bureau of Labor Inspections to oversee the inspections process. Currently, there are over 412 labor inspectors, 233 in Lima and the remainder working throughout the country. Additionally, the law redefines acts of union interference as administrative violations, allowing acts of union interference by employers to be punishable with fines. However, the government did not effectively enforce the law, and some employers engaged in antiunion practices.

Peru's Constitution prohibits forced or bonded labor. Despite government efforts to combat forced labor, the ILO's 2008 Committee of Experts observed that forced labor practices, including slavery and debt bondage, affected workers from indigenous communities. The ILO estimated that nearly 30,000 persons are involved in forced labor in Peru, particularly in the logging industry located in two departments of the Amazon River provinces. In January 2007, the Ministry of Labor created an interagency committee to combat forced labor and has chaired a multi-sectoral commission on the prevention of child labor since 2003. Also, in 2008 the Ministry of Labor trained its first group of labor inspectors specialized in forced labor. Laws exist to protect children from exploitation in the workplace and prohibit forced or compulsory labor; however, in practice, child labor remained a serious problem, and the laws were violated routinely in the informal sector. It is estimated that approximately 2.1 million children work in Peru, particularly in gold mining, brick and fireworks manufacturing, stone extraction, timber production, Brazil nut production, and coca production as well as domestic services and street vending. In January 2006, the Ministry of Labor created a special Office of Labor Protection for Minors, responsible for conducting on-site inspections to ensure that legal codes regarding child labor are enforced. The Office of the Ombudsman for Children and Adolescents works with the

Ministry of Labor and Employment Protection to document complaints regarding violations of child labor laws. More than 1,300 offices are located in communities throughout the country.

The Constitution provides that the State is responsible for promoting social and economic progress and occupational education. It states that workers should receive a "just and sufficient" wage to be determined by the government in consultation with labor and business representatives, as well as "adequate protection against arbitrary dismissal." The statutory monthly minimum wage is 550 soles ($192), which did not provide a decent standard of living for many families according to the ILO.

The Constitution also provides for a 48-hour workweek, a weekly day of rest, and an annual vacation. The law requires companies to pay overtime to employees who work more than 8 hours per day, to provide additional compensation for work at night, and to provide a 45-minute meal break to employees during their 8-hour shift. In 2006, the Ministry of Labor and Employment Protection issued a decree requiring businesses to maintain a register of hours that employees work in order to ensure that workers receive due compensation for working more than eight hours per day. The law also requires employers to document the 45-minute lunch break and to make these records available to workers and unions.

In 2009, a supreme decree was passed clearly stating what constitutes acts of discrimination against domestic workers. Employers have frequently required long hours from domestics and paid low wages.

Occupational health and safety standards exist, but labor advocates argue that the government lacks the resources necessary to enforce compliance. The Ministry of Labor and Employment Protection conducts random inspections, and receives and responds to workers' complaints regarding occupation safety and health. If a company is found to be in violation of the law, it is subject to fines and/or closure, although many fines went uncollected, in part due to the lack of an efficient tracking system.

In cases of industrial accidents, compensation is usually determined by an agreement between the employer and worker. The worker does not need to prove an employer's culpability in order to obtain compensation for work-related injuries. No provisions exist for workers to remove themselves from potentially dangerous situations without jeopardizing employment.

Economic Conditions

Over the past decade, Peru has been transformed by market-oriented economic reforms and privatizations that generated many of the conditions for long-term growth. Peru has posted stellar macroeconomic figures for the past seven years until 2008. Real GDP growth rate in 2008 was estimated at almost 10 percent, driven by investment, exports, and private consumption. GDP per capita reached an estimated $4,366 in 2009, up significantly from $2,047 in 2001. Mining, banking and retail services, manufacturing, agriculture, and fishing are key economic sectors.

Peruvian exports (balance of payments basis) of $26.9 billion in 2009 were 15 percent below the record $31.5 billion of 2008, with imports of $21.0 billion, producing a trade surplus of $5.9 billion. Peru's major trading partners in 2009 included the United States, China, Switzerland, Canada, Japan, South Korea, Chile, Colombia, Venezuela, the European

Union (led by Germany, Spain, and Italy), and Brazil. The United States receives approximately 17 percent of Peruvian exports and 20 percent of Peruvian imports originate from the United States (both Customs basis). Exported goods include copper, gold, zinc, lead, tin, iron ore, molybdenum, textiles, crude petroleum and petroleum derivatives, coffee, asparagus, grapes, fishmeal, and fishoil. Imports include petroleum and petroleum products, soybean residues for animal feed, soybean crude oil, corn, wheat, medicines, mobile telephones, automatic data processing machines, plastics, machinery, vehicles, sound/TV sets, iron and steel, fertilizers, and paper. According to Peru's Central bank, Peru's stock of foreign direct investment (FDI) was over $36.9 billion in 2009. The United States and Spain are the leading investors. Stock of U.S. FDI in Peru was $8.4 billion in 2008, a 12 percent increase from 2007. FDI is concentrated in privatized sectors such as metals mining, oil and gas, electricity, telecommunications, and finance.

Peru's economy is one of the better-managed in Latin America, but challenges remain. The Peruvian government still faces strong social pressures to reduce its poverty and underemployment rates. Maintaining long-term growth will require improving the investment climate, reducing corruption, and completing other reforms.

Market Access

The most recent extension of the ATPA/ATPDEA by the U.S. Congress provided benefits for Peru through 2010. The PTPA eliminated the tariff disparity between the United States and Peru. Following entry into force of the agreement on February 1, 2009, almost 90 percent of current U.S. agricultural trade enters the Peruvian market duty-free. These products include high quality beef, whey, cotton, wheat, soybean, and soybean meal, vegetables and fruits such as apples, pears, peaches, and cherries, and processed food products. In addition, Peru immediately eliminated its price band system on trade with the United States. Tariffs on other agricultural products will be eliminated gradually, most within five to fifteen years. Within seventeen years, all U.S. agricultural exports entering the Peruvian market will be duty-free.

Eighty percent of U.S. consumer and industrial exports to Peru were also duty-free upon entry into force of the PTPA in February 2009. Within five years of entry into force, an additional six percent of U.S. industrial products will become duty-free, and another four percent within seven years. Duties on the remaining 10 percent will be phased out over ten years. The PTPA will provide significant new opportunities for U.S. manufacturers of information technology products, industrial machinery, chemicals, remanufactured equipment, medical equipment, and electrical power generation and distribution equipment. Peru has also joined the Information Technology Agreement.

Additionally, the PTPA is enabling U.S. exports to compete more favorably with those from countries which already have preferential access to the Peruvian market through other trade agreements.

Participation in Free Trade Negotiations

On April 12, 2006, then U.S. Trade Representative Rob Portman and Alfredo Ferrero Diez Canseco, Peru's Minister of Foreign Trade and Tourism, signed the United States-Peru Trade Promotion Agreement in Washington, D.C. On June 28, 2006, the Peruvian Congress approved the PTPA by a vote of 79 to 14. The United States and Peru amended the PTPA in June 2007, to include provisions reflecting the May 10 bipartisan agreement with the U.S.

Congress. Congress enacted legislation approving and implementing the PTPA in December 2007. The PTPA entered into force on February 1, 2009.

Subsidies or Other Requirements that Distort International Trade

Peru has eliminated almost all non-tariff barriers, including subsidies, import licensing requirements, import prohibitions, and other quantitative restrictions. However, it bans the following imports for a variety of reasons: several insecticides, fireworks, used clothing, used shoes, used tires, radioactive waste, cars over five years old, and trucks over eight years old. Used cars and trucks that are permitted to be imported must pay a 45 percent excise tax – compared to 20 percent for a new car – unless they are refurbished in an industrial center in the south of the country upon entry, in which case they are exempted entirely from the excise tax.

Regional Trade Policies

Peru is a member of the Andean Community. According to the Peruvian government, Peruvian exports to Andean Community (CAN) countries reached $1.5 billion in 2009 representing 5.7 percent of Peru's total exports. Imports from these three countries were $2.3 billion in 2009, about ten percent of total imports. Exports to Brazil totaled $508 million (1.9 percent) and imports from Brazil totaled $1.7 billion (7.7 percent).

Peru is also a member of ALADI. Within the framework of ALADI, Peru has extended limited concessions to Argentina, Brazil, Chile, Cuba, Mexico, Paraguay, and Uruguay. Peru is in the process of negotiating free trade agreements with Mexico, South Korea, and Japan. Peru has concluded negotiations for free trade agreements with Thailand, the European Union, and EFTA. In 2009, Peru's trade agreements with the United States, Chile, Canada, and Singapore entered into force. On March 1, 2010, the Peru-China free trade agreement entered into force. Peru plans to pursue trade agreement negotiations with India, Russia, New Zealand, Australia, Morocco, and South Africa.

Narcotics and Counter-terrorism Cooperation

In 2008, Peru cooperated fully with the United States on counter-narcotics issues. Peru is the second largest cocaine producer in the world and a major exporter of high purity cocaine and cocaine base to markets in South America, Mexico, the United States, and Europe.

About 90 percent of coca leaf harvested in Peru is used to produce cocaine or its intermediate products. The remainder is used by the local population or for legal medical and commercial consumption in the United States and Europe. Coca cultivation is expanding to new areas while densities are increasing in the traditional source zones. With U.S. Government support, Peru eradicated 10,025 hectares of coca in 2009. Alternative development programs supported legal productive activities on almost 49,200 hectares since 2002.

Drug traffickers continue to move coca products, as well as some opium latex and morphine, out of Peru by land, air, and sea, to U.S., South American, and European markets. Mexican and Colombian trafficking organizations are implicated in using Peru as a primary source of cocaine base and cocaine hydrochloride (HCl). Maritime smuggling of cocaine shipments is the primary method of transporting multi-ton loads of cocaine base and HCl. Law enforcement efforts in 2008 focused on maritime and port investigations and interdictions. In 2009, approximately 19.7 metric tons of cocaine base and cocaine HCl were seized. The U.S. Government and the Peruvian government have cooperated to improve port security and to address increased maritime smuggling at key Peruvian port locations. Importantly, the National Port Authority (APN) made very significant advances in promoting the timely attainment of International Ship and Port Security (ISPS) requirements in 2008. The U.S. Government is continuing to work with the Peruvian government to enhance its capacity to identify and inspect suspect cargo shipments.

Peru is taking action against both international and domestic terrorism, and the government is seeking an integrated approach to eradicating the terrorism threat in the country. There continue to be indications that *Sendero Luminoso* (Shining Path) is directly participating in the various early stages of narcotics trafficking, and is attempting to rebuild its base through expanding its influence in universities throughout Peru. The Peruvian Congress created a national security system designed to improve intergovernmental cooperation and strengthen terrorism prosecutors. The National Police (PNP) Directorate of Counterterrorism works closely with the U.S. Embassy in counterterrorism activities. The PNP continues to break up Shining Path camps and capture leaders. Peru aggressively prosecutes terrorist suspects. After the Constitutional Tribunal overturned numerous provisions in Fujimori-era terrorism laws in 2003, then President Toledo issued new decree legislation and established the procedures for reviewing and retrying terrorism cases. Around 750 cases were retried in 2005. Peru is a party to all 12 of the international conventions and protocols relating to terrorism. Peru, Colombia, and Brazil signed a border cooperation agreement that addresses terrorism and arms trafficking, along with other issues.

A June 2002 law passed by Peru's Congress allows prosecution of money laundering related to terrorism and also created the Financial Intelligence Unit (FIU) as a means to identify money laundering. Peru further strengthened its anti-money laundering legislation in July 2004. The law: (1) included anti-terrorist finance activities among the FIU's functions; (2) greatly expanded the FIU's capacity to engage in joint investigations and information-sharing with foreign FIUs; (3) enhanced the FIU's capacity to exchange information and pursue joint cases with other agencies of the Peruvian government; and (4) required that individuals and entities transporting more than $10,000 in currency or monetary instruments into or out of Peru file reports with Peruvian Customs. The FIU has access to these reports upon request.

Government Procurement

Under the PTPA, Peru has agreed to provide U.S. goods, services, and suppliers with national treatment in the procurements covered by the Agreement. Peru is not a signatory or an observer to the WTO Agreement on Government Procurement.

SUMMARY OF SUBMISSIONS IN RESPONSE TO A NOTICE IN THE FEDERAL REGISTER

Pursuant to section 203(f) of the ATPA as amended, USTR requested the views of interested parties (74 Fed. Reg. 6440, February 9, 2009) on whether the countries designated as ATPDEA beneficiary countries in Presidential Proclamation 7616 of October 31, 2002, are meeting the eligibility criteria under the ATPA as amended.

USTR received twelve comments in response to its request. The full texts of the submissions are available at http://www.regulations, docket USTR-2010-0012. A summary of each submission follows.

The American Apparel and Footwear Association supports continued inclusion of Peru in the ATPA program despite the entry into force of a free trade agreement between Peru and the United States. The Association questions the WTO consistency of the duties Ecuador imposed on a range of goods while invoking the WTO balance of payments safeguard provision, and expresses concern about protective measures the Ecuadorian government may use to replace those duties.

The Association of Colombian Flower Exporters presents itself as a clear success story of the ATPA program. It notes that during the life of the program its workforce has grown tenfold, and that Colombian flowers represent 60 percent of U.S. cut flower imports. It states that its flowers are produced in an environmentally sustainable manner and with social responsibility towards its workforce.

The Association of Ecuadorian Pineapple Producers indicates that its members cannot compete in the U.S. market with other sourcing countries without the benefit of the ATPA program. It states that the Ecuadorian pineapple industry complies with international labor standards.

Chevron calls into question whether the Ecuadorian government is meeting the eligibility criteria of the ATPA program relating to the honoring of contracts with U.S. companies and recognizing arbitral awards involving U.S. companies. Chevron also states that the Ecuadorian government has demonstrated a lack of commitment to its legal obligations under the U.S.- Ecuador BIT.

The Colombian Government Trade Bureau describes the importance of the ATPA program for Colombia and the impact it has had on the Colombian economy. It states that, pending the entry into force of the United States-Colombia free trade agreement, the ATPA market access preferences are essential to support Colombia's continuing efforts to combat drug trafficking and improve the economic welfare of its citizens. The submission provides information regarding Colombia's compliance with the ATPA eligibility criteria.

CropLife America believes that Ecuador's Decree 183 of 2009, which provides for the granting of compulsory licenses for agricultural chemicals, falls short of the minimum standards provided for in the WTO Agreement on Trade-Related Aspects of Intellectual Property Rights (TRIPS). CropLife America points out that TRIPS Article 31(b) requires candidate licensees to first attempt to obtain authorization from the patent holder on reasonable commercial terms and conditions. The association indicates that although TRIPS Article 31(b) allows a government to waive this requirement in certain cases, such as a national emergency, Decree 183 requires no such circumstances for a waiver.

The Ecuadorian-American Chamber of Commerce describes the ATPA program as the cornerstone of an export promotion policy that has helped curb the production and trafficking of narcotics. The submission states that the program has promoted investment and stimulated employment in such sectors as flowers, textiles and apparel, broccoli, wood articles, tropical fruit, and tuna. It addresses Ecuador's recent balance of payments measures and describes steps the Ecuadorian government has taken to meet the ATPA eligibility criteria.

The Embassy of the Republic of Ecuador to the United States cites a number of positive benefits the ATPA program has provided Ecuador, including job creation, lifting people out of poverty, supporting counternarcotics efforts, and promoting political and economic stability in Ecuador. The submission reports on Ecuadorian government efforts related to a number of the program's eligibility criteria.

The Emergency Committee for American Trade (ECAT) strongly supports the ATPA program, believing it has promoted diversification and economic opportunities in the Andean region and strong economic relationships with Colombia and Peru. However, it states that a continued deterioration in the rule of law in Bolivia warrants its continued suspension from the program. ECAT questions whether Ecuador is meeting the program's eligibility criteria, stating that U.S. and other foreign businesses are experiencing expropriation and the repudiation of contracts in industries such as energy and construction. It says that Ecuador's judicial system often denies due process, notes that Ecuador has withdrawn from the International Centre for Settlement of Investment Disputes (ICSID), and states that Ecuador's recent issuance of a compulsory license may be inconsistent with Ecuador's WTO obligations.

The International Intellectual Property Alliance believes that it is critical for the four Andean countries, three of which are current ATPA beneficiary countries, to continue to take all appropriate actions in their respective territories to improve the protection of copyrights. It finds that for the most part the legal regimes are adequate but that enforcement efforts to combat copyright piracy are insufficient, and cites specific steps it believes each country should take to remedy the situation.

The National Business Association of Colombia details the trade benefits that have accrued to Colombian exporters under the ATPA. It also outlines areas in which the Colombian government has made progress in dealing with worker rights and the issue of violence against union members.

Oxfam America and the Center for International Environmental Law focus on Chevron's legal dispute with the Ecuadorian government. They state that the company bears responsibility for significant environmental damage in Ecuador and that the Ecuadorian government has complied with the ATPA eligibility criteria.

The U.S. Chamber of Commerce indicates that the ATPA has proven to be an effective tool to generate trade, growth, and jobs among the beneficiary countries, while also benefitting U.S. businesses. The Chamber expresses unreserved support for Colombia's continued inclusion until the United States-Colombia Trade Promotion Agreement is approved and enters into force; supports Peru's continued participation; and calls into question whether Ecuador is meeting the program's eligibility criteria. The Chamber states that the Ecuadorian government often fails to respect property and concession rights, particularly in the oil and gas sectors, exhibits systemic weaknesses in its judicial system, and failed to provide due process protections with respect to the compulsory licensing of a pharmaceutical product.

Operation of the Petition Process

Pursuant to the procedures outlined in Chapter 1 – Description of the ATPA/ATPDEA, USTR has administered a petition process under the program. A description of the earlier periods of operation of the petition process can be found in the previous USTR reports to Congress on the ATPA as amended posted at http://www.ustr.gov.

Since the last report, in August 2009, USTR published a notice in the *Federal Register* announcing the 2009 Annual Review of the ATPA. Seven parties filed submissions, but none of the submissions constituted petitions that were accepted for review. Submissions from the Embassy of Ecuador to the United States and the Ecuadorian-American Chamber of Commerce stated that Ecuador is meeting the program's eligibility criteria. The National Association of Manufacturers and the Emergency Committee for American Trade urged a reconsideration of Ecuador's eligibility, but did not cite specific violations of the eligibility criteria. Chevron updated its earlier petition concerning Ecuador and the Amazon Defense Coalition presented counterarguments. The U.S. Labor in the Americas Project (USLEAP) updated its earlier petition on Ecuador. The full texts of the submissions are available at http://www.regulations, docket USTR-2009-0024.

Following is the list of all petitions from prior years that remain under review: two petitions relating to worker rights in Ecuador (filed by Human Rights Watch and USLEAP), a petition involving gold trading company Princeton Dover in a dispute with Peru, one matter currently in international arbitration (Duke Energy versus Peru), and one involving Chevron Texaco and Ecuador.

The most recent notices in the *Federal Register* relating to the ATPA reviews can be found at http://www.ustr.gov.

End Notes

[1] Previously, USTR's reports on ATPA were submitted on April 30, however, the extension of ATPA enacted in 2009, changed the date for the report to June 30.

[2] President Bush suspended Bolivia's designation as a beneficiary country under the ATPA/ATPDEA, effective December 15, 2008, citing Bolivia's failure to meet the program's eligibility criteria related to counternarcotics cooperation.

[3] As noted above, the President submitted a report to Congress on June 30, 2009, regarding Ecuador and Bolivia's compliance or lack of compliance with ATPA/ATPDEA criteria,

[4] As noted above, in 2009 Bolivia did not receive benefits under ATPA/ATPDEA.

INDEX

A

B

C

D

E

F

G

Q

R

T

U